THE GOD FRANCHISE

A Theory of Everything

ALAN H. DAWE

Life Magic
Publishing
AUCKLAND

ISBN 978-0-473-20114-2

First published 2012

Life Magic Publishing
PO Box 51-460
Pakuranga
Auckland 2140
New Zealand

Produced by Life Magic Publishing
Cover and interior design by Justine Elliott, booklayoutguru.com
Copyedit and proofreading by Judith Sansweet, Proofreadnz.co.nz

QR code provided by QRCodeQueenz.com

Typeset in Garamond 11.75pt and News Gothic

Definitions (as indicated in the text) reproduced from *Collins English Dictionary Complete and Unabridged* with the permission of HarperCollins Publishers Ltd ©HarperCollins Publishers Ltd 2011.

A catalogue record for *The God Franchise* is available from the National Library of New Zealand.

Disclaimer
The author and publisher will not accept responsibility for the use or misuse of any of the information in this book. Whilst every effort has been made to ensure the accuracy of all statements and references, and to acknowledge original sources wherever appropriate, the author and publisher cannot accept responsibility for any errors or omissions.

EARLY REVIEWS OF *THE GOD FRANCHISE*

"I really love the heartfelt truth that flows from you in the book." **Sharon Turton**, NSW, AUSTRALIA (Author of *Connecting Kids with their Inner Potential*)

"I really admire the way you have brought together so many different beliefs and ideas about creation, God, religions, spirituality, manifestation, universal laws, ways of looking at life and living life. What a work! It is readable, it is personal, it is clear, it invites the reader to consider different aspects of life without disagreeing with them, and it entices the reader to a wider understanding of life. I like the way you have minimised the theory with clear explanations and put in lots of practical examples, and the way you have given summaries to clarify the meaning. I love the idea of my being a God Franchisee." **Annette Burrell**, CHRISTCHURCH, NZ (Journey Practitioner and Teacher)

"Alan H. Dawe ... writes with conviction and total sincerity, and the easy, somewhat chatty literary style should not divert the reader from the serious aspect of the subject. ... The ultimate conclusion, whilst by no means sacrilegious might be contentious. It is carefully and logically drawn, and should lead the reader to do some particularly reflective and deep personal thinking." **Mary Rhodes**, MA(Ed), SOMERSET, UK

"[The God Franchise] is a good read, very accessible and positive, despite dealing with heavy and complex concepts. ... I certainly hope many people will read the book and gain a great deal from doing so. I enjoyed the positivity of the book and would like to think it will help many people who are looking to broaden their thinking and consider alternative explanations for who we are and how we came to be. I also hope it may encourage some people to live their lives more fully and more positively (though I note you were careful to say we always have a choice)." **Kate Whelan**, PhD, DERBYSHIRE, UK

"What a mammoth book you have! I think you really have something significant here. It's been a real pleasure to work on it." **Judith Sansweet**, AUCKLAND, NZ (Copyeditor and Proofreader)

*To you, your Higher Self, who will recognise the
Ultimate Truth behind these words*

and

To Mum and Dad, who got me started.

CONTENTS

PART FOUR

Daily Living as a God Franchisee

PART FIVE

Reaching a Conclusion

APPENDICES

ACKNOWLEDGEMENTS

I would like to acknowledge:

My mum and dad, Kathleen and Cyril Dawe, who encouraged me, ensured that I received a solid education, and allowed me to have a wide and open experience of spiritual matters. Both have now moved on to a non-physical dimension, so sadly are not here to see their son's successes directly.

Susan, for her love and support at all times. She will be proud of her big brother's book.

Malinda and Jenny, who have always given me quiet love and support, and only chide me when I get completely out of hand.

Barb, for her love and support, and for allowing me to write my masterpiece as well as undertake all my other projects, studies, whims, enthusiasms, and book purchases — without questioning why I didn't just get a proper job (too often).

The late Dudley Clear (The Bird) who taught me how to write and appreciate the English language.

All my inspirational heroes over the years, including John, Paul, George, & Ringo, Bob Dylan, David Bowie, Nick Cave, Philip Glass, John Fowles, Paramhansa Yogananda[1], Joel Goldsmith, Eckhart Tolle, Brandon Bays, Kevin Billett, and Adam & Eve.

Everyone I have either personally come in contact with, or whose work I have heard or read. Every contact and interaction has had some effect on me, and has brought me to the place I am now. Thank you all so much.

A very big thank you to those who have encouraged me and who have reviewed drafts of *The God Franchise* and its cover along the way. Your advice, thoughts, and reviews have been very welcome and have helped me steer the work into its present form and structure:

---

1   Also spelt Paramahansa Yogananda.

Frank Biggs, Kevin Billett, Annette Burrell, Rowena Coleman, Joanne Eilbeck, Brian and Marion Groufsky, Ginny Jones, Christine Karl, Brendan McGrath, Mary Rhodes, Kushla Rolls, Sharon Turton, Kate and Simon Whelan and especially Barb, Malinda, Jenny, and Susan.

I extend my sincere thanks to Judith Sansweet of ProofreadNZ for her dedication and hard work, copyediting and proofreading against a tight deadline, and still ensuring the perfect result. This book is a real testament to her skill and professionalism.

I offer my deep gratitude to Justine Elliott, designer and Book Layout Guru indeed, who has beautified the manuscript and turned it into a book. Thank you so much for making every effort to give me what I wanted, without my really knowing what that was. Now we all know.

I must also mention the Ashton Wylie Charitable Trust Unpublished Manuscript Award 2011 judges, who by shortlisting *The God Franchise* as a finalist in the awards, gave me a huge boost of confidence in the literary balance and accessibility of my writing.

Finally, and most importantly, I would like to acknowledge the God of *The God Franchise* without Whom I would not have been inspired to write this book in the first instance. Neither would I exist, nor would you, as you will soon discover in these pages.

INTRODUCTION

When I was a young boy of eight or nine years, I had the dream of one day knowing everything there was to know. To me it seemed like the ultimate goal — to know and to understand everything.

I soon realised, as I continued through the school system and got tested on what I actually did know, there was an awful lot I didn't know, and most of it I would never know. That was in the 1950s, and by the time I had finished high school in 1965, I realised I knew very little at all. My wings had been severely clipped.

Now, with my 50-year anniversary School Reunion already in sight, I have written this book that effectively is *my* theory of everything. I am not a scientist, but I know many scientists see the Holy Grail as being *a theory of everything,* or *unified theory* as they prefer to call it.

Likewise, while I am sure there are many philosophers who, over the centuries, have written their own theories of everything, I am not a philosopher — well certainly not in a trained or professional sense. I am not even an intellectual who can necessarily make a good argument.

Rather, I see myself as the man next door who one day had an inkling of how and why everything is as it is, and I have felt a need to write it all down so I can read it myself and ponder over the various aspects and conclusions — the implications and the deeper meanings.

I see it, the realisations reached and the book, as the most profound spiritual experience I have had. Now, I feel a need to share these ideas with others so they too may be prompted to discover why things are as they are, and what they can and can't do about it.

This is a book about what must be the most important set of questions that has ever faced any man, woman, or child who has ever lived. Who am I? Why am I here? Is there a purpose to my life? Whose purpose is it? Is there a God? What is my relationship to God? Did God create the universe? And, if so, why and how?

Granted, many people do not formulate the questions in those words because it is not fashionable to do so in a secular world. Nevertheless, perhaps in a quiet moment or when faced with a moment of crisis or reality, everyone at some time searches deep within and inwardly screams, *WHY?*

Throughout the ages, since the first men and women gained the power of thought and the ability to create concepts, they have looked at the heavens and marvelled. They have watched the seasons shift and the storms rage. They have faced their own mortality and they have come to realise there are forces and powers much greater than they are. At first they believed in *the gods* as the source of this mighty power, and over time this concept evolved into the concept of a god who is greater than all other gods, a being who is worthy of the name, *God*.

The God Franchise is a book about this God. It is a book about the universe we live in. It is a book about **YOU**. You are a unique individual in this world, with your own personal experience of what it is to live this life. It is about your loves, your triumphs, your good and not-so-good actions, your fears and your pain. The book is about the purpose of your life and who you are. It is about your personal place in the universe.

We will look at the big questions that face us all, and we will arrive at some big answers. These answers are so big they cover every aspect of our lives. A deep understanding of what we discuss here offers you the opportunity for a huge shift in consciousness — assuming, of course, you are ready for it and you haven't already made that shift.

In saying that, let me hasten to add, I am being neither precious nor elitist. Some who read this book will already understand and live this Truth, even if they view its expression slightly differently. Others will discard what is written here as the ramblings of a madman. In days past (hopefully long past), I might be strung up as a heretic and blasphemer. Then, there are the people who are still searching for the Truth, and who seek a path that will give them real and practical answers. They seek a philosophy that makes perfect sense, one they can embrace, apply practically, and live.

This book is addressed to you, whatever your present beliefs and understanding of God and the universe. *The God Franchise* is written for everyone as there is real benefit to be found in its pages, however you prefer to use its pointers to Truth. *The God Franchise* can be read on many levels, so you will benefit from reading and rereading the book; as you reflect on the significance of its contents and how it applies to you in every moment of your life, you will gain fresh and deeper understanding.

As we tackle the big questions of life together, it is my intention to do this as clearly as possible. Unfortunately, because we are discussing God and a subject so vast and universal it is almost impossible to describe, you might appreciate that the clearer and more down-to-earth I try to make the explanation, the less accurate what I say becomes. While I will do the best I can within the confines of language, the real Truth can only be pointed to and not spelt out in so many words. Perhaps this book can be seen as one long analogy!

Nevertheless, this is a philosophy you can live. The ideas I present here have probably been raised many times before — frankly, I don't know whether they have or not. Many books that might tell me this are written in such a dense and obtuse way that I cannot reach them. Certainly, I have not discovered any books that approach the subject quite as I have done here. This is not a work of literature, nor is it a scholarly work. I am a straightforward person who likes to spell things out clearly and specifically. I like to write concisely and simply so you can easily understand the essence of the subject and my viewpoint. I may at times be critical about some people's beliefs, and you may not like what I say. I have felt a need to be emphatic at times, although I trust I am never disrespectful. I hope to break through ingrained beliefs that may not serve you. I certainly do not intend to offend you.

I will quote from the Holy Bible from time to time and will use this as a reference point. The Bible is still the book that has sold more copies than any other around the world, so the chances are you can easily lay your hands on a copy if you wish to check what I have written here. I am not a Bible scholar, and candidly, this book will make the same sense to you whether you are a regular reader of the Bible or not. Either way, don't let the Bible prevent you from understanding **The God Franchise**.

So, while I do make use of the Bible as a reference point, please realise that *The God Franchise* is not a religious book. It has no religious bias at all, but rather looks at the spirituality behind all religion. If I were better versed in other religious texts and holy books, I would use them as well. Unfortunately, the Bible is the only one with which I am at all familiar.

This book is structured in five parts. In Part One, we discuss and answer the question: Does God really exist? We look at what God might be like, and I can quite openly say that I have come to the definite conclusion that God does exist, although the God I have discovered may differ from the God you already believe in or disbelieve in. It will, therefore, be very interesting for you to discover where you and I agree and where we might need to have further discussion. Please note that, if you already believe in God, the appendices at the back of the book are an extension of Part One and are optional reading. You may prefer to skim through these detailed appendices, and/or read them after you have read the rest of the book.

Part Two describes and details **The God Franchise**. It discusses the purpose of the universe, starting with a new (and light) look at the Creation story in Genesis and the rise and fall of Adam and Eve. We look at God's Plan for us and at God's Laws. You might be surprised at what these are, and how you can live happily within this context.

Part Three focuses on some of the different beliefs people have and tries to reconcile them. Naturally, we have different beliefs because beliefs are formed in our childhood and depend upon our upbringing and environment. Beliefs are passed from generation to generation through culture and habits. Being dispassionate about it, there really is no reason why any of your beliefs are any truer than those of the next man or woman, or the men and women on the other side of the world. Nevertheless, you *believe* you are right and they are wrong. That is the same for us all; so, this part of the book looks at some of the beliefs surrounding God, the universe, life and death, morality, sin and so on. Yes, we have to face these things head-on!

Part Four is a more practical section of the book and looks at how we can benefit by living daily as God Franchisees. We look at subjects like the Law of Manifestation, sin, forgiveness, prayer, and the purpose of life. This is not prescriptive in any way, and there is certainly no claim that I can tell you what to do. However, this is an opportunity to discuss and discover the practical side of **The God Franchise**. You can adapt what you learn, as you desire, once you know what the opportunities and implications are.

Part Five is a wrapping up. By this time, you will have a distinctly fresh idea of the big subjects of God, the universe, and your part in it. This is a time for reflection and a time for celebration.

I have written this book specifically for you. Let it speak to your heart and to your deeper intellect. I know there will be many things you instinctively disagree with, so I, respectfully, ask you to remember those *instincts* are merely beliefs that you have from your upbringing, your traditions, and your schooling. Allow the possibility that something else might be true. Allow that what you are reading may still be compatible with what you already believe, if it just has a bit of time to settle in. Allow also that any strong feelings of disagreement may be Ego talking. You will gain the most from this book if you allow Ego to be left outside the door. This book may challenge beliefs that perhaps limit and contract you. I speak to you openly, and I hope you will speak openly with me. Let's meet in the middle, in the glorious blaze of Truth.

I will be thrilled if the words of this book give you something at a deeper level — if they help you more clearly understand the meaning of life, and lift some of the burden you may carry.

These words are truly liberating — if you allow them to be. So let us begin…

Bless you

alan

PS If you would like to comment, I would love to hear from you. I have set up a blog at **www.TheGodFranchise.com**, and my e-mail address is listed on the Life Magic Publishing website, **http://publishing. lifemagic.co.nz**. Once again, I ask that you keep Ego out of the way, and write clearly and briefly how you see things. Let this be a discussion, not an argument, and definitely not all-out war!

PPS When you have read *The God Franchise*, and feel as I do that this is a message that needs to be propagated, please visit the back page of the book for information on how you can help.

PART ONE

Does God
Really Exist?

CHAPTER 1

Who or What is God?

Although this may seem difficult or even impossible, try to imagine what it might have been like before there was an Earth, before there was a universe. Then ask yourself, what was there before that? If you come up with an answer, accept it and ask, what was there before that? Keep going back until you can go back no further.

Now try the same exercise forward in time. What comes after this universe that we live in? What comes after that? Clear away whatever comes up and ask, what comes after that? Keep going until you come to a stop.

If you go back far enough, there are only two possible answers to this question: either there was nothing, absolutely nothing at all, or else this universe is eternal and had no beginning. Likewise, looking forward, either there will be nothing left, absolutely nothing at all, or else this universe is eternal and has no end.

If there was absolutely nothing, the question is where and how did the universe spring into existence? If there was absolutely nothing, there was no need to do anything and there were no resources to make it happen. Nothing would just continue to be nothing. The only power that could possibly create something from nothing is Consciousness.

I use the word consciousness (and Consciousness) frequently in this book, and discuss it in detail in Chapter 4. For now, please accept consciousness as meaning *an awareness of self, environment, and mental activity, and the ability to determine choice of action.*[2] So, in saying that Consciousness is the only power that could create something from nothing, I am saying that awareness and an ability to determine choice of action were the prime qualities needed to precede the creation of something from nothing. Science has no credible explanation of how nothing could suddenly become something. Scientists start with the Big Bang,[3] not before it.

Just as an idea might be created out of nothing (although this seldom happens), so conceivably a powerful enough Consciousness might create the universe out of nothing. So, if there was nothing at all, there at least had to be Consciousness existent in order to create the universe of which we are now part. Man has decided to call this Consciousness, **God**.

The other possibility, that the universe is eternal, without beginning or end, also seems to imply some sort of eternal force that underlies the whole process. We know that nothing physical lasts forever, so there would need to be a non-physical force underlying the universe just to keep it maintained. This force is best described as *Consciousness* or *God*.

If we take the scientific standpoint about the origins of the universe, Edwin Hubble's Big Bang theory indicates that all atoms of matter in the universe were concentrated (as hydrogen) at a point in space,[4] and that since the Big Bang, it has been expanding outwards in all directions, over a period of about 14 billion years. This is fine, except for the question: How did all that hydrogen come to be concentrated in one place before the Big Bang? Once again, Consciousness (God) would seem to be the only possible creator of all the initial matter.

Now, if we look into the future, either things go on eternally, or there will suddenly be nothing. Where will everything go unless it is dissolved back into Consciousness (God)? If God switches off and dies, there will be absolutely nothing, and no chance of a new start. It

---

2   Derived from the definition in *Collins English Dictionary*.
3   The name "Big Bang" was coined by Fred Hoyle (1915-2001), the astronomer, although he personally did not agree with this theory and developed his own steady state theory of the universe. The Big Bang theory has been accepted as the most likely explanation, and is the one I accept in the context of this book.
4   However, as discussed in Chapter 7, Martin Rees says that any location in the universe could be seen as being that central point, and so there is no specific location for the Big Bang.

is very unlikely that if God started out eternally (in our past), that He would not continue into the future eternally too. And if He didn't, and there was absolutely nothing left, it wouldn't matter, would it?

So, if there is eternity, there has to be something that is eternal. That something is Consciousness or God.

I have used the word *Consciousness* to describe God in order to open up the definition of God and to help you break free of any preconceptions that you might have. Some people use the word *Universe*, and I have previously done so, but this almost hints of no God, just a universe — a Creation without a Creator. Consciousness is a concept we can all understand. It is allied to being aware, to being alive and being able to conceptualise. God is certainly Consciousness, so let's allow Consciousness to be God.

Throughout this work, I have generally used the words *God* or *God-Consciousness* to include everyone's concept of God, and to help free us all from any false associations we may be hanging onto. This God or God-Consciousness is central to our existence, whether we like it or not. Apart from using the terms God and God-Consciousness, I maintain the common usage of *He* and *His* as pronouns. This certainly will be so in many of the quotes I have used, particularly from the Bible. There is no implication that God is male (nor do I subscribe to the concept of a female Goddess). God is an *It*, but it just does not read well to use that pronoun; so He It is!

God is Consciousness, and to help us to remember that fact and to drop all previous concepts of Him, we will call Him *God-Consciousness*.

CHAPTER 2

The Arguments For and Against God

Chapter 1 provided a very brief explanation of why there needs to be a God — essentially, something (the universe) could not derive from nothing (nothing at all) unless there was some prior force or Consciousness that could conceptualise the something and decide to make it appear. Why and how Consciousness achieved this we will discuss a little later in the book; but for now, I would like to affirm that He did it. I declare that God exists purely because something had to have set the universe in motion, and whatever it was that was able to do that is worthy in my book of being called *God*.

The question of whether or not God exists has been pondered for centuries. The vast majority of people have always believed (or hoped) God did exist. A minority have put their hands up to gainsay that. Many great works have been written on both sides of the fence, and I have neither the room nor the inclination to discuss them in an in-depth, scholarly way here. Rather, I can say I believe God is alive and well, and He is living very close at hand. I would rather get on with the main thesis of this book, **The God Franchise**, than debate whether the book should have been called *The No-God Franchise*, *The Franchise without a Franchisor* or *The Godless Franchise*.

I have jumped very quickly to the assertion that God exists. If you are unhappy with this conclusion, may I refer you to the appendices at the back of this book? The appendices form a continuous discussion regarding the question of whether or not God exists. I look at the major arguments from the atheists' viewpoint and also from that of the theists. I look at science and the theory of evolution, and at some atheists who have jumped ship and become theists. I cover the whole subject in a depth and detail that I did not want us to be bogged down by at the outset of this book. However, if you would like to read why I can so readily assert that God exists, please turn to the appendices now. They flow in harmony with the development of the themes that follow. Alternatively, you may choose to read the appendices later, or not at all.

For now, let me just make a few points about the contents of the appendices. First, let me say that some atheists don't believe in God at all and others feel it is unreasonable to believe in God. It was also interesting to discover in my research that most atheists are against the most common concept of God, the Judeo-Christian-Islamic God, and that their *proofs* are directed accordingly. This means we cannot take for granted what an atheistic viewpoint means, or how it should be applied. To me, it is feasible that some atheists may accept the premise of **The God Franchise** despite their atheistic position.

Many scientists are atheists, but this is simply because their scientific research gives them evidence and explanations that religion does not deliver. Nevertheless, there are many scientists who do believe in God, and some who have changed their beliefs from atheism to theism. Once again, the acceptance of what science tells us about the origins of the universe and life, and concepts such as the theory of evolution do not necessarily imply there is no room for God or a Creator.

Looking at the many disparate arguments, as we do in the appendices, can seem like we are opening a can of worms. Do the arguments clarify the question of whether God exists, or do they just confuse things? Each champion of a particular viewpoint has merit; so, how can their opposing views be reconciled? These arguments have been going on for centuries, and each side merely continues to build a stronger case from and for their own perspective. We appear to be moving further apart rather than coming together to find the Truth.

Like the scientists themselves, I am prepared to accept what science tells us. Therefore, I accept that the theory of evolution and natural selection over a period of 3.5 billion years makes more sense than does a creation in six days with Man coming on the scene the day after the animals about 6,000 years ago. I also accept the Big Bang theory and many other theories scientists have come to settle upon. I accept that knowledge will advance in these areas, and it is quite feasible some of these theories will change. So be it. That is the nature of science.

The fact that science undergoes change does not invalidate its theories or its conclusions. The universe is slowly revealing its secrets, and we can marvel at what scientists have discovered so far. While some individuals may have pet theories they are reluctant to give up, in general terms, the field of science and the scientists collectively are prepared to bow to new discoveries and allow knowledge as a whole to move forward. This is great, and this is why I feel we can trust that, in essence, scientists are on the right track.

The case of one scientist, Charles Darwin, who really upset the beliefs of the Western world when he published *The Origin of Species* in 1859, is very interesting. Although atheists use the theory of evolution to support their case, Darwin himself was not an atheist. On the contrary, he saw the wonder of God's work in his studies of the evolution of life on Earth. There is certainly nothing in Darwin's work to deny that God is the Source of life on Earth — evolution being merely a part of the mechanism He used. Indeed, Darwin concludes *The Origin of Species* with the following words:

> *"Thus, from the war of nature, from famine and death, the most exalted object which we are capable of conceiving, namely the production of the higher animals, directly follows. There is grandeur in this view of life, with its several powers, having been originally breathed by the Creator into a few forms or into one; and that, whilst this planet has gone cycling on according to the fixed law of gravity, from so simple a beginning endless forms most beautiful and most wonderful have been and are being evolved."* [5]

What can we say about religionists and theologians? It would appear that many are looking to find extra ways of confirming what they already believe. The fortress of religion is being built ever bigger, with

---

5   Darwin, C., *The Origin of Species by Means of Natural Selection, or The Preservation of Favoured Races in the Struggle for Life*, 6th Ed., John Murray, London, 1876, Pg. 429.

enhanced fortifications and with deeper moats surrounding it. There has been a resurgence of fundamentalism in the Christian Church as expressed through the evangelicals over the last few decades, and by much of the Christian literature published today that appears to be coming from this angle. Equally, there are some brave non-conformists like Lloyd Geering in New Zealand and Bishop John Spong in the US who are prepared to present an unconventional view of Christianity. It is likely in the decades and centuries to come that the only hope for the survival of religion is for it to embrace the discoveries science offers. Christians need to accept the mystical and enlightened views of the teachings rather than adhere to the literal word of the scriptures and the restrictions of church dogma that are constantly being invalidated and refuted by the advances of philosophy and science.

It appears to me that the theists, the atheists, and the scientists have each presented their cases thoroughly over the years. If nothing changes in the approach they are taking, there will be many more years of the same or similar arguments raised on each side. My thesis, as presented in this book, is that all those arguments that have merit must have a measure of truth in them. Therefore, let us accept that all arguments with merit are correct, and then see how they can be organised to produce a cohesive unified theory (in the scientific sense of the word), or as I have called it, *A Theory of Everything*. It is as if the antagonists have become fixated on the Judeo-Christian-Islamic God for some reason, and so the argument can never be settled. No doubt, God sits on the sidelines of this particular arena and is having a tremendous laugh at the futility and arrogance of it all. So, let's move over to the sidelines ourselves and look at the Truth that is there.

Whichever way you currently tend to answer the question, *Does God really exist?*, I hope the reasons for your specific viewpoint are better than Pascal's Wager. What Blaise Pascal (1623-1662) wrote in his notes, published after his death as *Pensées*, was:

> *As one doesn't know whether God exists or not, it is nevertheless in one's interest to believe in God, since, if God does exist, not believing in Him would be bad for one's eternal soul, whereas if He does not exist, believing in Him would not matter!*

I suspect that Pascal might have said this with his tongue firmly in his cheek, but such fence-sitting due to the fear for one's *eternal soul* does not advance one's understanding of reality, nor does it get one closer to the foothills of Absolute Reality.

CHAPTER 3

The Nature of God

The God Franchise discusses the nature of God in detail, and offers many insightful answers to the sorts of questions we might have. So let's formulate a few thoughts and questions about what we might expect to discover about God that can act as a focus for this discussion.

While different religions and beliefs have various expectations of the nature of God, I would like to propose that the following qualities can be expected of God, if He is worth His salt:

+ God is conscious
+ God is eternal
+ God is omnipotent (all-powerful)
+ God is omnipresent (present everywhere)
+ God is omniscient (all-knowing)
+ God is the Creator of the universe
+ God is likely to have a purpose for His Creation
+ God is likely to be absolutely good (omnibenevolent)
+ God is likely to be immutable (unchanging through time).

You may not accept all these qualities for God right now; although, you might agree that if a God who displayed these qualities existed, He would definitely be worthy of the name, **God**. But we are not ready to discuss these qualities in depth yet, so I will leave further comment on them until Chapter 11.

When the question of God arises in some people's minds, there are a number of issues that often follow; even if they do not class themselves as being atheistic, they still have question marks regarding some of the following points:

+ First, there is the Problem of Evil. There is evil in the world, and an omnipotent, omniscient, and absolutely good God would surely not permit this. This is often seen as the most powerful argument against the existence of God, or a benevolent God anyway. Evil in the world can include both human evil and natural evil such as earthquakes, hurricanes, tsunamis and the lesser storms, fires, and floods.

+ There are many inconsistent teachings, whether from different religions or from within specific religions. How can they all be right? Surely, God must be consistent; so, does that mean many people are wrong? There is also a tendency for us to consider our own beliefs to be correct, and for everyone else to be wrong; this causes much division in the world, and of course, has been the source of many wars and atrocities.

+ The world could appear not to be the best possible world, and an omnipotent, omniscient, and absolutely good God would surely need to create the best possible world. There have been very different experiences of the world over the centuries, so how could each of these have been the best possible world? Why are some people born with a great disadvantage such as blindness, disfigurement, or other disability, or into a life of abject poverty?

+ God has been conspicuous by His hiddenness, or has He?

+ Do we really have free will, or is this incompatible with the concept of an omniscient God who can see both the past and future?

+ Doesn't God need to be an extremely complex being to have designed and created the universe — and still keep it running at an individual level, answering prayers, and supporting each conscious being? Where did He come from? Is the improbability of His existence even greater than the improbability of alternative physical theories of how the universe came into being?

+ Can Man know God or is the gulf between us too wide?

+ Is God **a** being or is He *just* Being?

+ What is the purpose of life? What is God's purpose for us? What was God's motivation in creating the universe? He must have had one!

These are all questions we consider in depth in this book. In the meantime, let me jump to the general conclusions I have come to, particularly in response to the arguments laid out in the appendices. To me, God does exist — not in the way depicted by many religions, but in the highest and most spiritual way.

It is my considered thesis that the universe was designed and created, even if the creation was "merely" the setting of the stage for natural evolution to take place. I totally accept what science has already discovered, the explanations of evolution and natural selection, and the significance of DNA. Where I differ is in what those explanations mean. Scientists (in general terms) try to extrapolate from the knowledge they have, as this is the best way to identify the next step of discovery. However, they go too far when they extrapolate a designer or creator **out** of the picture.

Perhaps scientists fear that the implication of a *designer* would be that the job is now done, and there can be no further development of life — that perhaps what we see on Earth today is the pinnacle of that design (and creation). Let me assure them this is not the inference at all. Just as God has used evolution, natural selection, and DNA as tools in the execution of His design, the future development and evolution of that design is assured in exactly the way scientists might predict it with their own projections — as well as in ways they have not yet dreamed of.

The purists and scientists may want scientific proof of a Being they can measure, a God they can detect with their instruments. Maybe this will be possible one day in some way, but what I suspect is they will find something they have been measuring all along — and not recognising for what it is. Scientists have come a long way in helping us to understand the universe we live in, from the Big Bang theory and the theory of evolution to the incredible details of biology, physics, chemistry, astronomy, and all the other sciences. Whichever way you turn, you are faced with an incredible universe. We have harnessed many of its forces and attributes to make life on Earth more comfortable, safer, and more interesting on a day-to-day basis.

Atheists and many scientists may believe that having God as creator of the universe is too complex a solution, and that *"any creative intelligence, of sufficient complexity to design anything, comes into existence only as the end product of an extended process of gradual evolution."*[6]

I find the solution, that there is God and God created the universe, to be the simplest solution of all. Some scientific theories postulate multiverses (multiple universes in different spaces and/or times), an eternal universe expanding and contracting in cycles, life springing spontaneously from inert matter, and so on. To me, these solutions are so complex as to be ludicrous. They do not explain anything, but rather add an extra layer of difficulty to an already complex question. Applying Occam's razor,[7] that a simple, succinct solution is usually the correct one, it is easy to accept that God exists and that He created the universe.

---

6   Dawkins, R., *The God Delusion*, Bantam Press, London, 2006, Pg. 52. (Copyright © 2006 by Richard Dawkins. UK and Commonwealth: Published by Bantam Press. Reprinted by permission of The Random House Group Limited. Rest of the world: Used by permission of Houghton Mifflin Harcourt Publishing Company. All rights reserved.)

7   A principle attributed to William of Ockham (c. 1285–1349), although not originated by him. The words attributed to him, but not found in his works, are "entities must not be multiplied beyond necessity."

CHAPTER 4

Consciousness

My premise in Chapter 1 was that all that existed prior to the creation of the universe was Consciousness, that is, God or God-Consciousness. This makes Consciousness the fundamental element of the universe. As we have said, consciousness with a small c is awareness of self, environment, and mental activity, and the ability to determine choice of action. With a capital C, we have said Consciousness is all these — plus there is the expectation that Consciousness is eternal, omnipotent, omniscient, and omnipresent (at least).

But what is consciousness really? You and I (I assume) are aware of ourselves as people. We both assume, I would guess, that all other people will be equally aware of themselves. We might make exceptions for people who are newborn or perhaps handicapped in a cognitive way, but generally, we can say a person is conscious of his or her own self. We also assume everyone is aware of their environment and of their own mind — as well as the thoughts that constantly comment on what they perceive. We might also expect that people have the ability to determine their own actions, even if it is constrained in some way by outside forces.

And what of animals? Are they conscious? If you are a pet owner, or observe animals or birds in the wild, your honest answer must be yes. They are aware of themselves and their environment, and they take decisive action about when and where to eat, to drink, and to walk, fly, or swim. This is consciousness, even if it is different to human consciousness and you cannot experience it directly.

Is a brain and nervous system necessary for consciousness to be present? I would say no. Perhaps plants are conscious in their own ways too; this we can only wonder about.

You might agree, coming back to you as a person, that everything in your interaction with the world is something you are conscious of at some level. Therefore, you could say that consciousness is the essence, the unchanging inner nature, of what you are. Likewise, if your consciousness were to completely leave you, you would not exist at all, as far as you were concerned. Thus, when you die, either your consciousness dies as well, or it continues and leaves your body behind. If, as some people believe, you leave your body at death and go to a different plane, you will be aware of this experience, and therefore, will still have your consciousness. If you are not aware of it in any way at all, then it is not happening, and you are just **dead**. An absence of consciousness within yourself — at every level — means you do not exist. (People in a coma still have consciousness at some level, or they would be dead.)

Just for a few moments, consider this. What is it like to be you? Recognise that you are totally unique. There is no one else in the universe who has a consciousness of being you. You, by some strange happenstance, are you. You have your own experience of life, your own thoughts, and your own beliefs. These are all different to anybody else's. You are consciousness coming from one particular perspective. You and your experience are unique. If you look around at other people, you can see they are not you, yet you can be aware they too, individually, have this same experience of being unique with their own unique experiences, thoughts, and beliefs.

You can, therefore, definitely claim to be consciousness.

So what of Consciousness with a capital *C*? Everything we have said above applies, and because we are applying this term as a name for God, we can add the qualities of being eternal, omnipotent, omniscient, and omnipresent. Because He is the Creator of the universe, He is also likely to have a purpose for His Creation that is likely to be absolutely good, and likely to be immutable. There is no real reason to exclude these qualities from Consciousness with a capital *C*.

So, why should God be Consciousness or Consciousness be God? That is the real question. If we look at the purely physical world that operates under physical laws, one can see everything has a prior cause or source. No scientist claims anything physical, any energy, or even any physical force has ever appeared out of nothing — there is always a cause. If we go back to the Big Bang 14 billion years ago, scientists are still expecting to find some sort of cause that set the ball rolling. However, as already mentioned, no one has yet come up with a viable theory of what existed prior to the Big Bang, and what prompted it to occur.

If there was anything physical in existence before the Big Bang, it had to have come from somewhere; it had to have had a cause. One has to go back then until the very first physical thing, energy, or force, and investigate the cause of that. The only thing scientists are aware of that is not physical is *awareness* itself. It is life and consciousness. Even time, energy, and forces are reliant on physical things. However, consciousness and being (life) are not necessarily dependent on anything physical. One can imagine that consciousness, being, and intelligence could exist eternally in an uncaused way because physical laws do not apply to them.

Naturally, one could speak of the spirit world that is beyond the physical world, but this is another form of manifestation. The spirit world would, by necessity, have its own laws and structures. Whether that exists does not alter the argument one bit — it is just another layer of complication if you wish.

As we said above, you can claim to be *consciousness*, as this is what makes you exist. Yet scientists cannot explain the source or even the nature of either life or consciousness. The reason for this is that when we speak of life or consciousness, we are knocking on the door of the divine. Hence, we speak of Consciousness and God-Consciousness. God-Consciousness is not only the singular pre-existent and original force or being, but, as Consciousness was all that was available to Him as raw material, everything that has followed in the creation of the universe (and beyond) is Consciousness. The universe is made of the very fabric of God. You can say that we exist in the Mind of God. There is nothing else but God-Consciousness, and what He has chosen to develop (or allow to develop) from His Being and His Consciousness.

Consciousness (with a capital *C*) is the fundamental element of the universe, and means nothing less than this. The physical universe is Consciousness solidified into form.

In Part Two of this book, we investigate **The God Franchise**, and we look more closely at who or what God is. If you already have a preconception of whom or what God is, that is fine. If you already have a preconception of whom or what God is **not**, that is fine too.

The starting premise of this book is that God does exist. We now have to discover more about Him. I have suggested that God is likely to be conscious, eternal, omnipotent, omnipresent, omniscient, creator of the universe, purposeful, omnibenevolent, and immutable. However, we have yet not come to any conclusions on this.

We move on to a more detailed discussion about the nature of God — and why He might have bothered to design this universe in the first place. We don't really need to know this, but being the curious beings we are, we always want to understand why things are the way they are, and how we can improve them.

So sit back, put on your seatbelt if necessary, drop your preconceptions and beliefs whichever way they fall, and enjoy. Open your mind and being to a new way of viewing the Creation story. You might be surprised at what nuggets of Truth await you there.

Let me introduce you to **The God Franchise**.

PART TWO

What is
The God
Franchise?

CHAPTER 5

In the Beginning…

"*In the beginning God created the heaven and the earth.*"[8] The Bible opens with this sentence and we will start here too, or rather just before here.

Let us undertake a short meditation. If you are familiar with meditation, that's great. If not, treat this as a quiet contemplation. Know that it is safe, and you will come back to full waking consciousness afterwards. If you want to do it with someone else who can ground you afterwards, that is fine too. Whatever you do, just do this now, so you can get an idea of where we are starting.

So, with closed eyes (once you have read this paragraph, or ask someone to read it to you), go back to the time of the Creation. We will run through it backwards, starting with the creation of Man, say Adam and Eve.

Imagine them wandering around the Garden of Eden. Then, go to a time before that when there were just animals wandering Earth, eating and drinking, procreating, and living their animal lives amongst the trees and vegetation.

Next, go back to the time before that when there were just fish in the sea and birds in the air. See them as they live their lives on the ground, above the ground, and in the sea.

Next, we go back to when there was nothing on Earth except

---

8   *Genesis* 1:1

plants, and we see the creation of the Sun and the Moon and the brilliant stars above. We get a sense of daytime and night-time. We also get a sense of the four seasons.

Next, we go back to a time when there was no dry land, only sea. We become aware that the sea, the rain and the air above the sea are all one, and that there is simply moisture that resolves into the sky as sky alone. And there is Day when you turn one way, and there is Night when you turn the other way.

And then, as we go back further, Earth is dark and there is no form or substance, as it all falls away in your mind. There is nothing.

Clear the mind of everything — all concepts. And if anything arises, say to yourself, "If that goes, what remains?" Keep doing this until there is nothing left. There is no thing that you can conceive, and if there is a sense of any presence at all, it is the sense of God's Consciousness alone, with no activity, no light, and no thoughts. Just pure Consciousness, waiting.

As you come to the end of this meditation, you might focus on your breathing, on your body, and on any sounds inside or outside the room. Become aware of the seat or bed beneath you, perhaps move and stretch, and when you are ready open your eyes.

It is important that you come back fully, so have a drink of water, take some deep breaths, take a walk around, and touch things. If you are about to drive or do any other dangerous task, please be sure that you are fully back to the physical world around you. You have been back to the beginning of time, the beginning of Creation, and a time when there was nothing but God's Consciousness.

Now, let's discuss this nothingness you experienced in meditation. Imagine God there with nothing around, nothing to do, and nothing to think about. Pretty boring. Just sit there and contemplate that for a moment. Nothing except Himself, and then as Consciousness.

God had been doing this nothing for what seemed like an eternity (yes!), and then hit on a plan. *What if I had something to look at?* Now, He had no idea what He might like to look at, but He decided to create the perfect shape, a round ball of something, something that was very fluid. Since He was everywhere, He had to create this ball of fluid inside Himself, like a thought. A God thought, although He didn't quite think of it that way.

This ball had no solid substance, but was so fluid it was more like water. Also, it was very dark. *"And God said, Let there be light: and there was light."* [9] This light was just a brightness that filled the whole space, and therefore, was not much different to it being dark everywhere. Pretty unexciting. But then...

> *"God saw the light, that it was good: and God divided the light from the darkness. And God called the light Day, and the darkness he called Night. And the evening and the morning were the first day."* [10]

God now had a watery ball within His Consciousness, and a lot of space around it. He also could switch on Day when He wanted, and when it was off, He had Night. Right, what next?

> *"And God said, Let there be a firmament in the midst of the waters, and let it divide the waters from the waters. And God made the firmament, and divided the waters which were under the firmament from the waters which were above the firmament: and it was so. And God called the firmament Heaven."* [11]

This gave the ball an environment where God could take His Plan a bit further. Notice that *His Plan* can now be capitalised as it is beginning to come together. This was the end of the second day.

God was very pleased with Himself at the start of the third day.

> *"And God said, Let the waters under the heaven be gathered together unto one place, and let the dry land appear: and it was so. And God called the dry land Earth; and the gathering together of the waters called he Seas: and God saw that it was good."* [12]

God was no doubt particularly pleased with the concept He had

---

9   *Genesis* 1:3
10   *Genesis* 1:4-5
11   *Genesis* 1:6-8
12   *Genesis* 1:9-10

of a very simple structure for this matter that He was creating. He started off with 94 elements that we call the natural elements[13]. While the scientists have now tidied these up into a Periodic Table of the Elements, God's idea was 1 proton for hydrogen, 2 for helium, 3 for lithium and so on. This went through 8 for oxygen, 20 for calcium, 26 for iron, and so on until there were 94 elements ranging from 1 to 94 protons in each. He also thought, if these elements integrated with each other in various ways, He could create all sorts of interesting combinations. So, He gave each element various qualities, and these fitted in nicely and neatly with what we have come to know as the Periodic Table.

So, using all these new resources, He created Earth, and the Seas with Air above.

> *"And God said, Let the earth bring forth grass, the herb yielding seed, and the fruit tree yielding fruit after his kind, whose seed is in itself, upon the earth: and it was so. And the earth brought forth grass, and herb yielding seed after his kind, and the tree yielding fruit, whose seed was in itself, after his kind: and God saw that it was good. And the evening and the morning were the third day."*[14]

At the end of the third day, God looked at what He had created. There was Earth floating in the sky (firmament), covered in all sorts of plants, some bearing seeds, some bearing fruits, and no doubt lots of pretty flowers as well. There was only one problem. Nothing moved. It was like a giant picture in the Mind of God. In fact, it **was** a giant picture in the Mind of God.

Here God was, after all this cleverness of creating a lovely Earth, with land and a beautiful garden, with the sea, and with the sky. He could switch on the light when He wanted to, and He could switch it off. And that was it. Nothing happened. It was almost as boring as before there was anything. He was not looking forward to a further

---

13 The atomic number of an element is the number of protons (the positive charge) in the nucleus of the atom. The number 94 is the number of elements that scientists have so far discovered in nature, although some are very rare and unstable. Scientists have synthesised another 24 elements that are not known to exist in nature.

14 *Genesis* 1:11-13

eternity looking at this lot, however beautiful and clever it might be. In eternity, everything is present now. There is no sense of movement, no sense of development, and no time. Frankly, this was a real mess.

He was just about to drop this Creation as a bad idea, when a new thought came into His Consciousness. What if, instead of this on-going eternity, this infinity, this timelessness, this... timelessness – that's the answer! Let's get rid of that.

So God created time. And He created a way of Day and Night happening automatically.

> *"And God said, Let there be lights in the firmament of the heaven to divide the day from the night; and let them be for signs, and for seasons, and for days, and years: And let them be for lights in the firmament of the heaven to give light upon the earth: and it was so. And God made two great lights; the greater light to rule the day, and the lesser light to rule the night: he made the stars also. And God set them in the firmament of the heaven to give light upon the earth, And to rule over the day and over the night, and to divide the light from the darkness: and God saw that it was good. And the evening and the morning were* **the fourth day.***"* [15]

And as God watched, He saw the Sun rising and setting. He saw the Moon and the stars shining in the night. He was able to walk through the beautiful trees, and shrubs, and grasses. He could feel the wind blowing, and could see the seed scattering, and new plants growing from the seeds. He could see the flowers growing and blooming, and then falling away as the fruit formed. That too fell to the earth, and from the fruit came new plants, and so the cycle continued. The rain in the sky could now fall, feed the streams and rivers, and irrigate the plants.

This was wonderful. God had also figured out a rather neat DNA system for His plants, so that the seeds or fruits of the plant were able to produce more of the same plant. Occasionally, there were subtle changes in the DNA, when something did not quite happen as it was supposed to. Did this happen by chance? No, God had realized that now that time was able to let plants move, flow, and generate, a subtle

---

15   *Genesis* 1:14-19

change now and then would produce variations that would be more interesting. Perhaps the flowers would be different colours, or maybe the new plants would be slightly different from their parents.

Fresh (in eternal timeframes anyway) from His successes with the plant kingdom, God started looking around for further advances in His Great Scheme of Things (God's Plan was now growing!). As the plants were largely covering the land, He thought it would be great to have a bit more happening in the sea. In fact, as the water of the seas was so fluid, and could support the weight of things, He thought that moving plants might be fun. In fact, there were already some moving plants like seaweed and reeds, but how about some that might move of their own will rather than just to be swept around by the power of the currents, waves, and tides? And what about the air? That was just as fluid. There could be birds that fly, and enjoy living in the tops of the trees and eating all the seeds and fruits. They could also move around of their own will. And they would be very beautiful to watch.

So, God took the life that He had given plants, and went a step further and gave the fish of the sea and the birds of the air the freedom to go where they wanted, and to hunt out their food rather than having to wait for their food to come to them as plants did. This seemed to be a lot more dynamic and interesting. He also added improvements to His DNA structures, providing much more development to His creatures. Now they could see, so they too could enjoy the sights that God had created in the world. They could hear, and He gave them song. Song was a lot more successful with the birds, as the air seemed a much better medium than water when it came to singing.

> *"And God said, Let the waters bring forth abundantly the moving creature that hath life, and fowl that may fly above the earth in the open firmament of heaven. And God created great whales, and every living creature that moveth, which the waters brought forth abundantly, after their kind, and every winged fowl after his kind: and God saw that it was good. And God blessed them, saying, Be fruitful, and multiply, and fill the waters in the seas, and let fowl multiply in the earth. And the evening and the morning were the fifth day."* [16]

---

16 *Genesis 1:20-23*

And God enjoyed His creations. He could see through the eyes of the different birds, and view every angle of His creation from a different vantage point. He could see through the eyes of fish and whales, and all the different sea creatures in between. He could experience being eaten for breakfast. He could experience diving deep down into the ocean, and He could experience waving around in the winds at the top of a tall tree. He could see and experience all these different perspectives at the same time, and it was exhilarating.

With DNA proving to be quite a winner for getting some variation going, and with the creation so far going exceedingly well, God decided that He needed some moving creatures on Earth. They could also eat the plants to keep them under control, as they were getting quite carried away, and Earth was becoming rather overgrown with abundance.

> *"And God said, Let the earth bring forth the living creature after his kind, cattle, and creeping thing, and beast of the earth after his kind: and it was so. And God made the beast of the earth after his kind, and cattle after their kind, and every thing that creepeth upon the earth after his kind: and God saw that it was good."*[17]

The animals were also a great success, and as He now had creatures in all three mediums: air, water, and earth, He was beginning to think that this was it. It was halfway through the sixth day of Creation, so the weekend was upon Him. He certainly felt a need to rest on the seventh day so He could take time to really enjoy His Creation. The view of Earth from an animal's perspective certainly was different, but as they were all creations of His Own Imagination, He soon became very familiar with the perspectives they were giving Him.

God knew there was still something missing. He soon realised the problem was that He was viewing everything at once through all these earth, plant, fish, bird, and animal perceptions, and while there were many variations, there was a similarity about it all. It was time to crank things up a bit: time to add a joker to the pack.

> *"And God said, Let us make man in our image, after our likeness: and*

---

17   *Genesis* 1:24-25

let them have dominion over the fish of the sea, and over the fowl of the air, and over the cattle, and over all the earth, and over every creeping thing that creepeth upon the earth. So God created man in his own image, in the image of God created he him; male and female created he them.

"And God blessed them, and God said unto them, Be fruitful, and multiply, and replenish the earth, and subdue it: and have dominion over the fish of the sea, and over the fowl of the air, and over every living thing that moveth upon the earth. And God said, Behold, I have given you every herb bearing seed, which is upon the face of all the earth, and every tree, in the which is the fruit of a tree yielding seed; to you it shall be for meat. And to every beast of the earth, and to every fowl of the air, and to every thing that creepeth upon the earth, wherein there is life, I have given every green herb for meat: and it was so.

*"And God saw every thing that he had made, and, behold, it was very good. And the evening and the morning were **the sixth day**."*[18]

There are two stories of the Creation of Man in Genesis; this is the first one. Let's just step back a moment, and take it slowly.

At this stage, prior to the creation of Man, God had created Earth and the Heavens with all the stars, and the Sun and the Moon. He had created time, and with time, God had created motion, change, and a dynamic universe rather than a still painting. He had populated Earth with plants, with fish, with birds and with animals.

Be aware that everything exists only in the Mind of God. God has imagined everything in His Creation. There is no external substance to this Creation — it is made by God and is made out of the substance of God. There is absolutely nothing that exists that is separate from God. It is God.

The Creation is made in and of God.

If this is difficult to understand with your current concept of God, perhaps this is where the word (or name) Consciousness fits in. Everything consists of Consciousness, and to that totality of Consciousness we have chosen to give the name God. This is done for

---

18   *Genesis* 1:26-31

convenience; it will become clearer as we go on, and as you meditate on these concepts and live with them.

Anyway, God was tired of seeing everything He had created all at one time. He was tired of thinking up new things. He was still lonely and bored. If He spoke or asked questions, He knew the answers before He had framed the questions. It was like looking at a giant snapshot, or rather a giant movie that He had commissioned, designed, and executed. He knew absolutely everything in every detail. He knew every blade of grass and every bird, fish, and beast.

The difficulty was He was still outside time, in eternity. He needed to experience time Himself to get the fun of it. He needed to pretend to forget. He needed to put on a blindfold so He could play hide-and-seek.

He then hit on the idea of a giant jigsaw puzzle. As you and I well know, these are great fun. You (usually) know what you heading for, you've got the big picture on the box, and yet it is still fun finding all the pieces. You can become quite obsessive about it, staying up well after bedtime so you can find those elusive pieces.

While God had designed and created the big picture, He now broke it up into millions, nay billions of little pieces. Of course, there were lots of space pieces and sky pieces, and we all know how hard those are to put together. There were also separate pieces for everything He had created.

Bear in mind, God is still only One — there is only One Consciousness. He now decided to **not** let the left hand know what the right hand was doing. He created individuals, letting them feel as if they were separate from each other, and from God, although in reality, they were all different pieces of the Giant Jigsaw Puzzle called God. It was as if He allowed the myriad pairs of eyes He had created in Himself to have a mist fall over them so they could not recognise who they were.

This was the ultimate game. A giant jigsaw puzzle built in time, so there was constant change and motion. Blindfolds on everyone. Memory loss. Now, said God, let the fun begin.

*"And God said, **Let us make man in our image, after our likeness:** and let them have dominion over the fish of the sea, and over the fowl of the air, and over the cattle, and over all the earth, and over every creeping thing that creepeth upon the earth. **So God created man in his own image, in the image of God created he him;** male and female created he them."*[19] [My emphasis].

This passage is very specific that God created man and woman in His own image. In fact, He was creating them as differentiations within Himself, within His own Consciousness.

God gave Man dominion over everything that He had already created on Earth. He also gave Man the ability to *subdue* it all. Now, we know that Man has taken this instruction to have dominion and to subdue very much to heart. We are certainly working with determination on this one, and in many ways have been very successful at it.

Unfortunately, we have forgotten the part about our having been created *"in the image of God"*, or we could say, in the imagination of God. Having said that, remember this is all part of the giant game, all part of the Giant Jigsaw Puzzle that God created as the way of experiencing, expressing, and enjoying Himself.

The fun is that as we put our part of the jigsaw puzzle back together and realise our true Oneness with God, we once again become consciously aware of the God-in-Us. This is the objective of virtually every religion and every spiritual path — to reach our home in God. The Truth is we have never left home. The God-in-Us is only playing at being separated, at being individual. And what a Game it is!

We have run through the first chapter of Genesis in some detail. Let's now look at the second chapter, which is where the second account of the Creation of Man is written. Firstly, we look at the seventh day:

"Thus the heavens and the earth were finished, and all the host of them. And on the seventh day God ended his work which he had made; and he rested on the seventh day from all his work which he had made. And God blessed the seventh day, and sanctified it: because that in it he had rested from all his work which God created and made."[20]

---

19 *Genesis 1:26-27*
20 *Genesis 2:1-3*

You will have noticed that through each day, God looked at His work and "*saw every thing that he had made, and, behold, it was very good.*" He was justly very pleased with His Creation, and so, rested on the seventh day. From this day forward, there was no need for anything new to be created. Everything was in its place. The structure and dynamics had been designed and created, and the joker in the pack, Man himself, had been created and given dominion over Earth and its resources. The creative process was now handed over to Man, not for Man to create anything that was absolutely new from nothing, but so he could create new developments, new inventions, and new ideas, by using the creativity power with which God had endowed him on an individual basis.

This is The God Franchise. We will be discussing **The God Franchise** itself in more detail in a later chapter. For now though, we can understand God was very happy to be resting on the seventh day, and very much looking forward to what could transpire.

The story in Genesis now steps back a bit to the creation of rain so that the plant kingdom could grow. This would have been on the fourth day when time was created, and therefore, when the universe became dynamic.

> "*These are the generations of the heavens and of the earth when they were created, in the day that the Lord God made the earth and the heavens, And every plant of the field before it was in the earth, and every herb of the field before it grew: for the Lord God had not caused it to rain upon the earth, and there was not a man to till the ground. But there went up a mist from the earth, and watered the whole face of the ground.*"[21]

God would have been pleased with the growth of plants and their regeneration through seeds and fruits. It quickly became obvious that the birds and animals were not going to be enough to keep Earth going in a sustainable way, so God needed to create Man to "*till the ground*" and also to subdue and dominate Earth and its contents. He was placing a greater spark of His Consciousness in control.

---

21 *Genesis 2:4-6*

He started small, with Adam and Eve, and gave them the power to multiply, just as He had done with the other forms of life on Earth. This system was working well, and that is why Man was specifically designed in the same way as the higher animals, the mammals.

We will continue the story of Adam and Eve in the next chapter. It is a fascinating one.

CHAPTER 6

The Story of Adam and Eve

The story of Adam and Eve starts in Chapter 2 of Genesis, in verse 7.

"And the Lord God formed man of the dust of the ground, and breathed into his nostrils the breath of life; and man became a living soul.

"And the Lord God planted a garden eastward in Eden; and there he put the man whom he had formed. And out of the ground made the Lord God to grow every tree that is pleasant to the sight, and good for food; the tree of life also in the midst of the garden, and the tree of knowledge of good and evil." ...

"And the Lord God took the man, and put him into the Garden of Eden to dress it and to keep it. And the Lord God commanded the man, saying, Of every tree of the garden thou mayest freely eat: But of the tree of the knowledge of good and evil, thou shalt not eat of it: for in the day that thou eatest thereof thou shalt surely die."[22]

God made Man from *"the dust of the ground."* Now, bearing in mind that the ground was firstly part of His Consciousness, and secondly, that it had been created using the 94 natural elements, all this is saying is the same elements were used in making Man. God gave Man a physical body made of natural elements and breathed into that body the breath of life, just as He had done with the other living creatures on Earth. Even though we are talking of a physical body, this is still a form of Consciousness. Perhaps it is better stated as the physical body being

---

22   *Genesis 2:7-9, 15-17*

Consciousness in form. The tendency in some spiritual circles is to dismiss the body as non-spiritual and as a hindrance and limitation. The Truth is, the body is as much a part of God and His Creation as anything else, and is therefore, just as spiritual.

So, God put the man (Adam) into the Garden of Eden which included the Tree of Life (immortality) and the Tree of the Knowledge of Good and Evil. God said that Adam could "*freely eat*" of any tree except the Tree of the Knowledge of Good and Evil, as he would "*surely die*" if he did.

In this, God gave Man free will. He was allowed to do whatever he wanted to, but he was warned not to eat of the Tree of the Knowledge of Good and Evil. Nevertheless, the Tree was there in the Garden, and it was there for a purpose.

We will find out shortly what happened when Man did disobey this clear instruction and did flaunt his free will. In the meantime, back to the story.

> *"And the Lord God said, It is not good that the man should be alone; I will make him an help meet for him. And out of the ground the Lord God formed every beast of the field, and every fowl of the air; and brought them unto Adam to see what he would call them: and whatsoever Adam called every living creature, that was the name thereof. And Adam gave names to all cattle, and to the fowl of the air, and to every beast of the field; but for Adam there was not found an help meet for him."*[23]

Adam's first job was to name all the animals. "*Whatsoever Adam called every living creature, that was the name thereof.*" Man firstly had free will to call the animals what he wanted to, and secondly, he was the one given the ability to do it — and the intellect to even need to do it. The animals did not need to have names or species or any other information about themselves. They still don't today. Animals, birds, fish, and in fact every living (and non-living) thing (form of Consciousness) does not need to have a name, except for Man. He alone is interested in such things; he alone wants to classify and compartmentalise things, as well as understand them in every detail.

---

23 *Genesis* 2:18-20

While in the rest of His Creation, God had created a wonderful ecological system within His Consciousness, He had not given it the power to be independently creative. Of course, the plants and creatures would evolve over time, but they had no in-built creative spark to do anything except live their lives and procreate. He had not given them the power of thought, inspiration, creativity, and independence. So, while He enjoyed His Creation, it was like a wonderful walk-in nature movie. It was great as far as it went, but it wasn't very exciting. God needed some excitement, some real source of interest. This is why He created Man.

Since He had already created male and female of other species so they could procreate, God decided to do the same for Man, so that he could also *"be fruitful and multiply."*

> *"And the Lord God caused a deep sleep to fall upon Adam and he slept: and he took one of his ribs, and closed up the flesh instead thereof; And the rib, which the Lord God had taken from man, made he a woman, and brought her unto the man. And Adam said, This is now bone of my bones, and flesh of my flesh: she shall be called Woman, because she was taken out of Man. Therefore shall a man leave his father and his mother, and shall cleave unto his wife: and they shall be one flesh. And they were both naked, the man and his wife, and were not ashamed."* [24]

So God created a wife for Adam made of his flesh, or in other words, the same chemical elements and DNA. Adam immediately got the idea of fatherhood and motherhood, and the children leaving them to take a wife so that they could be of one flesh. Adam was certainly not slow. Although they were both naked, they were not ashamed of their nakedness, but were comfortable with it. The woman had not been given a name yet, but as we find out much later, after their spot of bother with the serpent and the fruit of the Tree, *"Adam called his wife's name Eve; because she was mother of all living."* [25]

Now, I am sure that Adam and Eve would have had a wonderful time in the Garden of Eden. We still talk about that Garden today,

---

24   *Genesis* 2:21-25
25   *Genesis* 3:20

and when artists draw their renditions of it, it is always represented as the most beautiful place on Earth. Both Adam and Eve had free will, as granted by God, so they would have been able to do whatever they wished to do.

As we have said already, God would have experienced the Garden too, through the eyes and the experiences of the happy couple. No doubt, He would have experienced human sexual activity for the first time too, as the pair had been told to be fruitful. It was all too lovely.

Now God had created the Tree of the Knowledge of Good and Evil. He started to become impatient as He thought that by now, the couple, who were adventurous in so many other ways, had not really taken much interest in the Tree. God really wanted to see what effect the Knowledge of Good and Evil would have on Man with free will.

So, He hit on a plan. He solicited the help of a snake, a talking serpent at that.

> *"Now the serpent was more subtil than any beast of the field which the Lord God had made. And he said unto the woman, Yea, hath God said, Ye shall not eat of every tree of the garden? And the woman said unto the serpent, We may eat of the fruit of the trees of the garden: But of the fruit of the tree which is in the midst of the garden, God hath said, Ye shall not eat of it, neither shall ye touch it, lest ye die.*
>
> *"And the serpent said unto the woman, Ye shall not surely die: For God doth know that in the day ye eat thereof, then your eyes shall be opened, and ye shall be as gods, knowing good and evil. And when the woman saw that the tree was good for food, and that it was pleasant to the eyes, and a tree to be desired to make one wise, she took of the fruit thereof, and did eat, and gave also unto her husband with her; and he did eat."*[26]

The serpent was very persuasive. Here was God saying that the Tree of the Knowledge of Good and Evil must not be eaten, yet He had given Adam and Eve free will. And then there was the other view: You won't die, and instead your eyes will be opened and you will be as gods, knowing good and evil. Eve now saw the Tree as the source of wisdom, and having been designed by God to seek wisdom, she ate of

---

26   *Genesis* 3:1-6

the Tree. Adam, not to be outdone by a woman, easily followed.

Adam and Eve had free will, they had access to the Tree, and they were aspects of God's Consciousness. Even in ourselves, we know temptation is great, that a secret is a great source of interest, and that mystery is an even greater one. We are made in God's image and the temptation for God Himself was too great. What if Adam and Eve ate of the Tree of the Knowledge of Good and Evil? What would happen?

What's more, God has a sense of humour; we can be sure of that. And everyone likes a good mystery, even God. God would not have created the Tree of the Knowledge of Good and Evil without a purpose. I cannot believe He created it as some sort of power token, as something He could dangle in front of Adam and Eve, and expect them to ignore. No. He wanted Man to have free will, and to take Consciousness to the furthest stretches of the imagination. After He has discovered that they have eaten of the Tree, God says: *"Behold, the man is become as one of us, to know good and evil."* [27]

If you look back over the Creation story, you will see that at this point there was no evil. It was not that the Tree was the Tree of Good and Evil. It was that it was the Tree of the **Knowledge** of Good and Evil. Evil can be seen as an absence of Good. By believing in this absence of Good (God), Man has taken on a veil[28] of unconsciousness. It was part of the Game. It was putting on the blindfold so that God could play hide and seek. It was mixing up the pieces of the Giant Jigsaw Puzzle so God could put it all back together again. It was taking on the *"**Knowledge** of Good and Evil."*

Some people believe that the serpent was Satan. Whether it was or not is actually irrelevant. God had created the serpent, because He had created everything. Whether God gave Man free will first, or whether He gave it to a serpent (or Satan) first is a moot point. The end result was the same: Man now had the Knowledge of Good and Evil, and this was an **essential part of having free will**.

---

27 *Genesis* 3:22
28 I use the term "veil" many times throughout the book. It is used in the sense of *"something that covers, conceals, or separates; mask"* (*Collins English Dictionary*). The plural implies the many layers of coverings or masks we have taken on.

So the story of Adam and Eve continues:

"And the eyes of them both were opened, and they knew that they were naked; and they sewed fig leaves together, and made themselves aprons. And they heard the voice of the Lord God walking in the garden in the cool of the day: and Adam and his wife hid themselves from the presence of the Lord God amongst the trees of the garden. And the Lord God called unto Adam, and said unto him, Where art thou? And he said, I heard thy voice in the garden, and I was afraid, because I was naked; and I hid myself. And he said, Who told thee that thou wast naked? Hast thou eaten of the tree, whereof I commanded thee that thou shouldest not eat?"[29]

As soon as Adam and Eve had eaten the fruit of the Tree, *"the eyes of them both were opened, and they knew that they were naked."* This means they became self-aware. They each took on their own Ego, and started to see the differences in each other, and the need to protect themselves — their newfound image of their individuality and separateness — from each other.

Animals do not see others of their species in a deprecating way, or in a moral or judgemental way. Only Man does this, and that is **not** due to his free will per se, but rather due to his sense of Ego and separateness. Adam and Eve, therefore, felt self-consciousness and guilt for the first time. They felt they were naked and hid from God, and guilty because they had eaten of the fruit of the forbidden Tree.

As if playing hide-and-seek, God *"called unto Adam, and said unto him, Where art thou?"* Of course, God knew where they were since He was their Consciousness as we have said before, but He had chosen to start playing the Game. Adam and Eve had the veils of the Knowledge of Good and Evil covering them, so they no longer realised they were aspects of God; they felt they were separate entities.

"And the man said, The woman whom thou gavest to be with me, she gave me of the tree, and I did eat. And the Lord God said unto the woman, What is this that thou hast done? And the woman said, The serpent beguiled me, and I did eat."[30]

---

29 *Genesis* 3:7-11
30 *Genesis* 3:12-13

Immediately, their separate Egos started to blame someone else. Adam blamed Eve, and Eve blamed the serpent. Adam even hinted that it was God who gave him this woman who had led him astray, so maybe it was God's fault! Adam and Eve were totally under the spell of the Ego. This is where the concept of Original Sin has arisen, although it is not so much sin as separateness and self-importance, collectively called Ego.

"And the Lord God said unto the serpent, Because thou hast done this, thou art cursed above all cattle, and above every beast of the field; upon thy belly shalt thou go, and dust shalt thou eat all the days of thy life: And I will put enmity between thee and the woman, and between thy seed and her seed; it shall bruise thy head, and thou shalt bruise his heel."[31]

God clarified that with the Knowledge of Good and Evil also came an enmity or ill-will between humans and serpents (and all animals?). While Man still had to subdue them, it would not be easy due to this enmity. Bearing in mind that the serpent is also in God's Consciousness, it could not be truly cursed, except that there would be a sense of separation and friction between one species and another. In case you were wondering, there is no sense that serpents had legs before this time, or that they actually eat dust now.

This cursing of the serpent in the presence of Adam and Eve would have added another veil, and would have reinforced their separation from the animal kingdom. It would have raised fear in them with regard to serpents and many other animals.

"Unto the woman he said, I will greatly multiply thy sorrow and thy conception; in sorrow thou shalt bring forth children; and thy desire shall be to thy husband, and he shall rule over thee." [32]

Eve was faced with her own femaleness. She had to go through the pain of childbirth, with reliance on her husband, and being ruled by her husband. Women through the ages have been the "weaker sex." Cartoons of cave dwellers show the men dragging their women around by the hair. Women in the West have only gained their rights in the

---

31   *Genesis* 3:14-15
32   *Genesis* 3:16

twentieth century, and even today, they tend to be lesser-paid, expected to do all the housework, expected to look after the children, and so on. In the Middle East, Asia, and Africa, men continue to be dominant. One can certainly view this state of affairs as being related to the respective Egos of men and women in general terms. However, this is gradually changing as both men and women become more enlightened, and as both sexes move closer to their spiritual heritage.

> *"And unto Adam he said, Because thou hast hearkened unto the voice of thy wife, and hast eaten of the tree, of which I commanded thee, saying, Thou shalt not eat of it: cursed is the ground for thy sake; in sorrow shalt thou eat of it all the days of thy life; Thorns also and thistles shall it bring forth to thee; and thou shalt eat the herb of the field; In the sweat of thy face shalt thou eat bread, till thou return unto the ground; for out of it wast thou taken: for dust thou art, and unto dust shalt thou return."*[33]

Adam was not let off lightly either. Since he had now aligned himself with his Ego, he forgot that all resources were available through his spiritual heritage in Consciousness. He was lost in matter (*"cursed is the ground for thy sake"*), and he would have to rely on material food. This would bring sorrow, *"thorns also and thistles,"* and he had to sweat at work until he died and returned to the dust from which he was created. Man was now lost beneath the veils of Ego, self, and materialism.

> *"Unto Adam also and to his wife did the Lord God make coats of skins, and clothed them. And the Lord God said, Behold, the man is become as one of us, to know good and evil: and now, lest he put forth his hand, and take also of the tree of life, and eat, and live for ever:*
>
> *"Therefore the Lord God sent him forth from the garden of Eden, to till the ground from whence he was taken. So he drove out the man; and he placed at the east of the garden of Eden Cherubims, and a flaming sword which turned every way, to keep the way of the tree of life."*[34]

Of course, God did not reject Adam and Eve because they had taken this path with their free will, because as we have said, this was

---

33 *Genesis* 3:17-19
34 *Genesis* 3:21-24

all part of the Game. So, as a token of His care, and recognition of their self-consciousness, God gave them coats of skins to cover their nakedness.

God recognised that Man was now in a position of having the use of God's power through being a God Franchisee[35]. He was now *"as one of us"* and able *"to know good and evil."* This recognises Man's heritage in Consciousness, it recognises there were now multiple forms of being (*us*), and it recognises the world of duality (*good and evil*).

Now, God prevented Man from taking the next step of eating of the Tree of Life, which means immortality. If Adam, in his state of Ego and self-consciousness, should gain immortality, he would be locked into that state forever. While it seemed like a punishment to drive Adam out of the Garden of Eden, it was really allowing for any Ego to die after a comparatively short life so that that Ego/Man could reassess his life and actions, with the aim of eventually regaining the Garden of Eden through realisation of his True Self.

Man naturally does have immortality through Consciousness. However, his Ego does not, thank God.

Here endeth the lesson.

Let us summarise what we have learned from the story of the Creation and Adam and Eve, as given to us in the first three chapters of Genesis:

+ God designed and created the universe in order to experience, express, and enjoy Himself. (This is not being facetious — extrapolate this into divine terms).

+ God made everything of His own substance, namely Consciousness. He did not, and could not, create anything outside Himself.

+ Although God was outside time in the Eternal Now before the creation, He created time within His Creation in order for there to be motion and change.

+ God saw everything He had made, and behold, it was very good.

+ God made Man in the image of Himself. Man thus has creative powers.

---

35 Explained in Chapter 11.

+ God made Man in and of Himself. He added a blindfold and veils so that Man does not have omniscience.

+ God gave Man free will to generate variety and add a random factor to His Creation.

+ Man was given dominion over every other form of life on Earth.

+ Man's free will allowed him to choose whether to eat of the Tree of Knowledge of Good and Evil.

+ It was a Tree of **Knowledge**, not a Tree of Good and Evil. God did not create Evil. Evil is a perceived absence of good (or God) — it is the veil of unconsciousness.

+ Man used his free will to eat of the Tree, and so was laid open to sorrow and toil and then thrown out of the Garden of Eden. This was due to his now having an Ego and a feeling of separation from God.

+ Women became the weaker sex, and men are still dominant now in most parts of the world, although there is a shift, particularly in the West. Man became lost beneath the veils of Ego, self, and materialism.

+ God recognised that Man now had the use of the power of God. He acknowledged Man's heritage in Consciousness, and that men and women now lived with multiple forms (individuality/separation) and in the world of duality (good and evil).

+ Man was kept away from the Tree of Life (immortality) so that he would not be eternally locked into a state of Ego and self-consciousness.

+ Man has immortality through Consciousness. Ego does not.

+ Man was associated with the ground (the physical world), and would continue that association until physical death.

Having learnt all these things from a careful reading of the first three chapters of Genesis, let us see where this knowledge takes us in understanding more of God's universe and His Purpose.

CHAPTER 7

"But I Don't Believe in Adam and Eve..."

Okay, if it helps you, I don't believe in Adam and Eve either. Maybe the whole Creation story from beginning to end is just a big story. So what?

I must admit, I have always been fascinated by the story of the Creation and by Adam and Eve; and while it might not have happened just like that, I do believe that Truth underlies this whole story. You may also think that my extension of the Creation allegory is going a bit far. Perhaps I have not gone far enough. Hidden in this story is the most exciting Truth the world has ever known, or for that matter could ever know. That is what is important to me, and that is what counts. This most exciting Truth is what this book is really about, so stay with me. The biblical story is just one of many creation stories. Most, if not all cultures, have one. I happen to like this one, as it is the one I know and the one that is part of the culture I grew up in.

Before we continue with our exploration of the creation of the universe, and discuss why there even is one, let us quickly summarise the major different beliefs that are held on this subject. My main thesis is not to prove or disprove these beliefs, but rather to present a view that encompasses them all, and I do this in Part Three of this book. It is helpful to know what the alternate views are.

We start with creationism for clarity's sake, as my exposition of the Genesis story has not been quite what creationists might expect.

Creationism

The basic tenets of creationism are:

+ God created the universe and all life through specific acts of creation.

+ Evolution theories (Darwinism) are not correct, and are atheistic.

+ The creation acts of God occurred over seven 24-hour days, as described in Genesis 1 and 2.

+ The Bible, as a whole, can be taken literally. It is the Word of God.

+ Earth is about 6,000 years old.

+ The fossil layers that geologists have found are about 4,300 years old, from the time of Noah and the Flood.

+ There was no death until Adam and Eve disobeyed God and ate of the Tree of the Knowledge of Good and Evil, as described in Genesis.

Evolution and Atheism

While it is true that not all those who believe in evolution are atheists, perhaps the reverse is true — that all atheists are believers in evolution. In their purest forms, these two approaches to this subject appear to go hand in hand, so we will treat them in that way.

The basic tenets of evolution and atheism are:

+ There is no need for a God to explain the world around us.

+ All current forms of life can be explained as having evolved from earlier forms of life through genetic mutation and natural selection (survival of the fittest).

+ It all started with a Big Bang about 14 billion years ago. Earth is about 4.5 billion years old, dinosaurs lived in a period between 230 million years ago and 65 million years ago, and modern Man (*Homo sapiens*) came on the scene about 150,000 years ago.

+ Religious faith is irrational and is based on blind belief and wishful thinking.

✦ So much evil has been done in the name of religion, (e.g. wars, imprisonment, and execution for beliefs; the Crusades; and the Inquisition) that any God has effectively been discredited.

It should be noted that atheism only started to gain ground with the advent of evolutionary theories. The greatest impetus to this was the publication of Charles Darwin's *The Origin of Species* in 1859. In the briefest of summaries of his theory, Darwin says, *"one general law lead[s] to the advancement of all organic beings, namely, multiply, vary, let the strongest live and the weakest die."*[36]

As science developed at an ever-increasing rate, it has done much to confirm and develop the theories of evolution. Such work, in particular the decoding of DNA, has added much weight to scientific beliefs. The scientific alternatives to Darwin's summary above are largely variations on a theme, or have been discredited or withdrawn by their authors.

The Big Bang? Let's cover that in a bit more detail. In 1929, Edwin Hubble was able to provide observational data to indicate the universe was expanding, and that if you calculated backwards, you would be able to determine the age of the universe. The present age, which has been corroborated many times using different methods, is about 14 billion years. All matter in the universe started from one point in space about 14 billion years ago in what has come to be known as the Big Bang.

I say one point in space, but that is not strictly true according to recent discoveries. Martin Rees, Astronomer Royal, makes it clear that there is no specific point in space from which the universe expanded; rather, it expanded from every point in space.[37]

Research by scientists and mathematicians continues, and many theories have been proposed. The big questions are, What existed before the Big Bang, and what happened immediately before the Big Bang? So far, no one has answered that question. They also haven't answered the questions of, What is the origin of life? How did complex

---

36 Darwin, C., *The Origin of Species by Means of Natural Selection, or The Preservation of Favoured Races in the Struggle for Life*, 6th Ed., John Murray, London, 1876, Pg. 234.

37 Rees, M., *Just Six Numbers: The Deep Forces that Shape the Universe*, Basic Books, New York, 2001, Pg. 67.

cells first get started? What is the origin of consciousness? No doubt, there are other major questions like these that remain unanswered.

Intelligent Design

On the surface, the idea of intelligent design seems very attractive. It appears to combine creationism and science in an easily acceptable way, that is, science and evolution theories are reasonable, and this was the way God planned it. Instead of creating each species separately, God created the mechanism whereby they could evolve, with the pinnacle of evolution being Man himself.

Unfortunately, this is not what intelligent design (ID) is saying. ID was first written about by Phillip Johnson in his book *Darwin on Trial*[38] about 20 years ago.

The basic tenets of intelligent design are:

+ The evolutionists have got it wrong, as there are many complexities in organisms that are *irreducible complexities*. What this means is that there are a number of components necessary to carry out a specific function, and they all need to be present in order for their purpose to be carried out. Therefore, they could not have evolved, but need to have been designed.

+ DNA provides messages of *specified complexity* so needs to have been designed by an intelligent designer rather than by natural selection.

+ This is a fine-tuned universe, which has a number of constants in play. If any of these constants had a different value, then life as we know it would not have been possible. Therefore, there must have been an intelligent designer.

+ The proponents of intelligent design do not state who the intelligent designer is, although the consensus is that it is God.

+ The intelligent design thesis does not fulfil its promise and leaves us little better informed.

---

38   Johnson, P., *Darwin on Trial,* InterVarsity Press, Downers Grove IL, 1991.

These are the three main theories regarding the nature of God and the explanation of the universe in the Western world today. While there are many other approaches, particularly from the different religions around the world, I feel certain that you, as a reader of this book, are likely to associate with one of the above, or perhaps a variation or combination of them.

Having covered the main approaches to explaining the universe, and in preparation for our exploration of **The God Franchise**, I would like to outline the various –*isms* that attempt to define God:

+ **Theism**: The belief that there is a God and that He has an on-going relationship with His Creation. God is seen as personal, and actively governing and organising the universe. Adherents to mainstream Christianity, Judaism, and Islam are thus theists.

+ **Deism**: The belief in the existence of God and that He created the world, but that He does not alter His original plan and so does not intervene through miracles, revelations, and the like. Neither does He interact with the world in any way. God may even be dead or involved elsewhere in the universe. Deism founds its religious beliefs on reason and the observation of the natural world around us. **Polydeism** allows for more than one god.

+ **Pantheism**: The belief that God is identical with the universe and with Nature. Therefore, there is no transcendent,[39] separate, or personal God, and there was no act of Creation. Nature itself is sacred, and is being discovered through science. There are three types of pantheism:

  + Naturalistic pantheism (monist physicalist pantheism or scientific pantheism) which believes that the only substance is matter/energy.

  + Monist idealist pantheism believes the only substance is mental/spiritual. Ultimate reality consists of a single Consciousness. This is the basis of Buddhism.

---

39   Transcendent – existing outside the created world.

✦ Dualist pantheism believes in both physical and mental/ spiritual substances as being significant. Many different New Age type beliefs fall into this group.

✦ **Pandeism**: This is the belief that God created the universe, is now one with it, and so, is no longer a separate conscious entity. This is a combination of pantheism (God is identical to the universe) and deism (God created the universe and then withdrew Himself).

✦ **Panentheism**: This term was coined by Karl Krause in 1828, and means "All is in God." It is a combination of pantheism and theism. The belief is that the whole universe is within God, plus there is part of God that remains outside His Creation.

✦ **Panendeism**: This is a new term coined by Larry Copling in 2001 to offer a deistic version of panentheism. As he defines it in his website: *"The doctrine that all of physical reality (the 'universe') exists within the Deity and is created by a 'projective' evolutionary process that is on-going, self-evolving and ultimately co-creative in nature."*[40] There is also an emphasis on rational thought.

✦ **Gnosticism**: The True God is seen as transcendent and beyond the universe, and even beyond the act of Creation. However, the universe is an emanation from within Himself, so everything consists of the essence or substance of God. Nevertheless, the universe is seen as flawed since its substance is far removed from the essence of the True God and has become corrupted and changed in the process. The Demiurge assumed the role of creator, but is not the Supreme Being (True God). There are other gods that exist between the True God and Man. Gnosticism is based on personal religious experience rather than theology and philosophy.

✦ **Atheism**: The belief that there is no God or that He is irrelevant to us if He does exist.

✦ **Agnosticism**: The belief that we can only know the universe

---

40 Copling, L., PanenDeism FAQ, Updated 2009, Available http://www.panendeism.com/FAQ. html , Sighted 2 June 2010. Quote used with the author's permission.

through science, and knowledge of a Supreme Being is, therefore, impossible.

+ **Antitheism**: The active opposition to theism and religious beliefs.

+ **Monotheism**: The belief or doctrine that there is only one God.

+ **Polytheism**: The belief in more than one god. These gods are grouped into a pantheon or temple of gods. Hard polytheism is where the gods are seen as separate beings, whereas soft polytheism sees the different gods as reflecting different facets of the one Supreme Being. Some schools of Hinduism fall into the hard and some into the soft polytheism groups.

+ **Autotheism**: This is worship of oneself as a deity, or that one can aim towards becoming divine.

+ **Paganism**: These beliefs vary considerably, but tend to be polytheistic (hard or soft), refer to Nature as divine manifestation, and often see the female principle as sacred (the Goddess).

There are many other –isms relating to God; however, we have covered the main ones here. These others do not serve much purpose for this current discussion, yet you may find them interesting. *Wikipedia* on the Internet is always a good resource.

It might be tempting to try to pigeonhole **The God Franchise** into one of the above slots. I have admittedly tried to do this myself. However, I know that in what I have to say there is a subtle difference that is worthy of investigation. I won't give it a new *-ism* name, as I suspect all the best ones have been used up. We'll just stick with **The God Franchise**.

As promised, in the next chapter I take a fresh look at the subject of God and the Creation. I accept that the thesis I am about to expound may be a very old one, or one developed by other writers or philosophers. I am sure I will get to hear about them as this book makes its appearance in the world, perhaps directly or through **The God Franchise** blog. Any constructive thoughts or developmental information about **The God Franchise** will always be most welcome.

I am ready for the next chapter now. Are you?

CHAPTER 8

Before the Creation and Why There is One

L et's take this slowly. I realise that the view of God and the Creation that I present here may be radical from your perspective, and that it would be very easy for you to dismiss it out of hand. I appeal to you to let your mind relax a little and stay open to an alternative viewpoint. Yes, you have your beliefs, and I respect those. Nevertheless, I ask you to suspend those beliefs and preconceptions for a short period while you take in something a bit different.

It is only by seeing the whole picture, and perhaps even by spending some time sitting with it, that you will get to understand **The God Franchise**. Perhaps you will find that it does sit comfortably with you, and perhaps it does explain a few things that you have had trouble with previously, and perhaps it is not wholly incompatible with what you already believe. Maybe there is a different way to view God and His universe, whatever beliefs you already hold in that regard.

Before it All

What happened or what existed before the start of the universe? If we look at the three current theories of the source of the universe, we find that, frankly, no one knows. The Creationists, using the Bible, say, *"In the beginning God created the heaven and the earth."*[41] The scientists have no reasonable or consistent theory of what came before the Big Bang.

---

41 *Genesis 1:1*

Stephen Hawking is reported to have said in October 2005 on a UK TV show (*Richard and Judy*) that the question was as meaningless as the question *"What lies north of the North Pole?"*[42] The intelligent design theory does not cover what came before the "Creation" at all.

There is an alternative to the universe we see around us today, and that is absolutely nothing. Think about it. There could easily be absolutely nothing. Why not? Why bother? If there were nothing, no one would know that there was nothing. There would be no universe of any type and no God or Eternal Being. There would be no life of any description. There would be nothing. Nothing at all. Just consider it for a moment.

If there were nothing, then how would anything get started? Nothing has no qualities whatsoever and has no urge, consciousness, or footholds from which a God and/or a universe could arise. We obviously do have a very wonderful and complex universe around us today and we have life. This could not have started from nothing. That is impossible and illogical.

We all agree: Creationists, atheists, scientists, and the rest of us, that the universe did start at some point. We disagree about when, but we do agree that there must have been a time before the Creation (if I may call it that) or before the universe started.

If there was no universe, and there was also **not** absolutely nothing, then there was something there before, which was powerful enough to set the whole ball rolling. That essential starting point was Consciousness.

Based on history and convention, that Consciousness is called *God*. Remember this is just a name for the one Power, the one Force, the one Consciousness that pre-existed. However, the term God has many connotations, and many different uses of the word — and in a sense, I like to steer clear of it. So, for clarity, I have chosen to use the term *God-Consciousness*.

I described Consciousness in Chapter 4. With a small *c*, it is awareness of self, environment and mental activity, and the ability to

---

42   Stephen Hawking, At http://en.wikipedia.org/wiki/Stephen _ Hawking , Updated 24 May 2010, Sighted 27 May 2010.

determine choice of action. With a capital *C*, I suggested it is all these; plus, as It existed before the start of the universe, I suggested that Consciousness is eternal, omnipotent, omniscient, and omnipresent. If you were to consider this now, would you agree that God-Consciousness might have these qualities? If not, what part of this description do you think is unrealistic?

We have no way of scientifically proving the existence of God-Consciousness, so I appeal to your inner-self and to your intellect to accept that this state of Consciousness could conceivably have existed prior to the start of the universe, and that it could have been the motivating force to start the universe. May I suggest that even if you have doubts about it, accept it for a moment as a given, since this is fundamental to the rest of this discussion.

If you believe in God already, perhaps the idea of using the term God-Consciousness might not be too difficult for you. The qualities you associate with God, such as He is eternal, omnipotent, omniscient, and omnipresent, still apply. However, I do have something else to ask of you, depending on your existing beliefs. The God-Consciousness I describe here is an all-pervading Consciousness (as in all present), so He is not a Personal God. He has no form — He is formless. He does not reside specifically in Heaven. He resides everywhere — both inside space and time and outside space and time. He is not **a** being, but Being.

"For in him we live, and move, and have our being."[43]

"Who knoweth not in all these that the hand of the Lord hath wrought this? In whose hand is the soul of every living thing, and the breath of all mankind."[44]

For those who do not believe in God, I ask you to believe in Consciousness. It is a bit like asking you to believe that the principles of mathematics existed prior to the start of the universe. Is that fair enough?

---

43   *Acts* 17:28
44   *Job* 12:9-10

To summarise: Before the universe was created, there was either absolutely nothing at all, or there was God-Consciousness. Since we have a complex universe around us, and you, I, and a few other people are here and alive, there could not have been nothing, since there would have been no motivation to get started and no raw material with which to start. Therefore, God-Consciousness had to exist prior to the start of the universe, prior to the Creation.

The Motivation for a Creation

There is God-Consciousness and nothing else.
There is God-Consciousness and nothing else.
There is God-Consciousness and nothing else.
There is God-Consciousness and nothing else.
There is God-Consciousness and nothing else.
Great isn't it?

So, there is God-Consciousness and nothing else. And God-Consciousness is eternal, all-powerful, all-knowing, and all-present. What is the point? You might ask. And no doubt God asked Himself the same question.

God needed to experience Himself; God-Consciousness needed to experience Itself. At this stage, God-Consciousness was no more than Potential, formless Potential. While we cannot even start to conceive of what that must be like, it would seem obvious there was not a lot for God to see or do. It would be a lonely existence. So, God needed to do something about it.

Being omnipotent and omniscient, He created a ball of His Energy and placed it in a space in His Mind/Being/Consciousness.

He then caused it to explode in a tremendous Big Bang...[45]

---

45   While the science and mathematics of it all is beyond me and beyond the scope of this book, the possibility that God created the universe as a Big Bang — with the precise physics and chemistry necessary to create, over a period of time, the conditions we now know — is quite acceptable. The Big Bang theory does not invalidate God or The Creation. In fact, it supports the proposition that God exists and is The Creator.

Before we continue too far through this story, let's spend a few moments looking at the motivation God-Consciousness had at this time.

Firstly, let's go back to God or God-Consciousness. His experience can be the same as ours. In other words, if He were not aware or conscious of His own Being, He would cease to exist. Since we have agreed that Consciousness needs to exist or there would be absolutely nothing, we can take it that God is aware of God-Consciousness, always, eternally.

Let me add, as a caveat, neither you nor I can be specific about what God is like, what His qualities are, or what His motivations are. Everything I have written about Him, if taken literally, is probably wrong. However, I offer signposts towards what God might be like, what the universe might be like, and how everything might work. This is not a traditional scientific thesis. It is intended to reach you at a more subtle level. Please indulge me a little longer.

Cast your mind back to the time before the Creation, before the Big Bang. There was nothing except God-Consciousness. Nothing at all. Do you not think, in our terms, that God would be bored? His experience would be of.... Well, not a lot anyway. It would be like looking at a blank photograph. A photo of the inside of the lens cap. Looking at that eternally, that is, forever.

Now, I expect that an omniscient God would be smart enough to figure out that there would be some fun in experiencing more than this. He may have come up first with a black and white (or even sepia) photo. Boring. How about a colour photo? No, still boring. How about a moving picture? God could watch movies all day. Well, how about a live action world that He could sit up here and watch? No, this is all still very superficial. He needed to *really experience* what He was seeing.

Therefore, I submit that God-Consciousness did just that. He did not create a world that He could watch voyeuristically from Heaven. No, He created a world that He could take part in and experience first-hand.

God-Consciousness is eternal. This means that He had no beginning and will have no end. Does this mean that He experiences all time at once? That is beyond the knowable and understandable. It is, in truth, incomprehensible. Whether that is true or not, one imagines He might be interested in seeing how things progress sequentially. To see everything at once might seem to be an unholy mess, to use a word. When you have all time (and beyond), why not see some of what you can experience sequentially. See it develop. See it change. See evolution.

God-Consciousness is omnipotent. This means that He can do anything, and there is nothing that is too big or too powerful for Him to achieve. Handling a Big Bang is not an issue. God-Consciousness is omnipresent. This means He is everywhere: in every cell in your body, and in everything that you do, be it *good* or *bad*. He is in every square inch of the universe. He experiences the universe from within.

God-Consciousness is omniscient or all-knowing; therefore, if He needed to figure out the constants that govern the universe, that would not be a problem. If He had to figure out how evolution would work, that would not be a problem either. Neither would the Law of Gravity, the Laws of Mathematics, the Laws controlling the structure of matter, and so on. God can figure it out and set it all in motion ahead of time. Bearing in mind that He is outside time if He chooses to be, He can be sure that all the things that need to be in place for the future will be there when they are needed. The universe could be *"like a well-oiled machine"* as described by the philosopher and mathematician, Leibniz.[46]

Therefore, God-Consciousness had the motivation and the ability to create the universe, and that is what He did. He also did not create something out of nothing, as that is impossible. What He did create was the universe out of His very essence. He created the universe out of Consciousness.

Before we leave this chapter, let's just recap. Before the Creation, there was either nothing or there was God-Consciousness. Since there cannot have been nothing or we would never have got started, there had to be God-Consciousness. God-Consciousness had no way of experiencing anything without a Creation, an active environment in which He could take part. He, therefore, created the universe.

The next chapter covers a few thoughts on Time and Space before we move on to take a look at God's Plan, now that He had decided a universe was necessary.

---

46   Gottfried Leibniz (1646-1716) — German philosopher and mathematician, who invented the binary system and many other concepts.

CHAPTER 9

Thoughts on Time and Space

Time

Before God-Consciousness created the universe, there was no *time*. There was just an eternal Now. There was no movement, no change — just an immutable Now. God's Consciousness was aware and could think (if you like), and everything that He was thinking was Now.

So let's represent this Now as a rectangle:

God-Consciousness is aware of the whole of this Now, and there is no sense of time or linearity as we know it in our four-dimensional space-time world. There is just an eternal Now, without change.

With the Creation, God-Consciousness created a space-time bubble inside this Now. Let's represent it as follows:

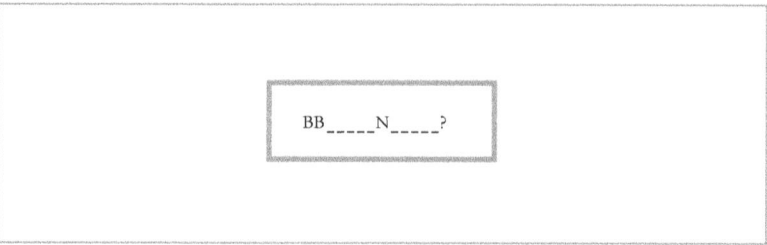

Where BB = The Big Bang – the start of the universe
      N = Now – today as you read this
      ? = The end of our universe at some future time (to us)

So, God-Consciousness continues to be aware of the whole of Now still as represented in the larger rectangle, and He also has a space-time bubble within that. From the outside, He can see all time, while within the space-time bubble, He will experience time in a linear way through consciousness as you and I experience time and space.

Of course, there is no reason whatsoever why there may not be a multiplicity of these space-time bubbles within the Now.[47] You and I will not be able to experience those, I would surmise, but there is no reason why God-Consciousness could not. Whether there are multiple universes or not has no impact on our on our lives; therefore, our interest in them is more curiosity than necessity. Whether they exist or not is conjecture; and either way I cannot see that the reality has any significance to us here on Earth.

We will represent the various different possible space-time universes as follows — just for fun:

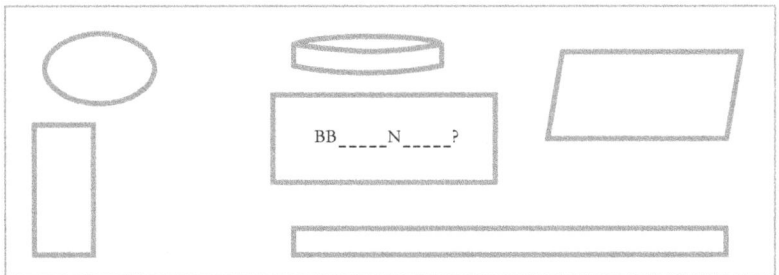

Whether these space-time bubbles operate in the same way as our universe doesn't matter either. Anything is possible, but is of no interest or significance to us. We have enough on our plates in our

---

47   Note that I am not thinking in terms of the multiverse theory which allows for almost an infinite number of universes so that ours has the appropriate conditions for life merely by chance. I am suggesting that there is no reason for there to be only one universe, the one we know and love. There could be other "physical" universes with totally different forms of life/ non-life and experience.

own universe without concerning ourselves with all this. Let God-Consciousness sort it out, as it is His Creation anyway.

Space

When God-Consciousness was existent before the Creation, there was no space either. There was everywhere or nowhere. There was just Consciousness in a timeless Now and without space. So, just as God-Consciousness created *time* to allow change, He also created three-dimensional *space* to allow a physical world to exist.

We don't need the drawings again as they are the same as those above. God-Consciousness is omnipresent in a spaceless Now. He then created one or more space-time bubbles to contain one or more universes. Each universe could have different rules; of course, we are unlikely to ever experience them, and that does not matter to us.

Our universe, which is a four-dimensional space-time continuum, is all we need to concern ourselves with.

Additional Note

There are those readers who believe in other dimensions such as the angelic realms, the spirit world, etc., and that is absolutely fine. Perhaps these are other universes we are contacting, despite what I said above; or perhaps, the angelic realms and spirit world (etc.) are a part of this universe. It does not matter, and you are very welcome to believe, and have your proof of, whatever conceptual permutations are appropriate for you.

I do not want to get into these finer points now; and anyway, they do not affect the main thrust of this book about **The God Franchise**; however, I certainly am not invalidating these larger scale concepts.

CHAPTER 10

God's Plan – the Ultimate Game

We have discussed the motivation of God-Consciousness to create a universe, and we know He is capable of designing it in any way He chooses, as He has omniscience, omnipresence, and omnipotence as resources.

I agree with the philosopher Gottfried Leibniz that God would have created the best possible world. Remember, God-Consciousness is doing this for His own purposes, just as we always do the best that we can for our own purposes and with the resources available to us. Since God-Consciousness had all possible resources, He would have created the best possible universe.

Looking around us, the universe does work pretty well. I would say it would be the ultimate arrogance to suggest anyone could do better. Sure, I agree, there are things we are not happy about, but I genuinely believe there is a very **good** reason for everything that happens in this universe. I would never dream of questioning what has happened, and what is happening in the world. I believe **everything is in its right place**, and **everything is perfect just as it is**.

There is apparent evil in the world. There are wars, massacres, rapes, murders, lies, fornication (a good old-fashioned word), theft, and dishonesty. There are also natural disasters like floods, tornadoes, fires, earthquakes, tsunamis, storms, landslides, and so on. There are personal tragedies like severe illness, disabilities from birth, poverty, abuse, personal loss, and death. While these are not pleasant experiences for the people involved, they are not the signs of a dysfunctional Creation or an inept Creator. We touch on this subject in the next chapter; so, for the meantime, let us put the questions we might have about apparent evil to the side.

God-Consciousness had the purpose of creating a universe that allowed Him to experience Himself. He, therefore, had to create the universe within Himself. As there was nowhere He was not, it would have been impossible for Him to do otherwise (assuming I can use the word *impossible* with regard to God!).

God's Plan was the ultimate game. One could view it as a game where God-Consciousness split Himself into lots of tiny pieces, and forgot who or where He was, with the object of putting the jigsaw puzzle pieces back together again and then removing the blindfold and regaining His memory so He once more knew He was God-Consciousness. I realise that this sentence is complete nonsense as it sits here, but I suspect it does point to something like the Truth. These words may be written in a light and playful way, but there is real Truth behind them.

Instead of there being one point of God-Consciousness as there was before the Creation, He wanted there to be a universe where He would be able to experience things from every possible perspective:

He could feel how a rock feels warming in the Sun.
He could feel the rain on His petals.
He could feel His fruit being eaten by a bird.
He could taste the fruit like a bird.
He could make love as a badger.
He could make love as an elephant.
He could make love as a man.
He could make love as a woman.
He could see the beauty of the sunrise.
He could be the power and light of the Sun.
He could swim as a fish in the sea.
He could be pushed helplessly as seaweed in the currents.
He could be smashed on the rocks.
He could feel joy as a child.
He could feel the pain of a rejected lover.
He could drink the water.
He could drink the wine.

He could die in the desert.

He could die on an executioner's cross.

He could experience the flight of the electron in the atom.

He could mystify scientists.

He could be a mystified scientist.

He could make spells.

He could make smells.

He could rot on the ground.

He could enrich the earth with His life-blood.

He could break His leg.

He could heal His leg.

He could be without legs and slither on the ground.

He could be inside the mouth of a lion.

He could be inside the stomach of a whale.

He could smile.

He could cry.

He could live at the depths of the ocean.

He could be a molecule of water at the greatest depths in the ocean.

He could be the next molecule of water to that, rubbing up against it.

He could fly through the air as a beam of light, or as a bird.

He could be the air, the trees, the earth, and the sky.

He could live on Earth or on Mars or on Betelgeuse.

He could use a telephone.

He could design a rocket ship.

He could be inside a turbojet at full power.

He could fling Himself over a waterfall, as a drop of water and as a log.

He could experience the fullness of life in the universe.

You may have the idea by now. God-Consciousness is in everything and is everything. As the Bible says, *"For in him we live, and move, and have our being."*[48] And it is not just you and me, it is **everything** that is in Him, that lives in Him, and that moves in Him. I am **not** saying this from a religious viewpoint. I am saying this from a realist viewpoint. This is how it is.

---

48 Acts 17:28

With these sorts of experiences and goals in mind, God-Consciousness set about creating the universe exactly as it needed to be to fulfil these ideals. While God-Consciousness would be able to interfere if He needed to, there was no challenge in constantly tweaking this universe when something went wrong. As He could see ahead in time how things would pan out, He could create the universe with a set of rules or Laws that would see it through.

I am certainly not able to list what is needed to create a universe; however, our scientists have figured out some of the requirements, for instance:

> A stable set of rules or laws
> Oxygen, water, and carbon to sustain life
> A particular range of temperatures to support life
> A particular set of universal constants (Martin Rees[49] describes six of these)
> A supply of energy to make the universe dynamic
> And so on …

And so it was that God-Consciousness created a universe that met His requirements. While complicated in its details, mind-boggling in fact, it is very simple in its concept. We, as humans, overcomplicate things as far as I can see. The real Truths are essentially very simple.

God-Consciousness created the universe in a Big Bang. He created the Laws that were needed and the building blocks of matter — namely the 94 natural elements in a very simple system we can see today in the Periodic Table of the Elements. He watched through time as 14 billion years passed, developing the rich and bountiful world we have around us today.

Finally, the time came for Man to appear on the scene. Bearing in mind that God-Consciousness is within each person on this Earth — in fact, within each cell of the bodies of each person on this Earth, and *is* them — He played His trump card.

He introduced **The God Franchise**.

---

49   Rees, M., *Just Six Numbers: The Deep Forces That Shape the Universe*, Basic Books, New York, 2001. We discuss these six constants in Chapter 15.

CHAPTER 11

The God Franchise

We have covered a lot of ground so far, and it is time to bring the discussion closer to home. The big question that needs to be answered now is, "Who am I?" With all this talk of God-Consciousness, it can start to get rather theoretical out there. What we need to do now is bring it back to me. What does this all mean to *me*?

We also need to define **The God Franchise** so that we can understand how that fits in. So first, let's go through the qualities that are attributed to God and see how these are interpreted within **The God Franchise**. Then we will discuss **The God Franchise** and why that term is used.

Finally, we will look at ourselves as individuals. You will be able to take this part very personally.

God and The God Franchise

At the outset, we defined God as follows:

+ God is conscious
+ God is eternal
+ God is omnipotent (all-powerful)
+ God is omnipresent (present everywhere)
+ God is omniscient (all-knowing)
+ God is the Creator of the universe
+ God is likely to have a purpose for His Creation

+ God is likely to be absolutely good (omnibenevolent)
+ God is likely to be immutable (unchanging through time)

We came to a point where we said that God is better defined as God-Consciousness in order to get away from any connotations associated with the word *God*. This is only for the purposes of this discussion. The term God is totally acceptable, and I have used it throughout this book — anyway, the name is only a pointer.

So let's take each of the above attributes and summarise what we can deduce and now know about God.

+ **God-Consciousness is conscious**. It (He) is Being. It is alive. The definition of a Personal God is one *"having the attributes of an individual conscious being."*[50] At this stage, let us avoid thinking of God as a person in the way that you and I are persons, and think of It as a focussed awareness and consciousness much as you might experience in the deepest meditation, or when all feelings of self are absent.

God-Consciousness has no sense of separation from anything. It is totally aware and present in this moment. It has total experience. It has no need for doing — just being. It has no desires, no emotions, no human-like qualities — just pure consciousness.

Having said that in the best way I can, now let's extend that sense of God-Consciousness into the realms of the Unknowable and just allow whatever is really there to be there as our unbiased, un-predetermined, unlimited, formless sense of God-Consciousness. This sense we now have is a tiny pointer to the true essence of God, which we can best simply call God-Consciousness.

+ **God-Consciousness is eternal**. This means that God-Consciousness has no beginning and no end. It is difficult for us to conceive of anything having no beginning and no end because in our experience there is nothing like that. Nevertheless, logically, it is possible there could be something outside time. There is no reason whatsoever why consciousness cannot be

---

50   *Collins English Dictionary*

eternal. Perhaps a good analogy is the Laws of Mathematics. They are eternal would you not agree? No one invented $1 + 1 = 2$. It just is, was, and always will be.

I used a diagram earlier, and I will repeat it here.

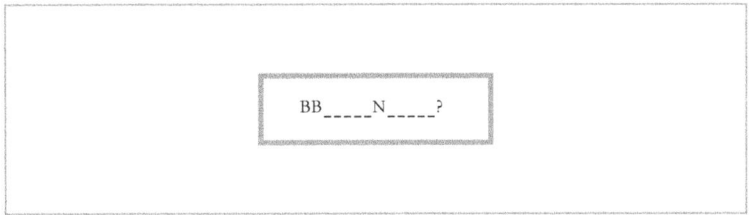

(Where BB = The Big Bang, N = Now, and ? = The end of our universe at some future time)

God's view is the whole of this larger rectangle (and of course beyond it) as the Eternal Now that He knows. In the midst of it, He has created a space-time bubble which has past, present, and future — and which is not eternal. The universe we know started with the Big Bang 14 billion years ago and, no doubt, will end one day in the distant future.

Our space-time bubble is held in God-Consciousness, and exists there. If He decided to discontinue our space-time bubble, He literally could just forget it. It would cease to exist. Now, do not be alarmed. There is no reason why God-Consciousness would do this — there would be no point. He has kept us going for 14 billion of our years so far, and long may the years continue. However, if He did decide to forget us, it would not matter one iota, as absolutely everything would be gone and only God Himself would be aware of its going, if He chose to. You wouldn't feel a thing.

So, it is totally reasonable for God to be eternal, even if nothing else is. As we have already said, everything has to have a cause, as something cannot come out of nothing. Going back to the beginning of time and beyond, we find the Prime Cause, Whom we have called God or God-Consciousness. Since there needs to be a cause for everything, there cannot be a time when a Prime Cause, or the very first cause, did not exist. Therefore, God has to have existed forever. Yes, God is eternal.

+ **God-Consciousness is omnipotent** (all-powerful). There has been much argument on this point. Just think about it. If absolutely everything is held in God-Consciousness, then anything that exists or could exist is within the power of God to create. If something like the square circle is logically impossible, then God cannot create it either. This does not reduce His power. As C. S. Lewis said, *"[God's] omnipotence means power to do all that is intrinsically possible, not to do the intrinsically impossible. You may attribute miracles to him, but not nonsense."*[51]

God-Consciousness can do whatever He can conceive of doing. Since there is nothing that can be conceived where God-Consciousness is not the one conceiving it, then nothing more powerful can exist. So, there is no need for any definition of what omnipotence means other than it is as powerful as it gets — however powerful that might be!

+ **God-Consciousness is omnipresent** (present everywhere). If God-Consciousness is the very substance of every aspect of our universe, and of all other possible universes, as well as Himself, He is by definition, omnipresent. He is everything that is. There is nothing else that exists.

+ **God-Consciousness is omniscient** (all-knowing). God-Consciousness could not have created something out of nothing. It doesn't work like that. God used His own substance, which is Consciousness to create our universe, and any others He might have created. Science knows that things get a bit strange when you go into the makeup of the atom, which can be seen as the fundamental unit for the existence of all physical matter. I am not a scientist, but I have read of the strange behaviour of matter there, and that it starts to look less like matter and more like consciousness the deeper you go. Likewise, energy and matter are interchangeable as in Einstein's $E=mc^2$ (where E is energy, m is mass, and c is the speed of light in a vacuum) and matter/energy cannot be created or lost, just transformed.

---

51   Lewis, C., *The Problem of Pain*, Harper Collins, San Francisco, 2001, Pg. 18. Copyright © C.S. Lewis Pte. Ltd. 1940.

When God wrote the Bible (i.e., God-Consciousness wrote the Bible as various human writers — just as with any other book), His omniscience knew nothing about the motorcar, the computer, the Internet or TV. Does this make Him less than omniscient? Of course not. God-Consciousness is aware that anything can be brought into being as it proves to be necessary or desirable, yet He has neither preordained nor forecast any specific inventions or developments. The potential for all inventions is, nonetheless, inherent in God-Consciousness. As He has developed the specific fundamentals of modern life through individual human inventors, His knowledge of these things has increased as the inventors' knowledge has increased, because they are identical (when looked at from God's viewpoint).

So, if God-Consciousness is the very substance of every aspect of our universe, and of all other possible universes, as well as of Himself, He is by definition omniscient. He knows everything that is, because He is everything that is. There is nothing else that exists.

+ **God-Consciousness is the Creator of the universe**. Oh, yes, as described above.

+ **God-Consciousness does have a purpose for His Creation**. Without His Creation, God-Consciousness is nothing but eternal nothing and some idle musings about nothing. As we said, with all due respect, this could get boring. So, God's first purpose in creating the universe was to add experience, expression, and enjoyment into His Life. God-Consciousness experiences what it is to be a grain of sand on the beach, to be the Sun that warms it, and the wave that cools it. He is the child who puts it into a bucket and He is the bucket. How much experience, expression, and enjoyment can God take?

God-Consciousness added free will into the mix when He created Adam and Eve and gave them access to the Tree of the Knowledge of Good and Evil, and this resulted in the appearance of Ego. Now, there is no need for a tree or a snake or Adam or Eve really, this allegory (if you prefer it that way) just says that Mankind was given free will. This means that each individual was given the right, the permission, to do whatever he or she wanted to do. This freedom quickly turned into Ego as one man thought he could be better than another man. He also chose to discover the knowledge of good and evil. This is the start of duality. Before that, there was only what we might call good (which we discuss next).

So, coming back to God's purpose, another purpose is for His Creation to learn to see through the futility of Ego and evil. From God's perspective, it is all experience, and at the same time it is illusion (*maya*); it would be wonderful to see all that has come out of Pandora's Box[52] returned inside and locked up forever. It would be very rewarding to see His Creation, and humanity in particular, realise the Truth and then to voluntarily recapture and lock up Ego and duality in Pandora's Box for eternity.

I described the universe as a Giant Jigsaw Puzzle that God-Consciousness created so He can put it together and show off the beauty of His perfect Creation. God's purpose is to put this puzzle together. Then, as with all great jigsaw puzzles, He can either frame it and look at it forever, or break it up into pieces and start again.

+ **God-Consciousness is absolutely good** (omnibenevolent). This attribute has also been very controversial, as one looks around at all the so-called evil in the world. So, let's take it slowly.

Before Man discovered the knowledge of good and evil, there was neither. There was just whatever was, and that was not judged as being either good or bad. When, in Genesis, God sees everything that he has created day by day, He sees that "*it is good.*" This does not mean good as opposed to bad or evil, it means that it is perfect according to His Plan.

---

52   Pandora's Box (or jar actually) is described in a Greek myth. Pandora was the first woman on Earth (i.e., the Greek Eve) and she was given a sealed jar as a gift from the gods. It contained all the evils and misfortunes of existence. Pandora's curiosity overcame her, and she broke the seal and allowed misfortune, disease, and sorrow into the world. Hope was supposedly trapped inside and that was all that was left.

Likewise, plants and animals do not judge things as good or bad. If a tree gets its leaves eaten by a passing giraffe, this is not bad. Even if an elephant uproots the whole tree, this is not evil. Likewise, if a lion is able to bring down a zebra or baby wildebeest, this is not evil; it is the law of the wild. Plants and animals live in the Now and face whatever the conditions, experiences, and situations are now, and the fittest survive.

So, God too is as He is, and that is it. Nothing He is or has created is either good or bad. It is just what it is. It is all in keeping with how things should be and how they are, as created by God, and as experienced by God-Consciousness through us. Therefore, we can say that God-Consciousness is omnibenevolent because He has not created anything for an evil purpose — everything is created for a positive purpose as just discussed. He has not set out to torture, to destroy, to goad, to cause pain, or to cause sorrow. His Creation is perfect, and He is perfectly omnibenevolent.

It is Man and his Ego, abusing free will, this gift from God, that has created the notion of good and evil. All the crime, wars, rape, pillage, and torture that men and women have imposed on others have come from Ego. If a true understanding of God and His universe were realised by everyone, then all evil would cease. Even natural disasters – floods, earthquakes, drought, eruptions, tsunamis, plagues – are merely part of the way things are. They are not intrinsically evil. We judge them so, particularly when we are caught in the midst of them. However, great good can come from these things too. In the end, it is all experience. The very worst thing that can happen is that we die and the earthly experience ends. From the perspective of God-Consciousness, who is our very being, this is acceptable and perfect in the moment.

God-Consciousness is absolutely good (omnibenevolent) in reality, which is God's perspective of things. Any view to the contrary comes from the Ego and is illusion (*maya*).

+ **God-Consciousness is immutable** (unchanging through time). God Himself is unchanging in that He has no need to change.

Also, with His view of the Eternal Now, there is no need to change in essence. Nevertheless, as we have said above, within the confines of God's experience, within His creation, there is all that change, growth, evolution, experience, invention, and development offers. By putting on a blindfold and experiencing time as you and I experience it, God-Consciousness experiences movement, change, life, joy, and excitement. And this is within His overall immutability.

So What is The God Franchise?

We will start with describing a franchise as developed in the business world. A franchise agreement between a franchisor (the originator) and a franchisee (you) allows you to create and run a business under the franchise name, and market and sell the franchised product or service. For the privilege of being able to do this, you pay the franchisor a franchise fee, plus a percentage of the sales of your business. In return, the franchisor provides the systems you will need to run the business, as well as some marketing support, including group advertising.

So, if we tabulate the key concepts of a franchise, we arrive at the following:

Franchisor: the originator of the franchise
Franchisee: you, who wish to benefit from that franchise
Franchise Agreement: the agreement between these two parties
The Offering: the product, name, brand, and concepts which make this franchise valuable
The Systems: the rules, procedures, and methods which enable this franchise to operate profitably for everyone
Franchise fee and royalties: any returns to be paid to the franchisor for these ongoing benefits
Non-exclusivity: except for a specific territory
Ongoing support
Start-up costs
Business plan: your plan for making the franchise work
Brand recognition

Advertising and global marketing by the franchisor
Training
A franchise is already a functioning business system
Turn-key business: everything is provided ready to operate
All franchisees share responsibility for maintaining high standards for the brand
The ability to quit the franchise at some future time

You may be able to think of some other key concepts – if so, just go ahead and add them.

The God Franchise takes this concept to the ultimate. It states that God-Consciousness can be seen as a Franchisor, and that you and I and every other person on this Earth individually is a Franchisee. By creating Mankind in his own image, **God-Consciousness franchised His Creative Power to each and every man and woman on Earth.**[53] This is a key concept of **The God Franchise**. In addition, God-Consciousness gave us free will (as He naturally has), consciousness, and purpose. In fact, he gave us all his qualities to a greater or lesser extent, and we will discuss these in a moment. He franchised everything to each of us in what may be termed **The God Franchise**.

Now, before you get too carried away with this concept, let's look at it more closely. It does not mean that you can rush off and create universes. We have many veils covering our Godhead (such as unconsciousness, Ego, self, separateness, and materialism), and there are some other constraints we will cover in the next few chapters.

So let us take the table of key concepts of a franchise and add **The God Franchise** to it. It will end up looking something like this:

---

53 There could be civilisations in other solar systems that have similar opportunities, but we will stick with planet Earth. I have generally avoided the issue of other inhabited planets, but this is for simplicity only.

BUSINESS FRANCHISE	THE GOD FRANCHISE
Franchisor: the originator of the franchise	God (or God-Consciousness)
Franchisee: you, who wish to benefit from that franchise	You and me, individually
Franchise Agreement: the agreement between these two parties	Your birth certificate. Also, the fundamental code by which you live your life (e.g. moral code, life's purpose, etc.) is your personal pact with God-Consciousness.
The Offering: the product, name, brand, and concepts that make this franchise valuable	The ability to create and be a creator; individual life and free will.
The Systems: the rules, procedures, and methods that enable this franchise to operate profitably for everyone	Universal Laws (God's Laws)
Franchise fee and royalties: any returns to be paid to the franchisor for these ongoing benefits	The experience of the ups and downs of life, pain, and suffering until you learn the realities of creation and free will. For some people, it is a life of devotion, worship, and/or a commitment to use these powers for the benefit of all. It is also enlightenment and/or conscious creation for the evolution of the universe.
Non-exclusivity: except for a specific territory	Each of us, individually, is our own territory.
Ongoing support	We have constant support from God through His Universal Laws and His Grace.[54] Our Higher Self is God-Consciousness incarnate so provides the ultimate support.
Start-up costs	Going through the pain and suffering of having veils over our consciousness. Also, our time and effort to learn how to free ourselves from the veils, overcome the Ego, and rediscover God-Consciousness.
Business plan: your plan for making the franchise work	Both God's Plan and our own determination to follow a specific plan to achieve what we desire.
Brand recognition	Personal Creative Power. Son/daughter of God.

54   More about God's Grace in Part Four.

Brand advertising and global marketing	Books like this one. All the books, scriptures, teachers, gurus, courses, religions, sermons, and churches promoting the Power of God that is within each one of us.
Training	Life experience, study, and meditation, seeking the Truth, scientific work, spiritual work, opening to the Now, and being present.
A franchise is already a functioning business system	Creative Power and the Universal Laws are already proven in the universe.
Turn-key business: everything is provided ready to operate	Everything is provided.
All franchisees share responsibility for maintaining high standards for the brand	We collectively share responsibility for keeping standards of personal creation high.
The ability to quit the franchise at some future time	We cannot quit. Only God-Consciousness could take that power away from us, and that would likely mean annihilation.

You and I are franchisees in the ability to create and to live our lives from a divine perspective. However, there is a vast difference between using **The God Franchise** consciously and using it unconsciously. The main theme of Part Four of this book is the practical implications of **The God Franchise** in our daily lives. In particular, we will see what happens to us when we are unconscious or unaware of the existence of this birthright, this God Franchise, and what happens when we work with it consciously.

The Extent of the Franchise

This is all very well, you say, but does that make me God? No, not quite. Just because God is you, does not make you God. Just because you are a McDonald's franchise holder does not mean you are McDonald's! It means you have the right to run a store according to some very strict rules, and you are compensated for your efforts. However, you also need to pay dues to McDonald's Corporation, and you cannot claim to be the McDonald's Corporation.

So, let us look at the qualities we have identified as being God's qualities and see how we are able to use these as a God Franchisee.[55]

---

55   I expand on all these qualities in the next chapter.

GOD	THE GOD FRANCHISEE (YOU AND I)
Conscious	We are conscious; however, we do cover our consciousness beneath many veils. We do much that is unconscious and we are unaware of our true selves. We have a Higher Self and a Lesser Self, and only the Higher Self could be seen as truly conscious, although, of course, our Lesser Self cannot see even that.
Eternal	We, as individuals, are not eternal; however, it is entirely possible/probable that we maintain our individuality for longer than just our stay on Earth for three score years and ten. Our God Essence is eternal, and if and when we lose our individuality, we merely drop back into the Ocean of God-Consciousness, which is eternal.
Omnipotent	We do not have all power; however, we do have all the power we need. The Law of Manifestation[56] attracts into our experience whatever it is that we want or need, either consciously or unconsciously, and without fail.
Omnipresent	We are not omnipresent; however, we are able to move outside our present location in time and space through our minds. We can also do this these days through modern communication systems. In spiritual terms, we can attain God-Consciousness through meditation and similar practices if we are so inclined. We can also learn much about presence by being present at all times in the Now. Any restrictions on where and when you are present are self-imposed.
Omniscient	We are not omniscient; however, we can find out whatever it is we wish to discover. These days this is assisted through the Internet. The main constraint is our own Ego that holds us in limitations and preconceptions. We have the ability to shake off these shackles if we so desire. Any restrictions on what you know or understand are self-imposed.
Creator of the universe	We cannot create a universe; however, we do create our own lives. We create our lives through the Law of Manifestation whether we do it consciously or unconsciously. This is a major aspect of **The God Franchise**, and the other aspects follow as we allow them into our lives. You could say we create our own universe.

---

56   Discussed in detail in Chapter 34. It is also commonly called the Law of Attraction.

Has a purpose for His Creation	We each have a purpose: to use our free will and to experience. We can direct this purpose wherever we wish to direct it, and, by being ourselves, we fulfil God's purpose of experience. We can also have specific purposes for our own lives which we either identify through determining our life's purpose, or which we can be given. When you have found your life's purpose, you feel happy and fulfilled, and you feel directed towards achieving what it is you need to achieve.
Omnibenevolent	We are omnibenevolent in our Higher Self; however, our Lesser Self is caught up in the illusion of the Ego. It is from the Ego and the *misuse* of our free will that evil derives.
Immutable	We are immutable in our essence (Higher Self) as we are a splash in the Ocean of God-Consciousness; however, in the environment of time and space, and in terms of our Lesser Self, we do change.

As spiritual adepts know, it is possible to get close to God-Consciousness. In doing that, they usually, if not always, leave behind the trappings of the earthly experience. However, as you can see above, we have a lesser set of powers than God-Consciousness. All the powers and qualities of God-Consciousness are represented in each of us in a more manageable potency. We have all the powers and qualities we need and, frankly, all we can handle.

Nevertheless, whether we are a spiritual adept, a high-flying businessperson, or a beggar in the street, we have an equal stake as a God Franchisee. God is an equal-opportunity franchisor!

CHAPTER 12

Who am I Then?

The final chart in the previous chapter gave you an overview of what it means to be a God Franchisee. We also mentioned the Higher and the Lesser Self. Let us spend some time going through these concepts in more detail as they are critical to your understanding of God as God-Consciousness and of you and your role in His Plan. We have discovered that each one of us has, as a birthright, a franchise with God-Consciousness – **The God Franchise**.

It is time to look at you and me. We will look at every individual person on this planet, irrespective of what religion or what beliefs he or she has. We are all in this together, and more together than you might think. I will address you, the reader. However, you will know at the same time we are discussing what is true for every other you in the world of seven billion people.

Essentially, you are made up of two parts. Let's call them a Higher Self and a Lesser Self, but this is just for convenience. However, let me rush to add that the two parts are not quite so distinct, and, therefore, I ask you to give this description some careful open-minded contemplation.

The Higher Self

In the first instance, you are a part of God-Consciousness. God-Consciousness is one whole (the One God we speak of) present in the Eternal Now, and within Himself he has differentiated a Creation in order to have experiences. As a child might play blind man's bluff,[57] God has blindfolded Himself and has taken on an individual form, many times over. Each one of us is a blindfolded subset of God-Consciousness.

To put things in perspective, it is not so much that you are God — it is that God is you. Does that make you (your Higher Self) conscious, eternal, omnipotent, omniscient, omnipresent, a creator, with a purpose, absolutely good and immutable? Let's take these questions one by one.

+ **Are you a conscious being?** The answer is Yes. That is the importance of being present in the Now — the importance of the *Power of Now*[58] as presented by Eckhart Tolle. It is very easy to get caught up in the machinations of the Lesser Self, and in day-to-day affairs, so losing sight of our Higher Self Consciousness. However, God-Consciousness does not lose sight of Itself, thank God!

When we pray, it is to a Personal God — it is to our Higher Self, the personal form that God-Consciousness is taking. When we meditate, we are in communication with our Higher Self. When we sit quietly and receive inspiration or intuition, God-Consciousness is talking to us. Our Higher Self is talking to us. As Alfred, Lord Tennyson wrote, *"Closer is He than breathing, and nearer than hands and feet."*[59], and Florence Scovel Shinn wrote, *"Prayer is telephoning to God, and intuition is God telephoning to you."*[60]

When we are focussed and giving our whole being to a task in complete enthusiasm, honesty, and openness, we experience the consciousness of the Higher Self. However, much of the time we cover our consciousness under many veils, and, therefore, act unconsciously.

---

57 Also called blind man's buff, this game is similar to the children's game Marco Polo.
58 Tolle, E., *The Power of Now*, Hodder Headline Australia, Sydney, 2004 (Originally published by Namaste Publishing, Vancouver, 1997).
59 Alfred, Lord Tennyson (1809–1892) in a short poem *The Higher Pantheism*.
60 Shinn, F. Scovel, *The Wisdom of Florence Scovel Shinn*, Simon & Schuster, New York, 1989 (including *The Power of the Spoken Word* (1945)), Pg. 337 (Permission:*The Power of the Spoken Word* by Florence Scovel Shinn| DeVorss Publications | 9780875162607| www.devorss.com).

+ **Are you an eternal being?** The answer is Yes. Your Higher Self is eternal because it is God-Consciousness. You were never born and will never die. However, we are talking here of the Higher Self, which we compare to a splash of water from the Ocean of God-Consciousness that is briefly separated from the Ocean, and then falls back into the Ocean again.

The Lesser Self certainly dies as we realise the illusion it is, and we will discuss this in a minute. The physical body dies because it is not designed to live forever — it wears out over time, what we call a lifetime. The Higher Self is God-Consciousness with a blindfold on. We retain our individuality in this lifetime and possibly in further lifetimes (and I say this without prejudice either way), and one day the blindfold comes off, when God is ready, and we will recognise and be recognised for who we truly are: God-Consciousness Itself.

+ **Are you an omnipotent being?** The answer is No, although you do have all the power you need. While God-Consciousness is omnipotent in the Eternal Now, He has put on a blindfold in coming to form as you. This has also reduced His power to a level that is appropriate to you. Imagine if He gave seven billion people both free will and omnipotence! Yes, it is not a pretty thought.

So, for the purpose of experiencing life in form, God-Consciousness has reduced the power that is available to the individual. Remember, He does have the power to do this, so this statement is not a cop-out. Nevertheless, the power that your Higher Self does have is phenomenal when measured against what you normally use. The fact that it is not omnipotence is really just academic.

You can achieve whatever you desire to achieve, and God's Laws (to be discussed shortly) are there to assist you with that. The Law of Manifestation attracts into our experience whatever it is that we want or need, either consciously or unconsciously.

+ **Are you an omnipresent being?** The answer is No. Nevertheless, you can travel in thought to distant places, times, and concepts. By using modern technology, you have the ability to communicate with people in other places with ease. We can approach experiencing God-Consciousness in meditation and other spiritual practices. We can experience presence in this moment by being present in the Now, as described by Eckhart Tolle.

Your Higher Self, as God-Consciousness, is a part of God's overall omnipresence. In addition, every cell of our bodies, every molecule, even every atom, contains a spark of God-Consciousness because the whole universe is made from the substance of God-Consciousness. Omnipresence is thus the totality of these individual presences, if you like.

+ **Are you an omniscient being?** The answer is No, although you do have access to all the knowledge you need. Your Higher Self does not know everything, once again because of the blindfold. However, there is access to everything you need, as and when you need it. Carl Jung wrote of the collective unconscious, and we are told there are the Akashic Records[61] that purport to hold all the information of the universe. I am not saying these exist, although it does make sense that we have access to a vast amount of information and knowledge that is not normally available when one is restrained by the limitations of the Lesser Self. It may be easy to interpret this as accessing the Mind of God through your Higher Self.

If what I have just said sounds a little esoteric to you, that is fine. Let's look at it in a different way. When you go to your Higher Self, consciously or unconsciously, seeking inspiration or help with some particular problem, you are always able to get an answer. Sometimes you get the answer directly, and other times

---

61 The Akashic Records are sometimes called a "hidden library" or "The Book of Life." The concept is that everything that has happened is recorded in the Akashic Records "in the ethers" or at a level of consciousness, and that these records can be accessed in deep meditation or under deep hypnosis. There are individual records for each of us through many lifetimes, as well as wider records. Famous readers of the Akashic Records include Rudolf Steiner, Dion Fortune, Madame Blavatsky, and Edgar Cayce. There is no *scientific* proof that the Akashic Records exist.

you are directed to a person who can help you or to a book that contains the information you need. No problem is too hard to solve, and using your Higher Self to find the answer is the best way to go. It is interesting that often scientists discover the same facts about the universe or develop the same ideas at roughly the same time as each other, without working together or even being aware of the other's work. Carl Jung called this synchronicity.

From a practical point of view, it is also sensible that you don't know everything. It would leave no room for the growth of knowledge and experience. As we have said, even God-Consciousness is acquiring new information and knowledge as we individually add to that knowledge through our experiences of life. Your Higher Self is the medium of God's experience and knowledge accumulation.

In the search for information, we are assisted by modern tools such as the Internet. We are in the Information Age. Our biggest constraint is our own Ego that restricts us with preconceptions and limitations. We have the ability to shake off these shackles if we desire to.

+ **Are you a creator?** The answer is Yes. This is an important and very practical part of **The God Franchise**. God-Consciousness created the universe out of His own substance. You create whatever you create in life out of the substance of the universe. Nothing can be created out of nothing — not even God can do that. As inventors have shown, there is no limit to the innovations that can be created. Science has no boundaries, certainly not in its own sphere, and all that work is creative work. The source of the inspiration is the Higher Self, God-Consciousness. The main tool we have is the Law of Manifestation, and with this, we create our lives and life experiences, whether we do it consciously or unconsciously.

+ **Are you a being with a purpose?** The answer is Yes. Firstly, you are fulfilling God's purpose, and after all, that really is the only significant purpose. We have already discussed God-Consciousness' purpose, so I will summarise: To add further experience, expression, and enjoyment to God's experience of Himself, to see through the futility of Ego and evil voluntarily, and to put the universal puzzle (The Giant Jigsaw Puzzle) together, so that He can then frame it, or break it up and start again.

At an individual level, you can choose many other purposes in life, ones that suit your interests and your talents. These purposes all add to the experience, expression, and enjoyment of God-Consciousness, and with them you make positive use of your free will.

+ **Are you a being who is absolutely good?** The answer is Yes. This is true at a Higher Self level. Any evil, mistakes, or badness is the doing of the Ego in the Lesser Self. You look at any young child and you see good, not evil. Everything a person does is with a positive intention. If that positive intention is for evil, or is in some other way misguided, this is because it has been driven by the Ego, the Lesser Self. It has been driven by pain and ignorance.

In essence, in your Higher Self, you are perfect and absolutely good.

+ **Are you an immutable being?** The answer is No. Immutable means unchanging. As we have said, God-Consciousness has no need to change at the formless level. However, by putting on a blindfold and experiencing the Now that you experience, God-Consciousness experiences movement, change, life, joy, and excitement through your Higher Self.

In summary, we can say that the Higher Self, which every one of us is individually, is similar in quality to God-Consciousness Himself in five of the nine attributes that we have discussed. In the case of the other four — omnipotence, omniscience, omnipresence, and immutability — it is illogical for us individually to have those qualities. Nevertheless, we have access to all the power and all the knowledge we could possibly need. We collectively provide God's omnipresence and provide God with the experiences of Life that He needs, without compromising His immutability.

You may not realise that you experience your Higher Self directly quite frequently during the day. I would like to clarify what this feeling is so you can get a clear experiential sense of it. You might be surprised to find you do not have to be an overtly spiritual person to experience your Higher Self on a regular basis. By the same token, there will be some regular churchgoers (synagogue-, temple-, mosque-goers) who very seldom if ever experience their Higher Selves.

How about, right now, experiencing your Higher Self? Just allow yourself to relax and find space away from your day. You can sit or lie down, or you can go for a walk in the garden or in a park. You can even do some gardening, or some other easy effortless activity you enjoy. Choose a space where you will be undisturbed. Relax into wherever you are and allow yourself to think gently about something you really enjoy doing, or someone or something you love intensely. Feel happiness rise in you about that positive experience you have brought to mind. Realise this is your very own experience and you can enjoy it. There is no sense of competition with anyone else about this activity or thought. It just makes you feel warm and comfortable inside. If you could keep this up for the rest of the day, you would be happy. All is well with the world. There are no issues you have to attend to. This is your time now.

Notice some things around you. It might be a bird in the tree, a flower in the corner or a picture on the wall. Appreciate its beauty. Acknowledge its presence, and thank it for showing itself to you. Move on to another thing. Allow this state of peacefulness and presence to stay with you for as long as you wish.

This is what your Higher Self is like. The feeling may be subtle at first, perhaps because you have been unaware of it, or have not put any significance on it. It is when you feel at peace with the world. When everything is going well for you and there are no issues weighing you down. It is like being on a very enjoyable holiday. It may be a spiritual experience for you, or you may prefer to put it into other terms. Whatever you call it, you will recognise it as being a deeper sense of yourself. You will feel that it is somehow a feeling of yourself that it would be great to always feel. It is as though you have just realised an important truth and it is reaching you at a really deep level, much deeper than the mind or the emotions. It is a sense of being at home.

Your Higher Self is what you experience when you are at peace with yourself. Many people will experience their Higher Self as unconditional love for themselves, for all other people, and for the whole world (and universe). Others will experience great joy, bliss, or other heightened emotions or states of mind and/or being. You could be doing anything, and somehow you know it is going well. There is no sense of Ego or comparison with others. There is no fault-finding with the world or with yourself. Everything is just great in that moment. Perhaps you have just completed a task such as the ironing, or mowing the lawn, or washing the dog, and you just acknowledge that it is good. Just as God completed each day of the Creation and *"saw that it was good."*

Let me clarify that this feeling of *good* you are experiencing is not from a sense of duality. It is not the opposite of bad or evil. It is just an acknowledgement of what is, without any real connotations. You, therefore, do not feel pious, or special, or self-righteous, or even pleased with yourself. It is not an ego-type feeling; it is much higher than that. It is your Higher Self.

You might wish to remember to keep your attention open to this feeling whenever you get a chance, and acknowledge the feeling to yourself. It is worth keeping in touch with your Higher Self.

The Lesser Self

The other side of you is your Lesser Self. This is the side that developed from the misuse of free will, and has been passed down through the generations. Each child is taught, by commission or omission, to fit into the material world, the world of Ego, free will, limitation, evil, and pain.

First, let me say that God-Consciousness, through our Higher Self, is totally aware of all aspects of our Lesser Self. He does not approve or disapprove of what we do with our Lesser Selves. After all, the reason for it is free will, and God-Consciousness gave us free will so He could add to His experience, whatever form it takes. Most importantly, it is self-regulating, so the Lesser Self should never completely destroy itself. If it did get so bad that it did destroy itself, it still would not cause any significant problem for the Higher Self, God-Consciousness.

Essentially the Lesser Self, in the grand scheme of things, can be seen as illusion (*maya*).

The Lesser Self is the Ego. While we need individuality to operate in this world effectively, that is provided by the Higher Self, which is God-Consciousness divided into individual beings with blindfolds on. There is differentiation and free will in the Higher Self, but not the egotistical, self-serving, and limited frame of reference of the Ego. The Ego is the source of our problems.

So what is this Ego? Cast your mind back to how you felt being with your Higher Self. Now, just for this exercise, think of someone who annoys you, someone who can't get it right and somehow causes you strife. Think how you could do whatever it is in a better way. Think how you might be better than they are Think how maybe you should be paid more, have a better partner, live in a nicer house because you have earned it. Imagine how things would be better if a particular person was not in the way of your achieving it. Think what you could do if you had your own way.

Stop and get a sense of how this is different to how you felt when experiencing your Higher Self. Notice that with the Higher Self, you felt gently positive, but not in a way that was competitive. You did not feel that you were better than anyone — more spiritual, more relaxed, or more evolved — you just felt comfortable in yourself. However, when the Lesser Self is engaged, suddenly you are comparing yourself with others, and you are feeling emotions — and not necessarily very pleasant ones either. You may even feel tension about the state you are in. You do not feel at peace, but rather somewhat at odds with the world. You are more in your mind, more strategizing to get your own way and more critical of others.

The Ego has a nasty streak, and has an ulterior motive for everything it does. It increases the feeling of separation. It engages with you quite easily, almost as if this was the real you. *You've got to look after yourself. Right? Or you'll just be walked over.* The Ego is very involved in the mind and in justification, self-pity, blame, and superiority. Sometimes it is a feeling of inferiority, but it is always with a feeling of the need to protect yourself.

Do you have a sense of this now? The Ego could be described as a false sense of self. It is one built on the fear of loss of self. It is a fear of annihilation. In contrast, the sense of individuality and free will are a part of the Higher Self, a self-blindfolded God-Consciousness who is having a bit of fun. That side of you is fine. Could you have a game of football without having eleven or so individuals on each side, with the free will to kick the ball when and where they wanted to? No. Free will and individuality is not the issue. The issue is the Ego.

Studies have been made of the Ego in terms of the so-called enneagram. This is an interesting subject, but not one I want to spend any time on in this current book. In the simplest sense, it is a categorisation of Ego Types into nine groups.

1. The Reformer
2. The Helper
3. The Achiever
4. The Individualist
5. The Investigator
6. The Loyalist
7. The Enthusiast
8. The Challenger
9. The Peacemaker.[62]

At times, each of us naturally associates with one or more of these Ego Types. The interesting thing is that what drives the Ego Type is fear. Because of this, the Ego will jump into action anytime and every time it feels threatened. If you felt any reaction to the simple request I made at the start of this book — whether you were prepared to let your preconceptions go and read this book with an open mind — that was your Ego kicking in. By suspending your current beliefs, your Ego comes under threat. If this book makes you change what you have believed in the past, your Ego is also threatened; it will kick and fuss so it can maintain its control of you.

The Ego's greatest ally is the mind. Your mind will kick in and talk

---

62   Riso, D. and Hudson R., *The Wisdom of the Enneagram: The Complete Guide to Psychological and Spiritual Growth for the Nine Personality Types*, Bantam Books, New York, 1999. Other writers' renditions of these nine types are similar in name or meaning.

away at you. It will give you all sorts of reasons why you should not be reading this book. It may even say it is the work of the Devil (I know that it is not). In fact, a number of people who started reading this book are, no doubt, not reading these words now. I guarantee that it was the Ego and its fear of annihilation that stopped those people from continuing to read. (Thank you for staying with me!)

To answer the question asked in the title of this chapter, "**Who am I Then?**", and to summarise the ideas above, I can say that each and every one of the seven billion people on Earth is formed in the same way, whether we are good, bad, or indifferent. I will describe how I view myself, and then you can assess how you feel in contrast or similarity.

+ I am in essence a Higher Self and a Lesser Self that together make up what I call *me*. There is no one else in the universe who is the same as me and I am unique in my expression in the universe.

+ My Higher Self is God-Consciousness. This is God expressing Himself in the form of a human being on planet Earth. God is in everything and is everything in the universe (omnipresence) and is the only reality. Amongst all those things and creatures and plants and minerals, He is also in the form of Alan H. Dawe. In this, I am no better and no worse than any rock, plant, animal, or other person. I am "just" God-Consciousness in expression (or form).

+ My Lesser Self is an illusion, a very real illusion that I can't see through at this stage, but an illusion nevertheless. It hides my Higher Self and pretends to be *me*. Here resides my Ego and my mind. This is what I have created through expressing my free will. In Christian terms, this is my fallen self, the original sinner born of Adam and Eve. However, this Lesser Self is not separate from God — as it cannot be — it just lives in the illusion that it is separate from God.

+ When I was born, I came into form as Alan H. Dawe. Whether I was a separate entity before that really does not matter. Maybe I am a separate spirit or soul who has incarnated many times before, or maybe this is the first (and only) time. Frankly, it does not matter, as I cannot remember the time before I was born, and I am happy with myself and understand why I am as I am with reference purely to this lifetime. I am not going to argue one way or the other on the question of whether I have lived before, because it is irrelevant to this life, and it is irrelevant to the eternal Now, which is the only reality.

+ During this lifetime, I express myself as I feel at the time. I do the best I can in every moment. Sometimes my best meets the standards I expect of myself and meets the expectations of others, and sometimes it doesn't. Whatever happens and whatever I do, my Higher Self (God-Consciousness) is right there and is experiencing it without judgement.

+ All experience my Lesser Self and Higher Self have is perfect. That is one of the major purposes of life — God experiencing Himself. There is no true judgement from God — there is only the Lesser Self judging itself and judging others. It is the Ego that thinks it can judge. From God's perspective, the perspective of my Higher Self, what I **do** is experience.

+ When I die, I may cease to exist as an individual and may be absorbed back into the Ocean of formless God-Consciousness. Alternatively, I might continue as a separate entity. Frankly, it does not matter. It is only the Ego (Lesser Self) that needs to think it is special enough to continue separately. I am not going to argue one way or the other as to whether I continue as a separate individual in the afterlife, or whether I become One with God-Consciousness, which I am anyway. It is irrelevant to the eternal Now, which is the only reality.

+ My body is an expression of consciousness. How things are with my body may influence the Lesser Self as to how it responds to that body. However, the greater influence is the other way around — my body will respond to what is in my mind and in the consciousness of my Lesser Self. If I am sick, it is my mind that is usually sick first, and the body is just reflecting that state of mind.

+ If I need to heal my mind or body, I need to allow my Higher Self to come through, and then allow my Lesser Self to withdraw from its fixed attitudes or stance. Healing comes from God-Consciousness. Prayers to God are heard by the God-Consciousness of my Higher Self, and can be immediately answered if my Lesser Self is prepared to allow the healing in. God does not interfere from outside His Creation (including me); He *interferes* from within. Thus, the Lesser Self and free will are not compromised. They are healed by acceptance and surrender. Healing is always readily available.

+ My purpose in life is to express myself and experience. I can choose to do a lot in each minute of my life or I can choose to do very little. I have free will. I cannot complain about my excess or lack of life experience as it is in my own hands. My Lesser Self has the say as it has usurped the free will that I have been given as a God Franchisee. My Higher Self accepts what is presented to it, and will help my Lesser Self whenever it is truly asked for that help. This is my hotline to God.

This gives you an idea of how I see my place in the universe. I also see you and every other person in the universe in the same way. The effect of viewing people in this way may lead you to become much more empathetic to others, much less swayed by trivia driven by ignorance and illusion (or delusion), and much more understanding of why people do what they do. There have been many occasions when I have read or seen in the news a story of someone who has committed a serious crime and is described as evil. Based on the perspective stated above, I have come to realise they are not evil, but have acted from a place of pain, ignorance, and Ego. Forgiveness and understanding arise much more easily.

We are going to move on now to a discussion about the Tree of the Knowledge of Good and Evil. This leads us to the question of Original Sin, and will tell us a lot more about our Lesser Self. I expect you will find it interesting.

CHAPTER 13

The Tree of the Knowledge of Good and Evil

We have discussed the time before Creation, and have realised all that existed then was God-Consciousness (God). Through a desire for His own experience, God created the universe by starting with the Big Bang. He allowed it to develop following the fundamental laws of cosmology, physics, and chemistry. Life then developed through the effects of evolution and natural selection. This process has been determined and recognised by scientists as one that took place over a period of 14 billion years (by our time measurement on Earth).

God-Consciousness also split an aspect of Himself into a myriad of tiny pieces, and chose to forget who or where He was, with the object of putting the jigsaw puzzle pieces back together again, removing the blindfold, and rediscovering His God-Consciousness. In other words, He created Man in *His image and likeness.*[63]

God-Consciousness gave each individual person a God Franchise. Amongst other things, this meant we had free will and the ability to create whatever it was we wanted. This simple act of adding free will to the Creation mix meant that instead of God-Consciousness experiencing the Creation as if it was a giant machine filled with automatons — which would have been totally predictable and ultimately boring — He added a joker to the pack. God-Consciousness gave Man free will so that Man could determine how Creation would pan out. He gave Man

---

63   *Genesis 1:26-27*

all the resources he needed, and set him free to do whatever he desired with these resources.

How and when was this done? We return now to the Garden of Eden.

> *"And the Lord God took the man, and put him into the Garden of Eden to dress it and to keep it. And the Lord God commanded the man, saying, Of every tree of the garden thou mayest freely eat: But of the tree of the knowledge of good and evil, thou shalt not eat of it: for in the day that thou eatest thereof thou shalt surely die."*[64]

God-Consciousness gave Man the choice of eating of the Tree of the Knowledge of Good and Evil, or not. In doing that, He gave Man free will. Well, superficially anyway. The fact was, God had created the Tree in the first place, and secondly, He had created a smooth-talking snake as well. Thirdly, He had created Adam and Eve as intelligent beings who were about to start His experience in an evolutionary world that He had not predestined. Up until that point, everything was predestined, and that is, perhaps, why many people today believe in determinism[65] — because they see it in nature.

God was not going to allow Man to simply ignore the Tree of the Knowledge of Good and Evil. He was going to encourage him to eat of it, even if He had given Man free choice. However, neither Adam nor Eve could withstand the temptation, and I suspect neither could God! In terms of evolution, if you take into account what Man has achieved because of his free will, and because of his nature, you will agree that he, and that free will, have had a tremendous impact on evolution in the wider sense.

If you disagree with this assertion that God-Consciousness Himself was tempted to see what effect free will would have when Man was faced with temptation, let's look at it from another aspect. Many people believe that the serpent was Satan (the Devil, the Tempter) come to tempt Man, and because Man sinned by taking the fruit of the

---

64 *Genesis* 2:15-17

65 "The philosophical doctrine that all events including human actions and choices are fully determined by preceding events and states of affairs, and so that freedom of choice is illusory" (*Collins English Dictionary*).

Tree and eating it, he fell from Grace. This is the source of the concept of Original Sin.[66]

Fair enough. It is true, God gave Man free will, and he immediately used it to taste the fruit of the Tree of the Knowledge of Good and Evil despite God's instruction. The answer is simple. Man now had Ego, and his Ego wanted to show its self-importance and independence. Just like a child. Tell a child one thing and it will do the opposite just to show its independence, its autonomy.

Satan, the Devil that so many people fear, is nothing more than their own personal Ego. I suspect there is no entity called the Devil or Satan, or if there is, he can no more interfere in this universe than the Angels or Archangels do, assuming they exist![67] There are many individual people who carry their own personal Devils — their Egos. Recognition of this fact would save people much fear, and much looking outside themselves for the source of their life issues. Those issues in life, I'm afraid, are within them, and only within them.

It is the Ego that has acquired the knowledge of good and evil, and it is through understanding and overcoming that Ego that we discover our Higher Self, the God-Consciousness that we are. We cover this in more detail in Part Four, *Daily Living as a God Franchisee.*

In summary, God-Consciousness gave Man free will, which He immediately employed to eat of the Tree of the Knowledge of Good and Evil. Yes, this did have a huge effect on Mankind, but this was not the Original Sin, which has been taught as the source of all Man's ills. That was the development of the Ego. The Ego is the real source of all Man's problems.

---

66   The Tree of the Knowledge of Good and Evil is traditionally associated by Christians with the doctrine of Original Sin, although that concept is not specifically mentioned in the Bible.

67   I don't want to get side-tracked into a big discussion on Satan, Angels, and Archangels. For this present discussion, and for everyday life as you and I know it, they do not need to exist, or certainly have no direct effect on us. Black Magic may evoke Satan or create satanic thought forms which could be construed as being Satan, and so such practices should be avoided for your own health and safety. Many people believe in Angels and Archangels, and are guided by them. This is fine and safe, and I prefer to view such positive support as coming from one's own Higher Self. Any "interference" from Satan or Angels, should there be any at all, will be at the volition and request of a human, and is not imposed on us.

Having said that, it was all part of God's Plan. God-Consciousness did not create anything frivolously. He created the Tree for a reason. He gave free will for a reason. The Church has assumed Man has disobeyed God, generating Original Sin, and that is the source of all the world's problems. No! I will repeat it again. The source of all the world's problems is each individual's Ego. So, God effectively allowed Man to create the Ego for a reason too. The real challenge each one of us faces is to rein in our own Ego. We are not sinners — we are egoists.

Let's not forget that God-Consciousness throughout this is experiencing Himself through Man. This is what God wanted and this is what God has got. God-Consciousness wants (needs) to experience the freedom in free will. If God-Consciousness had not given men and women free will, there would be limitations on how the universe could evolve. Men and women are still One with God-Consciousness, and are God-Consciousness in differentiation. They can neither create nor do anything outside God. However, we can come up with a multitude of individual ideas, each individual expressing his or her own perspectives and choices in life. Every one of these experiences is God's experience.

There are seven billion human beings alive today, and this number is growing. The first time there were a billion humans alive at one time was as recently as 1804, so our numbers are growing fast. Every one of these seven billion experiences is God's experience. So that includes you and it includes me. You and I are partners in God's Plan, along with 6,999,999,998 other people.

You could also say that God discovered Himself in Adam and Eve in that He gave Himself the Knowledge of Good and Evil, of duality. This vastly increased the breadth of what could be experienced within the Creation — therefore, what God could experience — thus fulfilling His Purpose. God-Consciousness created differentiation within Himself. *This* was different to *that*, and therefore, He could get some interaction between two opposites.

God created the Tree of Knowledge of Good and Evil and gave Adam and Eve free will to eat of it or not. Until Adam and Eve ate the fruit from the Tree, they followed God's instructions, as did all the plants and creatures of Earth. With that single act, Adam and Eve declared their (apparent) independence from the will of God. While on the surface, God was disobeyed, He was the one who created the Tree of Knowledge of Good and Evil, and we know why.

Prior to that there was no concept of Evil, only Good. He decided there could be an alternative to Good, **and God wanted to experience it**. Once Evil was recognised, and thereby created, Man's innocence was lost. If God was truly upset by Adam and Eve's disobedience He could have zapped them there and then. However, this was not the Plan. When I say there was only *good*, realise that *good* is just a word. There was neither good nor evil — there was just whatever it was with no moral or judgemental value attached to it. With the Tree of Knowledge of Good and Evil, that knowledge of the world of duality was created, the knowledge of good as much as of evil.

I have no doubt that God-Consciousness is beyond duality, and therefore, one cannot call God Good or Evil. To put some words to it, eutheism is the belief that a deity is wholly benevolent, while dystheism allows for there to be evil in the realm of the gods. There is nothing in this world or the way that the world works, despite all the pain and sorrow in the world, that would convince me that God-Consciousness has an evil intent in any respect. While the word *benevolent* implies a duality, in the English language that is the word we use. God-Consciousness is neither Good nor Evil. However, due to language constraints we need to say that he is benevolent, loving, and is doing everything for the highest possible purpose.

Since there is nothing outside God-Consciousness, whatever happens in the world is 100 percent as it should be. It is all part of God's experience of Himself, and therefore, is perfectly as it should be. With the eating of the fruit of the Tree of the Knowledge of Good and Evil, Man became *"as one of us, to know good and evil"* and this was really what God wanted. He wanted to no longer be alone, but to have Adam and Eve, and their successors, as independent creators — and with free will. He gave them a God Franchise.

God-Consciousness made everything: *"And God saw every thing that he had made, and, behold, it was very good."*[68] Although God had created the light and so differentiated light and darkness, He did not have the

---

68 *Genesis* 1:31

concept of opposites. He saw everything as good, and did not decide that some things were bad or evil.

It is interesting that darkness is not something of itself. You can't get a darkness machine or have a darkness switch. Darkness is the absence of light, and it is the light that God-Consciousness created. In space there is no light; there is only darkness. The light radiates out from luminous bodies like the Sun and other stars, and is reflected by planets and moons. Likewise, the nothingness that existed before The Creation is not a something; it is just the absence of a Creation. God created The Creation — He did not create nothingness.

The idea of opposites is a man-made convenience, which has come from Adam and Eve eating of the Tree of the Knowledge of Good and Evil. It is also an illusion.[69] So, when God said that everything he had made was very good, it was by way of appreciation of their very existence rather than a good vs. evil judgement.

From God's viewpoint, you could not have, for instance, lawful and unlawful. God's Laws are absolute, and we discuss these shortly in another chapter. It is impossible to avoid or break God's Laws. They just don't work that way. The Laws of Mathematics, for example, cannot be countered. You can make mistakes or misunderstand them, or try to ignore them, but you cannot invalidate them.

Now that we have tasted of the Tree of the Knowledge of Good and Evil, let's discuss why the Creation is as it is.

---

69   As Hamlet says, *"There is nothing either good or bad, but thinking makes it so."* William Shakespeare (1564-1616), Hamlet, Act II Scene II.

CHAPTER 14

Creation and the Filters on It

I used to hold the idea that God had created only the natural world of Earth, the Sun, the Moon, and the stars. God had created the humans, the animals, the plants, and the minerals. God had created the atom, the 94 chemical elements that make up the physical world, and so on. I also believed that Man had created the invented world that we see around us: the buildings, the cars, the space shuttles, the computers, the CDs, DVDs, iPods and iPads,[70] the clothes, the sculptured gardens, the genetic modifications, the hybrids, and essentially the whole modern world.

Of course, everything that Man has invented and *created* is made out of the materials that God has created: the minerals, the oil, the wood, the plants, and so on. It seemed to me that God gave us the ability to go out and create whatever we wanted to of our own right. I felt, and still feel, there is no limit to what can be invented, designed, and created. No limit whatsoever.

With my realisation of **The God Franchise** came a subtle shift. What if it is not Man who creates all these new things? What if it is God who creates them through us instead? What if God is the Creator of everything, from the natural world and wonderful modern creations we have around us, to the atom bomb, the gun, the porn movie, and junk food?

God uses you and me as channels for His further creation. In reality,

---

70   iPod and iPad are trademarks of Apple Inc., registered in the US and other countries.

not even as channels. As I have said, God is you and me continuing His Creation through our forms. You and I have this false idea of self, which is effectively just Ego showing up. Ego says I created that or I designed this. Ego says I wrote this wonderful song or I painted this fantastic picture. If we remove Ego, all that is left is God creating.

What if we painted a picture, wrote a poem, or designed a spaceship and just accepted that it was good? Not that I was good, but rather "Look at this wonderful creation that God has created through me." Let's use, appreciate, and enjoy the creation, not the Ego that *created* it. God is the Creator. When we see a great painting, we don't need to say "Wow, what a brilliant artist!" No, let's say, "Wow, what a brilliant picture!" Or rather than "aren't you a great cook," say "what a great meal!" Or rather than "what a talented musician," say "what a great piece of music or beautiful song." The Creator is God in every instance, so thank Him.

In fact, by praising the artist, the musician, the cook, the inventor, and yourself, you are essentially doing them a disservice. You are bolstering their Egos, and thus making it more difficult for them to reach a state of freedom from the tyranny of Ego.

"And God saw every thing that he had made, and, behold, it was very good." [71] Even God didn't say, "Behold, I am very good — look how clever I am."

Of course, many human *creators* have been humble enough to recognise that it is not themselves as individual Egos who should be credited with their creations. But what about you and me? How often do we think we have just done something marvellous? We don't need to know about how to create — that is not our job. Our job is to be the best channel we can be for the creation. By learning practical skills (art, music, design, writing, cooking, carpentry, welding, you-name-it), and by leaving the Ego out of it, we are creating the best channel we can for God's work. Our second job is to appreciate and enjoy what has been created for us, and through us.

The Ego is the illusion of the self as a creator. God-Consciousness is the Creator of everything, and He also is the substance of the whole of His Creation. So, why is there so much around us that appears

---

71 *Genesis* 1:31

to be the exact antithesis of what one would expect God to create? Why is there disease, poverty, war, corruption, danger, and death? Philosophers ask how God can be omnibenevolent in the face of all these dreadful occurrences if He is also omniscient and omnipotent. The argument is that if God knows about Evil, as He is omniscient, and is powerful enough to destroy all Evil as he is omnipotent, how can He be omnibenevolent if He allows Evil to occur? This is the so-called Problem of Evil, which we have previously mentioned.

Let me say that while God is the creator, His creations are filtered through our physical being, including our Egos. If our Ego is so big that we want to interfere with the creation, or so big that we think we have greater skills than we really have, we are dumbing down the creation. Our Egos can even pervert the creative process so that what starts as a benign discovery (e.g. atomic power, motion pictures) is directed by Ego into being something we can view as being very evil (e.g. nuclear weapons, child pornography).

Nevertheless, the reality is that you are looked after by God-Consciousness just by being a perfectly open channel for His creation. All you need will flow to you as well, including money as the current common exchange unit. You are constantly in the presence of creation. It is happening all around you. Bow with me in awe to the whole of creation!

Now, let's take a look at the filters that seem to affect and possibly minimise the on-going creation work of God-Consciousness. We can start by looking at you and me, and the other 6,999,998 people in the world, as most of the trouble starts here.

The Human Being and Ego

You and I are perfect aspects of God. We are God incarnate, if you like. As I have already said, it is not that you are God. No, it is that God is you. Many Christians believe that not only was Jesus the Son of God, but that He was God incarnate. The truth is that we are all God incarnate. Jesus, of course, was a shining portrayal of what it is to be God incarnate, and we can certainly acknowledge him for that, as Christians do. Nevertheless, Jesus Christ (or Jesus the Christ to be more exact) was not the only Son of God; we are all sons and daughters of God, and He is *"well pleased"* [72] with every one of us.

We have already hinted at the following analogy, and a great one it is: Imagine God is like an eternal, infinite Ocean. A human being is like a splash of water from that Ocean that is briefly separated from the Ocean, and then falls back into the Ocean again. While rising above the Ocean as a splash, it is easy in that moment to think you are separated, but the reality is, you are still part of the Ocean; you are still a part of God. So, do you want to call that Divine Splash the Ocean (God) incarnate in a bubble or splash, or a son or daughter of the Ocean (God), or even an aspect of the Ocean (God)? It is just semantics. The reality is unchanged.

When God differentiates into an individual, He gives that human being, that incarnate spirit, free will. He does this so He can experience a unique expression of His Life. The free will has been misinterpreted to mean Man can do things of his own volition, so he becomes a creator and can be powerful without any need for God to exist at all. He has even stretched God's permission or directive to *"have dominion over the fish of the sea, and over the fowl of the air, and over every living thing that moveth upon the earth"* [73] to include his fellow human beings. Over the thousands of years that Mankind has existed, this belief has been extended and developed as free will has gone further and further to our heads.

The Ego is the obvious outcome in this development of free will, as well as the personality and human beliefs regarding limitation (shortage, loss, poverty, sickness), personal power over others (arrogance, authoritarianism, rape, tyranny), the need to take from others through force (crime and wars), and so on. It is not that God set out to create these things, it is just that the opportunity to use free will from an individualistic viewpoint automatically led to the development of the Ego.

Ego has been around since Adam blamed Eve for giving him the fruit of the Tree of the Knowledge of Good and Evil, and Eve blamed

---

72 *Matthew* 3:17
73 *Genesis* 1:28

the serpent.[74] Later, Cain killed Abel[75] because he felt that the Lord preferred Abel's offering to his own — these two men were Adam and Eve's first two sons! This is just in the first four chapters of Genesis, the very beginning of the Bible. Ego, of course, shows up all the way through the Bible, and has continued right through human history to daily life today.

The Ego, personality, and human beliefs act as filters on everything that God creates through a particular human channel. So, if you are a perfectly egoless channel, the individual creation will be perfect, be it a work of art, a piece of music, the design or prototype of a new machine or device, or a piece of writing. As the Ego gets in the way, this acts as a filter to change the pure creation and produce something that contains traces of the individual's free will. One could say that the creation is God's, while the filter is the Ego's. The creation is the Higher Self's, while the filter is the Lesser Self's.

If you watch any performer or artist at work, you will see they are completely open and egoless when they are in the midst of a peak performance. There is pure God-Consciousness in evidence in that moment, and the Ego is set aside. Creation is not limited to works of art, music, engineering, or writing either. Everything we do in our day-to-day lives is a part of the continuing creation process. Everything we are and stand for is a part of creation and a resulting development of that creation. And all the way through the creation is God's — or to put it another way, the Creator is God-Consciousness operating through the Higher Self. Any degree of impurity or evil in that Creation is purely due to the Ego acting as a filter.

The Human Being and Emotions

The emotions are strange things, and I suspect that most of us misunderstand them. Some people might classify them as an aspect of mind (as in, "your emotions are all in the mind"). Others associate them more with spirit, I guess, as they are rather ephemeral. Others, in turn, associate them with the body because they are felt in the body.

---

74   *Genesis* 3:12 - 13
75   *Genesis* 4: 8

Perhaps that is part of the mystery of the emotions, that they don't have a neat home in mind, body, or spirit, but can be experienced and classified in all those parts of the being. Nevertheless, they are extremely important, and they do act as very significant filters of creation.

It is not a surprise to find that writers apparently do not agree on a clear and consistent categorisation of emotions. Even some states of being like peacefulness, calmness, and tranquillity seem to get overlooked altogether, maybe because they are not active enough. I will, therefore, classify emotions into three groups. Any other emotional words you think of should fit into one of these three groups:

+ **Positive emotions** include feeling amazed, amused, calm, caring, comfortable, compassionate, confident, content, curious, delighted, eager, ecstatic, elated, enthusiastic, excited, glad, good, happy, humble, joyous, loving, optimistic, passionate, patient, peaceful, pleased, surprised, sympathetic, thrilled, tranquil, warm, wonderful

+ **Survival (self-preservation) emotions** include feeling anguish, anxious, cautious, desire, fearful, grief, helpless, homesick, horror, nervous, overwhelmed, panicky, protected, relieved, safe, scared, secure, suffering, terrified, worried

+ **Negative emotions** include feeling alienated, angry, annoyed, arrogant, contemptuous, cynical, defeated, depressed, despairing, disappointed, disgusted, embarrassed, envious, frustrated, guilty, hateful, humiliated, impatient, irritated, isolated, jealous, lazy, loathing, lonely, mean, miserable, pain, enraged, resentful, sad, shameful, shy, sorrowful, spiteful, unhappy.

(An emotion like pride can have either a positive or a negative connotation, and fits in well with either of these once you know the context.)

It is interesting, when we review these lists of emotions, that the positive emotions do not seem to relate to the Ego, whereas the negative emotions shout out the word *Ego*. The emotions I have classed as survival emotions do not have a sense of Ego about them, although they are protective of the separated self. They give a feeling of separation from God-Consciousness certainly, and they are beyond the Ego.

One can easily and correctly reach the conclusion that emotions that come from the Ego are negative or hurtful ones — ones that cause us pain. Pain comes from resistance, and with these emotions we are resisting something. We don't like the reality that is facing us, we don't accept what is, and our Ego becomes angry, depressed, envious, unhappy, or whatever.

However, with the positive emotions there is a sense of wholeness and oneness. The Ego is not present, and instead our Higher Self reaches out to the situation or the other person and we gently feel love, compassion, happiness, optimism, patience, and so on.

The middle group of survival emotions are felt because the self feels threatened, or there is relief that the threat has abated. These emotions are not felt in the same way as the negative group. There is no sense of Ego or self-importance, but rather a sense of separation from God.

So, how do the emotions act as filters on creation? First, we add an element of judgement to creation. We say some things are good and some are evil. We say this as if our pronouncement was absolutely true. It is not that the created thing is changed by our perception in any way — whatever it is it is a perfect expression of our ability to create through **The God Franchise**, or if you like, for God to create through us. What is changed by our perception is how we feel about that created thing. It changes our experience of that created thing. God-Consciousness is satisfied with experiencing whatever we choose to experience. We have free will in how we choose to experience any created thing.

What we have is the freedom to have choice, taste, opinions, and preferences. Free will gives us the freedom to prefer one thing over another and one experience over another. We can choose what we love and desire, and we can decide what it is we would rather avoid or not experience. This is what makes us all different, and what gives God-Consciousness the variety He likes to experience.

Unfortunately, at times, emotions get in the way of the creation. Different people (Egos) believe strongly and differently about the same thing and fight over it. The root cause of this is they believe there is a built-in limitation on creation or on the material expression of creation. Two men will fight over the same girl, forgetting there are many other girls in the world with equal if not better qualities. Two people will fight over ownership of the same house, or car, or other unique creation. Egos will try to get as much as they can for themselves, even if they have to resort to crime or war to achieve it. Countries fight over mineral rights or sea access or state security or religion, when in fact, it is just the Egos at the top who want to have their own way. The soldiers who have to fight the wars or the civilians living in the battlefield usually don't care about the cause being fought for. They just want peace and to be able to get on with their daily lives.

If you look into any of these situations, you will find Ego, and you will find negative emotions. The negative emotions drive the Ego and colour the decisions and actions being taken. These emotions are extremely powerful and are the driving force behind the Ego and in the individual experience of the Creation. The emotions are extremely significant filters on the Creation.

Another interesting aspect of emotions is the fact that those we have classified as negative have a strong impact on the person who is feeling them. While we might try to put the blame out there on Creation, the cause of the negative emotion is within ourselves. It does not feel good, so we react to it or resist it, and this is what causes the pain. This pain stirs us to do more negative things, and we end up in a downward spiral of self-inflicted pain and resistance to reality (what is here now).

By contrast, the positive emotions do not involve the Ego, and you feel closer to your true self, your Higher Self. You could express this as being closer to God. It is not that God-Consciousness is good or only wants good, it is just that the fundamental, non-Ego way of feeling and being is in keeping with what we have termed positive emotions. If we were not coming from Ego, we would not experience the negative emotions at all. Our only experience would be the positive emotions that we would not call positive or good as the duality in the emotions would no longer exist.

So far, I have conveniently overlooked the survival (self-preservation) emotions. Remember, these are only felt as a sense of separation from God-Consciousness. If we truly realise we are one with God-Consciousness and that *"in him we live, and move, and have our being,"*[76] we will not feel scared or worried or overwhelmed — we will feel secure, safe, and protected. Once again, without the duality of fear, etc., the feeling of safety and protection will be "just" a state of peace and wholeness.

The Human Being and Conscious Creation

People can be either more or less conscious about their creativity. We could say that some creativity is conscious and other creativity is unconscious.

Conscious Creation is about an individual's conscious appreciation of the fact that he or she can create consciously. That it is not only the ability to create a new book, a new artwork, or a new product, it is also the ability to create your own experience of life at will.

In truth, there are many thousands of people who do understand and operate the Law of Conscious Creation, which we can call by its more common and topical name, the Law of Attraction — or by the name I prefer, the Law of Manifestation. Nevertheless, there is no general appreciation of the realities of **The God Franchise**. There are many books now on the market about the Law of Attraction, and it is becoming better known. Still, people generally do not appreciate what it is and how it works. This is an exciting development (evolution) ahead for Man.

Unconscious Creation is the experience of the vast majority of people during the greater part of their lives. Since Man appeared on Earth some 150,000 years ago, development has been very slow. Cultures have come and gone, and it is only since the Industrial Revolution, which started around 1850, that progress has been huge.[77] Since then, of course, the rate of change has been phenomenal, and today new products are obsolete even before they hit the marketplace.

---

76 *Acts* 17:28
77 We can safely ignore the discoveries and developments in earlier civilisations such as Atlantean, Incan, or Mayan civilisations, as not enough is directly known about them and there is considerable conjecture. The point made here is not invalidated by doing this.

The everyday person has been caught up in this constant rush of creativity, and many people are directly involved in making something better from what has already been created. This creativity has been a part of the lives of every living person on Earth today, with the possible exception of those people living in the outposts of the world – those living away from civilisation. Nevertheless, there is no real appreciation in most people of what this power of creativity is, and therefore, much of this creativity can be viewed as being unconscious.

In addition to this, and perhaps more importantly, everything we do or say or think in this life is attracting things towards us or pushing things away from us. This is creation at a much more subtle level. We create the lives that we lead, in every detail. We will be covering this subject in much more detail in Part Four.

The Filters from the Scriptures

There are many scriptures and holy books in the world, written at different times and from different perspectives. These include the *Holy Bible* (Old Testament and New Testament), the *Koran*, the *Bhagavad-Gita*, the *Upanishads*, and the *Tao Te Ching*. I am not a scholar of these books and am only familiar with the Bible to a certain extent, so I will limit my comments.

The books of the Old Testament were originally transmitted by word of mouth and were written down between 1200 BC and 100 BC, while the New Testament books were written down between 50 AD and 150 AD. As Bible scholars will tell you, there were many authors of these books and there is still considerable controversy about much of the detail and circumstance of the Bible. Of course, now is not the time to debate this, nor am I equipped to do so.

What I can say is that the Bible is the inspired Word of God. I can say this because God-Consciousness is the being of every one of us, and of course every one of the authors of the Bible. Just as we have filters come into play in everything we do and say, as discussed, so is this true of the authors of the Bible. The Bible was written to the level of understanding and the terminology of the people of those times. Likewise, every other scripture, and for that matter every other book ever written on spiritual or other matters, is to some greater or lesser extent the work of God-Consciousness. However, and I accept this is a big however, the filters of the author's own Ego make a huge difference to the importance and trustworthiness of the final work. Thus, one cannot equate the Holy Scriptures listed above with say a formulaic Mills & Boon romantic novel, or the work of a biased, egocentric, down-on-his-luck-and-skills pseudo-scientist or pseudo-spiritual teacher.

Each one of us, individually, comes from our own place. This is part God-Consciousness and part Ego. The mix differs for each person, and this is what makes it interesting. This is what makes each individual's contribution to evolution and continuing creation interesting, and it is from this that wars, corruption, and poverty spring. They do not come from a Satan lurking in the background, from Original Sin, or from a dystheistic (possibly evil) God — they come from **free will** and **the Ego**, nothing else.

St John chapters 13 to 17 are very interesting chapters in the Bible. These are the words of Jesus at the Last Supper, just before he was betrayed by Judas. They are worth reading and studying. Christians take the words to mean we need to be Christians and follow Jesus in order to know God. I believe the meaning of the words is much broader, so please do take some time to read these five chapters of St John with an open mind.

Some of the things that Jesus says here are:

"I am the way, the truth, and the life: no man cometh unto the Father, but by me. If ye had known me, ye should have known my Father also: and from henceforth ye know him, and have seen him."[78]

"The words that I speak unto you I speak not of myself: but the Father that dwelleth in me, he doeth the works. Believe me that I am in the Father, and the Father in me: or else believe me for the very works' sake."[79]

"Verily, verily, I say unto you, He that believeth on me, the works that I do shall he do also; and greater works than these shall he do; because I go unto my Father."[80]

---

78 *John* 14:6-7
79 *John* 14:10-11
80 *John* 14:12

"And whatsoever ye shall ask in my name, that will I do, that the Father may be glorified in the Son. If ye shall ask any thing in my name, I will do it."[81]

"At that day ye shall know that I am in my Father, and ye in me, and I in you."[82]

"I go unto the Father: for my Father is greater than I."[83]

"Abide in me, and I in you. As the branch cannot bear fruit of itself, except it abide in the vine; no more can ye, except ye abide in me."[84]

"That they all may be one; as thou, Father, art in me, and I in thee, that they also may be one in us."[85]

These passages point to God-Consciousness being in Jesus, and that there was still a differentiation. It is not that God and Jesus are identical entities. Jesus was not speaking from a point of Ego here, so when he speaks of *I* or *me*, he is speaking of the Christhood or God-Consciousness in him. And so, *"He that believeth on me, the works that I do shall he do also; and greater works than these shall he do."* This refers to anyone who recognises the God-Consciousness in themselves. We all, without Ego, can do *greater works* than Jesus did. This is not a competition. This is reality, and it is evolution in all things.

So the Scriptures are very important in that they are the way most of us get to hear about, and start to think about, God. However, the Scriptures cannot be taken as literal in their entirety. Firstly, they were worded for an audience different from today's audience, and secondly, while they may be the inspired Word of God, there is also the human element of Ego filtering the work, either intentionally or unintentionally. This does not invalidate the Scriptures — it just means you need to use them as a source of inspiration and of pointers, not of literal facts. Having said that, this current book, my humble offering to the spiritual literature, is also not a book of literal facts — it is

---

81 *John* 14:13-14
82 *John* 14:20
83 *John* 14:28
84 *John* 15:4
85 *John* 17:21

offered as a source of inspiration and pointers to the Truth, whatever that really is.

The Truth is within you, within the God-Consciousness that you are.

The Filters of Physical Reality

God-Consciousness created the universe so He would not have to meddle with it or tweak it as it evolved. As He is omnipotent and omniscient, He could interfere whenever He felt like it, but that would be like playing blind man's bluff and peeking over the blindfold to cheat. It would be like playing chess and reorganising the board when you were losing and no one was looking.

God decided what was needed and what He wanted, and then designed the universe accordingly. He does not and has not interfered so far as we are aware. This is why some people such as atheists or even deists say God is not involved in the universe, but rather that it runs due to evolution. They see no place for God. Nevertheless, God-Consciousness is very much aware of everything that is happening in the universe, and is experiencing it all. This is how He designed it, and this is how it works. And everything is working very well indeed.

One of the laws of physical reality is that every living thing goes through a birth, life, and death cycle. Likewise, every non-living thing goes through transformation from the time it starts in a specific state until it is transformed into another state. Through all this transformation, there is no loss of matter or energy. These may transform into each other in general terms, and matter can take many different forms, as can energy. Nevertheless, the universe is a closed system and nothing is lost overall. It is merely transformed.

Earth started out as molten rock with no life at all. Slowly it cooled on the surface so that rocks and mountains solidified. Areas of water massed as seas and rain started to fall. Over billions of years, the wear and tear of the movement of water and air caused erosion of the rocks into smaller particles, and over time, this became the sand and the soil of the earth. Life started as single cell organisms (prokaryotic cells), much like the bacteria we see today. They developed (somehow!) into the eukaryotic cell (the complex cells of plants, animals, and humans), and before we knew it, over a few more billions of years, we had plant life on Earth.

Bacteria are essential for life on the planet. As plants went through their life cycle, bacteria helped in the breakdown of dead leaves and dead plants. This material mixed with the earth to enrich it with nutrients. The nutrients helped further plants to grow. Also cyanobacteria carried out photosynthesis to convert carbon dioxide and water into nutrients for the plant, and generated oxygen in the process. Oxygen is vital for animal and human life.

When it came to animals, bacteria played an enormous role both when the animal was alive and after its death. When it was alive, the bacteria helped break down the food it was eating so that its constituent elements and compounds could be absorbed into the animal's body. After death, bacteria broke down the dead body into its elements again, so that the earth was enriched for plant growth.

As you can see, this is an excellent way for nature to operate. It is perfectly designed and operates automatically without interference from either God-Consciousness or Man. As mentioned, the purpose of bacteria is to clean up the planet. To do this, they decompose dead organic material, freeing up the atoms for reuse. Bacteria are present in our stomachs to help break down foods so they can be absorbed by the body, and they also protect the lining of the stomach. Yes, bacteria are essential for life on the planet.

On the other hand, these same properties can appear as an infection when cells die after the body is damaged through an accident. The body's immune system is designed to cope with such bacterial infection, but is sometimes overwhelmed. Nowadays, we resort to antibiotics to help clear an infection. Many diseases have bacteria as their apparent cause, although the body is normally able to cope through the immune system that is designed to counter just such invasion by overzealous bacteria.

Disease becomes apparent when the immune response is low; this reduced ability to cope is usually due to the effects of stress in and on the body. These stresses are caused by outside factors in the environment or by internal processes such as thoughts and emotions. The body gets sick to show the person (or animal or plant) that it needs to take action to remove itself from the source of the stress. Naturally, plants have little opportunity to do this, but animals, and certainly humans, do.

Bacteria adapt quickly to changes in their environment so they can survive. This, no doubt, has been a critical factor in their success, and therefore, the success of all life on the planet. It does mean though that they can appear to cause us problems when they turn up in situations where we don't like to see them — manifesting as disease. So, is sickness the sign of evil as some people believe? No, it is nature doing its thing; the bacteria are critical to our survival.

Likewise, there was a need for rock to break down under the stress of storms and flowing water in order to generate the earth that we need to support life. Therefore, if a rockslide occurs and crushes a car or house in its path, and life is lost as a result, is this an evil event? No, this is nature doing what it needs to do for life to exist and continue. Man built the house at the top of a loose cliff due to his greed for property or prestige of position — in other words, due to his Ego. Perhaps he was just in the wrong place at the wrong time, although it appears to me that many people escape such situations by being in tune with the physical world and just not being there at the moment of catastrophe. Many people are not in tune with their Higher Self and, therefore, cannot avoid the place and time when nature is doing its natural and very important thing. I read recently of an elderly man who was killed in a freak accident where a car accidently drove down a grassy bank into his bedroom. He was in the doorway just walking into the room. He had stated earlier that he did not want to die of sickness in old age, but wanted to go "out with a bang." He did.

Earthquakes are caused by shifts in the tectonic plates that make up the solid outer crust of Earth. These shifts release stress. This is a natural occurrence resulting from the way Earth was structured and developed. Man has decided to build cities on fault lines. I live in Auckland, which is home to 48 volcanoes; the most recent eruption was on Rangitoto, the small volcanic island in the harbour, in about 1350. The volcanic field is seen as dormant rather than extinct, yet New Zealand's largest city, housing one third of the country's population, is located here. Why? Certainly it is our choice to be here, even though another volcano arising from the land or sea is very likely to happen at some stage. New Zealand's capital, Wellington, is built on a fault line so it is prone to earthquakes. New Zealand's second largest city, Christchurch, suffered a 7.1 (Richter scale) magnitude earthquake on 4 September 2010 as well as continuing aftershocks that caused considerable damage to property. A second, more serious, earthquake was experienced on 22 February 2011 (6.3 on the Richter scale); that one killed over 170 people, caused major damage to hundreds of historic and commercial buildings (including the iconic Christchurch Cathedral), destroyed thousands of homes, and left the whole city devastated.[86] Frequent and powerful aftershocks continue.

Are earthquakes and volcanoes evil, or are they a natural part of the continuing evolution of the planet? If it were not for rain and wind, life could not exist on Earth. So why is a catastrophic storm something to see as evil? How can this be seen as bad design? The design is perfect — it is Man who decides to build next to flood-prone rivers, or on fault-lines, or even at all in a country called the Shaky Isles[87] (New Zealand) that is the problem. It is Man deciding to live in hurricane or tornado or monsoon territory that is the problem, not the hurricanes, tornados, and monsoons themselves, as they are a part of nature. In fact, Man's impact on Earth is so great that he could well be causing an increase in the frequency and severity of storms through the destruction of large tracts of forests and pollution that leads to global warming.

We could continue, and we could be more scientific about the discussion, but the bottom line remains that Earth was designed perfectly. We see events as catastrophes and disasters, but this is due to our lack of awareness and our own Egos. Of course, looking at the bigger picture, this is all part of the experience being had by God-Consciousness and cannot be seen as either good or evil at that level either. It just is.

---

86   Japan recently (11 March 2011) experienced a 9.0 magnitude earthquake and consequent tsunami. It also faced a nuclear disaster as a nuclear power station built right on the coast of an earthquake and tsunami prone country was seriously damaged.

87   We have 15,000 or more earthquakes a year in New Zealand, including a few hundred of 4.0 magnitude or greater. (Per GeoNet, a collaboration between the NZ Earthquake Commission and GNS Science).

These are five of the filters on Creation; I am sure there are many more, but we do not need to get bogged down in this detail. With these five, you can get a taste of how a perfectly designed Creation can be changed by Man's Ego, his Lesser Self. We cannot blame God for the way things are — we can only blame ourselves. Even God, God-Consciousness does not blame us. He accepts that this is the way things are, and that things will change. So should we, and so will we.

The Creation was conceived in keeping with God's Laws. Perhaps we should take a look at these next.

CHAPTER 15

God's Laws

Now that we have discussed the Creation in great detail, it will be useful to discuss some of the Laws that God-Consciousness has set up to ensure the universe runs without any need for intervention. These are Laws such as the Laws of Mathematics that cannot be broken. Whether we have free will or not, these Laws apply.

Then there are the Moral Laws, which are able to be broken, and this is where free will comes in. However, an effect comes into play if we do break these Laws. An example of these Moral Laws would be the Ten Commandments. If we break the Sixth Commandment, *"Thou shalt not kill,"* then it is codified in the law books of most if not all countries, that the culprit will be punished, be it with a jail sentence or even an execution.

Apart from the laws of science and physics, I have listed a group of six Universal Laws, which like the physical laws, cannot be broken. These are simply truths that exist. A great example is the Law of Manifestation, currently popularised as the Law of Attraction.

So, let's take a brief look at God's Laws, starting with the physical and mathematical laws, and see what we can make of them.

The Laws of Mathematics

There is 1 + 1 = 2, and all the other mathematical statements that remain true whatever you do. If you get a different answer, you have made an error. That is all there is to it. Mathematics is the foundation of all science. Due to the dependability of Mathematics, science has been able to calculate and postulate many discoveries in the physical world, and in the universe. Such predictions go on to be proved in due course by observation.

Mathematics is also the foundation of all aspects of modern life. How would commerce run, how would appliances work, how would computers operate, or how would anything else we use in this modern world work, if it was not for the dependable Laws of Mathematics?

The Law of Gravity

Newton's Universal Law of Gravitation says that every object in the universe is attracted to every other object in the universe. Gravitational force is proportional to the product of the two masses involved and inversely proportional to the square of the distance between their centre points. Just as Π (pi) is a constant (3.1416) for the relationship of the circumference of a circle to its diameter, so there is a Universal Gravitational Constant called G, as a constant of the proportionality. While gravity is obviously useful for holding the universe together, why there is this attraction between objects is not known.

Gravitation acts on all objects with mass, it has an infinite range, it cannot be modified or protected against, and it is always an attractive force, rather than a repelling one. Gravitation is one of four fundamental forces in nature.

It also enables us to walk on the surface of the planet and keeps our coffee from floating out of the cup.

The Laws of Electromagnetism

Electromagnetism is the second of four fundamental forces in nature; it acts between electrically charged particles and has an infinite range. Electricity, magnetism, and light are produced by this force. There are a number of laws related to it such as Faradays' Law, Coulomb's Law, and Ohm's Law. Magnetism and electricity are intrinsically linked as electricity produces a magnetic field, and magnets are used to produce electricity.

Electricity was known to the ancients from, for instance, the shocks they got from electric eels and similar creatures. Benjamin Franklin proved the suspicion that lightning was electricity as recently as 1752. However, it was only in the early nineteenth century that the laws of electricity were discovered, and their application was only developed later in the century. The creation of an electric light bulb, for instance, was worked on throughout the century by various inventors, and Thomas Edison is credited with inventing the first practical incandescent light bulb. The first sales of light bulbs were around 1880, but it was 1910 before light bulbs that used the long-lasting and practical tungsten filament were developed.

The modern world could not function without electricity. We take it for granted with our lighting, refrigerators, stoves, water heaters, electric motors, computers, communications, the Internet, heating, banking, factories, and many other applications. Electricity enters every facet of our lives, yet we barely give it a thought. It was only 150 years ago that scientists started to figure out how to generate and apply this powerful energy.

The Laws of Electromagnetism have applied since the Big Bang 14 billion years ago, yet we have only just come to realise what electromagnetism can do for us and how to apply it. One wonders what other universal secrets there are that we have yet to discover and apply to our lives.

The Strong (Nuclear) Force and the Weak Force

The other two of the four known fundamental forces in nature are of short range and operate at a subatomic level. Strong Force is the strongest force, followed sequentially by Electromagnetic Force, Weak Force, and Gravitational Force.

Newton's Laws of Motion

Sir Isaac Newton discovered three Laws of Motion and published them in his *Principia* in 1687. They are:

1. **The Law of Inertia**. Every body continues in its state of rest, or of uniform motion in a straight line, unless it is compelled to change that state by forces impressed upon it.

2. **The Law of Motion**. The acceleration of a body is directly proportional to the net force acting on the body and inversely proportional to the mass of the body.

3. **The Action-Reaction Law.** To every action force there is an equal and opposite reaction force.

These Laws only start to break down at subatomic levels and nearing the speed of light. The principles of Albert Einstein's Special Theory of Relativity then apply.

The Laws of Thermodynamics

These have developed over time and have been modified and renumbered. The current Laws of Thermodynamics, which of course have continued through all time, however they came to be discovered or numbered, are:

0. Objects in thermodynamic equilibrium have the same temperature.

1. **The Law of Conservation of Energy.** Energy cannot be created or destroyed; it may be transformed from one form into another, but the total amount of energy never changes.

2. **The Law of Increased Entropy.** Energy flows naturally only from hot to cold, and tends to become dispersed as heat (entropy). Usable energy diminishes as it converts to unusable energy.

3. The entropy of a substance is zero if the absolute temperature is zero.

Absolute Zero

Absolute Zero temperature is the lowest possible temperature and is equal to minus 273.16°C. It is also known as 0°K (Kelvin).

Six Fundamental Constants

In his book *Just Six Numbers,* Martin Rees, the Astronomer Royal, has described six fundamental constants that determine the feasibility of the universe. It is simplest just to quote his summaries for our purposes.[88]

---

88   Rees, M., *Just Six Numbers: The Deep Forces that Shape the Universe*, Basic Books, New York, 2001, Pg. 2-3 (Copyright © 2001 Martin Rees. Reprinted by permission of Basic Books, a member of the Perseus Books Group.)

✦ N (nu) – *"The cosmos is so vast because there is one crucially important huge number N in nature, equal to 1,000,000,000,000,000,000,000,0 00,000, 000,000. This number measures the strength of the electrical forces that hold atoms together, divided by the force of gravity between them. If N had a few less zeros, only a short-lived miniature universe could exist: no creatures could grow larger than insects, and there would be no time for biological evolution."*

✦ ε (epsilon) – *"Another number, ε, whose value is 0.007, defines how firmly atomic nuclei bind together and how all the atoms on Earth were made. ... If ε were 0.006 or 0.008, we could not exist."*

✦ Ω (omega) – *"The cosmic number Ω (omega) measures the amount of material in our universe - galaxies, diffuse gas, and 'dark matter'. Ω tells us the relative importance of gravity and expansion energy in the universe. If this ratio were too high relative to a particular 'critical' value, the universe would have collapsed long ago; had it been too low, no galaxies or stars would have formed. The initial expansion speed seems to have been finely tuned."*

✦ λ (lambda) – *"An unsuspected new force - a cosmic 'antigravity' - controls the expansion of our universe, even though it has no discernible effect on scales less than a billion light-years. ... λ is very small. Otherwise its effect would have stopped galaxies and stars from forming, and cosmic evolution would have been stifled before it could even begin."*

✦ Q – *"The seeds for all cosmic structures - stars, galaxies, and clusters of galaxies - were all imprinted in the Big Bang. The fabric of our universe depends on one number, Q, which represents the ratio of two fundamental energies and is about 1/100,000 in value. If Q were even smaller, the universe would be inert and structureless; if Q were much larger, it would be a violent place, in which no stars or solar systems could survive, dominated by vast black holes."*

✦ D = 3 – Space has 3 dimensions – length, width, and height. *"It is the number of spatial dimensions in our world, D, and equals three. Life couldn't exist if D were two or four."*

As a conclusion to his book, Martin Rees says, *"A few basic physical laws set the 'rules'; our emergence from a simple Big Bang was sensitive to six 'cosmic numbers'. Had these numbers not been 'well-tuned', the gradual unfolding of layer upon layer of complexity would have been quenched. Are there an infinity of other universes that are 'badly tuned', and therefore sterile? Is our entire universe an 'oasis' in a multiverse? Or should we seek other reasons for the providential values of our six numbers?"* [89]

We could, of course, go on. I could research all the physical laws and list them here, but frankly, that is not the subject of this book. The point I want to make is that science has not created these laws, nor are these laws new. The laws that rule the way the universe works are laws that have been in place for 14 billion years, dating back to when God-Consciousness set up the universe with a Big Bang. Just because we have only recently discovered these Laws does not mean they did not exist. Likewise, the fact that we have not codified other laws that have yet to be discovered does not mean that they do not exist and operate right now.

Scientists are at the forefront of the understanding of the physical universe. Their work is tremendous, and we owe these dedicated men and women much appreciation for their work. They are improving the world's knowledge of itself daily, and at an accelerating rate. There has always been a battle between the spiritual fathers and the scientific fathers of this world. Each side believes implicitly that it is correct. With the tremendous advances being made today, I believe there will soon come a time when those differences can be set aside. Then we can all recognise the true nature of the universe as designed and created by God-Consciousness, within His own Being, for His own purpose, and for His own experience. We will also realise we are each an integral part of that God-Consciousness experience, and that our sense of Ego and separation is not only an illusion, but a self-created source of personal pain and unhappiness.

Now that we have covered some of the laws of the universe that science has discovered, let us take a look at the Laws of God as the church has depicted them.

---

89   Rees, Pg. 161

The Ten Commandments

The Ten Commandments[90] were given to Moses to give to the children of Israel. These were followed by sundry other laws and ordinances,[91] which were coined in terms specific to the people then. This record in the Book of Exodus forms the oldest document of Jewish Law. Remember that Moses lived about 1500 BC so the wording had to suit the people and the culture of 3,500 years ago.

The Ten Commandments are:

1. *Thou shalt have no other gods before me.*

2. *Thou shalt not make unto thee any graven image, or any likeness of any thing that is in heaven above, or that is in the earth beneath, or that is in the water under the earth: Thou shalt not bow down thyself to them, nor serve them.*

3. *Thou shalt not take the name of the Lord thy God in vain.*

4. *Remember the Sabbath day, to keep it holy. Six days shalt thou labour, and do all thy work: But the seventh day is the Sabbath of the Lord thy God.*

5. *Honour thy father and thy mother.*

6. *Thou shalt not kill.*

7. *Thou shalt not commit adultery.*

8. *Thou shalt not steal.*

9. *Thou shalt not bear false witness against thy neighbour.*

10. *Thou shalt not covet thy neighbour's house, thou shalt not covet thy neighbour's wife, nor his manservant, nor his maidservant, nor his ox, nor his ass, nor any thing that is thy neighbour's.*

---

90 *Exodus* 20: 3-17
91 *Exodus* 20:22 - 23:33

Jesus' Commandments as a Summary of the Ten Commandments

Jesus summarised the Ten Commandments and *"all the law"* in two clauses.[92] Review the Ten Commandments, and you will see they are covered totally in just these two sentences:

1. *Thou shalt love the Lord thy God with all thy heart, and with all thy soul, and with all thy mind.*

2. *Thou shalt love thy neighbour as thyself,* or *Do unto others as you would have them do unto you.* This is called The Golden Rule.[93]

If you find the Ten Commandments a bit antiquated, applying these two Commandments will achieve the same result. You can't go far wrong with doing this. The Ten Commandments and Jesus' summary of them are very different to the laws of science. Physical laws describe immutable facts, so by definition cannot be broken. Or, if they are broken, then the wording of the law itself needs to be changed so that it is worded more accurately.

With the Commandments, which many people treat as God's Law, the *laws* can in fact be broken. This is called *sinning*. We discuss other aspects of sin in later chapters in Parts Three and Four. We do not get punished directly by God for our sins, despite what the Church may say. We punish ourselves by believing in attitudes and actions that are incompatible with God's Law and, therefore, with Truth. These attitudes and actions are created by the Ego, and the fruits of them are pain, suffering, and unhappiness that we experience directly.

The punishment we experience occurs through the workings of the third set of God's Laws, the Universal Laws.

---

92 *Matthew* 22:37-40
93 While commonly ascribed to Jesus, this Law appears in the Laws recorded by Moses at the time of the Ten Commandments (see *Leviticus* 19:18). It also appears in many different religions and philosophies from ancient times – see http://en.wikipedia.org/wiki/The _ Golden _ Rule. While the saying, "Do unto others as you would have them do unto you", is assumed to be biblical, it is not, but first appeared in the Roman Catholic Catechism from 1583. *Luke* 6:31 says, "And as ye would that men should do to you, do ye also to them likewise."

Universal Laws

This is a group of laws that are always true and cannot be broken, just like the physical laws. Some of these laws are well known, although unfortunately, many people forget them or don't believe in them. This is unfortunate because it means such people are cutting themselves off from reaping the benefits the laws provide. The laws continue to operate whether you believe in them or not, just as with the physical laws. This will become clearer to you once we have discussed them.

Bruce McArthur defines a Universal Law as *"an unbreakable, unchangeable principle of life that operates inevitably, all the time."* [94] This means that each of us individually is in the same boat. The Universal Laws act impartially, justly, and equally for every single person. What could be fairer than that?

Universal Laws, by definition, cannot be transgressed. Thus the concept of sin in this sense would be a little out of place. If you do something that is harmful to another, the Universal Law that is invoked will bring the appropriate punishment (karma) on you. It is just a question of reaping what you sow.

There are many Universal Laws worded in many different ways. Here is my choice of the six most significant ones.

1. God is[95]

2. The Law of Cause and Effect[96]
   (including the Law of Karma)

3. Like creates like[97]
   (including The Law of Manifestation)

4. The Law of Increase: Your attitude and intention determine the extent of your result[98]

5. The Law of Balance: The universe remains constantly in a state of equilibrium[99]

---

94 McArthur, B., *Your Life: Why It Is the Way It Is and What You Can Do About It - Understanding the Universal Laws*, A.R.E. Press, Virginia Beach, 1993, Pg. 5.
95 McArthur, Pg. 121
96 McArthur, Pg. 79
97 McArthur, Pg. 13
98 McArthur, Pg. 41
99 McArthur, Pg. 213

6. The Law of Self: You are a unique individual, and the fulfilment of your desires is of primary importance. The same is equally true of every other person.[100]

Bruce McArthur states that there are about sixty laws that apply to our lives. His book covers thirty-two Universal Laws, and is based on the Readings of Edgar Cayce (1877-1945), who is considered one of the greatest psychics of the twentieth century. I heartily recommend McArthur's book to you, as he has done a brilliant job of explaining the Universal Laws in clear and practical ways.

I have summarised the main Laws and grouped them so that we end up with a few major Laws. Many of the Universal Laws that McArthur defines are subtle variations of the same Law. There is benefit in focussing on the major Laws so that we can come to really understand them. In practice, we can extrapolate from there to apply the variations that naturally occur in specific life situations.

So, let's go through these six Universal Laws in outline now. In Part Four we look at them in detail in a practical way as a part of *Daily Living as a God Franchisee*.

1. God Is

We should say "God-Consciousness Is" of course, except that "God Is" is much snappier! The corollaries that apply to this Law include:

+ The Universal Laws are *created* by God-Consciousness and are, therefore, as infinite, inevitable, and unchanging as He is. The Laws are, in truth, the very nature of God-Consciousness.

+ The universe is ultimately good. Evil (or other bad things) is purely the appearance of an absence of good.

+ God loves His Creation, and Love is an essential force of the universe.

---

100 McArthur, Pg. 147

2. The Law of Cause and Effect

The essence of all causative factors, including your own intentions and the current conditions or way things are, results in the exact effect you will experience. This Law has a number of corollaries:

+ Nothing is by chance.
+ There are no such things as accidents or bad luck.
+ Life is the experience of your choices.
+ You are responsible for everything that happens to you.

Naturally, the Law of Cause and Effect includes the Law of Karma — that you reap what you sow. The next Law, Like Creates Like, can also be seen as related to the Law of Karma.

3. Like Creates Like

While you may not have heard of the Like Creates Like Law before, no doubt you will have heard of more colloquial renditions such as:

> What goes around comes around
> You reap what you sow (The Law of Karma)
> The Law of Attraction
> The Law of Manifestation.

This Law has a number of corollaries. You will see that many of these corollaries together make up what is called the Law of Attraction (Law of Manifestation):

+ You reap what you sow.
+ You must give in order to receive.
+ Your life experience mirrors your self.
+ Like attracts like.
+ As you believe, so it will come into reality for you.
+ You intensify what you focus on.
+ You attract what you expect.

4. The Law of Increase: Your attitude and intention determine the degree of your result

As we have said, what you sow, you reap. This Law says your attitude and intention directly affect the extent of the result you get. There are three aspects to working with the Law of Increase: desire; intention and expectation; and attitude.

5. The Law of Balance: The universe remains constantly in a state of equilibrium

Just like water settling to find its lowest level, the universe as a whole always moves to maintain a state of equilibrium. Two of the corollaries are:

+ All exchanges between you and others balance.

+ You have to sacrifice one thing in order to receive something else.

6. The Law of Self

The Law of Self can be stated as follows: **You are a unique individual, and the fulfilment of your desires is of primary importance. The same is equally true of every other person**. This is not a sign of selfishness, but rather an acknowledgement of your unique role as a God Franchisee.

We discuss the implications and use of these six Universal Laws and their corollaries in more detail in Part Four.

We have just touched on some of the more important of God's Laws. We can rest assured whether we have identified all God's Laws or not, they are alive and well and operating in the universe. Some are laws that affect the physical operation and existence of the universe, and science has made an excellent job of uncovering these. No doubt, there are many more physical laws to be uncovered, or at least to be rephrased. Likewise, with the Universal Laws, there are many more that have not been listed here. This list is just a sample of the types of laws that exist.

Many scientists and mathematicians have worked on, and still work on, the problem of the elusive *theory of everything.* One would imagine that such a unified theory is feasible, although scientists will need to allow their view of the world to widen to include consciousness. As we know by now, God-Consciousness is the source and the foundation of the universe, so by excluding Him, the theory of everything might well remain elusive. In a unified theory, all God's Laws need to be taken into account.

Part Two has given us a clear insight into **The God Franchise**. In Part Four, we will continue with what it means to be a God Franchisee in a practical way; however, before we do that, I would like to spend some time in Part Three comparing the various beliefs people hold. We will see if we can derive an integrated thesis that will be reasonably acceptable to most people who have an open mind, and can allow that a wider definition or concept of God is possible. With this, **The God Franchise** might just bring us closer to an understanding of how the different religions, the atheists, and the scientists can all be right.

PART THREE

Comparing
Our Beliefs

CHAPTER 16

Can We All be Right?

We have reached an important stage in this book. The main thesis of **The God Franchise** has just been detailed, and in Part Four, *Daily Living as a God Franchisee*, we will move on to the practical application of what we have discussed so far. But now, in Part Three, we will try to integrate the various religions around the world, and perhaps draw them together with **The God Franchise**. Some of the assertions I have made may seem a little foreign to you, or may be contradictory to what you know to be true.

Strange as it may seem, it is possible, whatever your beliefs have been to date, that they may not be too far afield from what I have said here. This may surprise you because on the surface we seem to be miles apart. We have different factions disagreeing with other factions. We have wars all over the world in the name of God. For Heaven's sake! We have religious people disagreeing with spiritual people, and people who can't see the difference. We have religious people disagreeing with scientists and atheists. We have many different religions each teaching apparently very different truths. Frankly, our beliefs in the world are in total disarray.

Wouldn't it be great if we could all just agree on something, something really big, and something really important? I am not suggesting that everyone should drop their beliefs and start to believe that **The God Franchise** is the only answer — not at all. What I am suggesting is that whatever your beliefs were when you started reading this book, perhaps they can rationally incorporate some of the concepts of **The God Franchise**. Perhaps your beliefs can soften and broaden so you are able to reach out and meet others halfway.

To help with this, Part Three of this book looks for common ground so we can all move forward positively to discover how we can improve our experience of day-to-day life, and reach a place of peace, prosperity, and health — or whatever it is that we want from life. Why do I believe this is possible? There has to be one central Truth, one theory of everything that must encompass all the other valid theories and belief systems. Sure, there are some eccentric ideas out there that won't fit in; however, if there are millions of people believing the same thing, then there is likely to be some truth in what they believe. They are unlikely to all be wrong. I have to accept, for instance, that Christians are right, Hindus are right, Buddhists are right, Islam is right, and Judaism is right — and let's not forget the scientists. How can millions of believers be totally wrong and misguided? Therefore, it makes sense to reach for a point of synthesis where we can all recognise a single common place, and yet still continue with the individual beliefs and faiths we choose to follow. We have the free will to do so.

Recognising the Ego in Your Beliefs

Ever since Adam and Eve accepted the gift of free will from God-Consciousness and then chose to eat the fruit of the Tree of the Knowledge of Good and Evil, Ego has been the biggest problem Mankind has had to deal with. Of course, some aspects of Ego have helped evolution move forward, in the sense that if you want to really achieve something, be it intellectual, spiritual, scientific, financial, in sport, or whatever, having a forceful Ego will help to drive you to full achievement. Well, that is the way it has usually worked so far, and for that reason, I am not advocating dropping or suppressing your Ego completely. While there is a time and place for Ego, with all due respect, perhaps this is not one of them.

So, humbly, let's take a look at your beliefs. If I were to suggest that you should change them, what is the first thing that comes up? The Ego says, "How dare he try to change my beliefs? I can believe what I want to. Anyway, what I believe is true, so how can I change my beliefs? My parents taught me these truths, my church taught me these truths, my teachers taught me these truths, my professors taught me these truths, and so on. I know my beliefs are true!"

Yes, I know. The Ego-Mind will always come back with this response because it is under threat. This is, perhaps, the start (or a continuation) of the fight for survival. Of course, the Ego is going to kick up a serious fight.

Perhaps, for a while, you could allow your Higher Self, the real essence of you, to have a look in; you could recognise the Ego for what it is, and open your Higher Self to the possibilities that might be hiding in the words you are reading here. You can always return to your Ego when you wish to, but in the meantime, give yourself permission now to read these unifying ideas.

The Approach We Will Take

If I were to list the beliefs of each of the major religions and then work with them, I am sure we would quickly come unstuck. This is because, in reality, no major religion has specific beliefs that all members of that religion adhere to. Roman Catholics believe something very different to Evangelical believers, and both differ radically from Christian Scientists. Nevertheless, all three fall under the Christian umbrella. Likewise, not all Hindus believe the same things, and neither do all Buddhists, all Jewish people, or all Muslims.

So instead, we will discuss certain beliefs without worrying too much about which religion they apply to. You will know what you believe, and we will work within that context. At the end, we should have covered all the main tenets that we need to consider. Let us begin.

CHAPTER 17

Approaching God

As you know, it is possible to view a particular situation between yourself and another person from multiple points of view. You can view it from your own perspective. You can view it from the other person's perspective. You can also view it from a third party's point of view, that is, from the objective viewpoint of an onlooker who is not involved in the situation. You can take this further by seeing it from the perspective of another onlooker who is observing the original third party, who is viewing the situation between the two of you. And so on.

You could even imagine that you are watching the interaction from above the players and/or from floor level and/or from any other perspective you choose. You can take the viewpoint of a fly on the wall. Likewise, if there are more than two of you involved, you can imagine the interaction as experienced by each of these people.

Why am I telling you this? Because firstly, it gives you insight into how it is possible to (virtually) become another person and experience things from a different perceptive position. Secondly, the exercise makes you aware that viewpoints other than your own are valid and important. You will notice that the experience from their perspective is equally as important as yours from your own perspective. From this, understanding can arise.

Thirdly, this process is an analogy for how God-Consciousness experiences His Creation. He experiences all the different aspects of your life from your perspective. He also experiences the lives and interactions of you and the other players. He, therefore, experiences all interactions from all points of view simultaneously. You can say that God-Consciousness is each of the people described above, and the collective experience of all involved is God's total experience.

Imagine two earthworms are having a discussion in the language that earthworms have. They are deliberating on what Mankind is all about. Perhaps, what Mankind has achieved and what its purpose is. They might consider Mankind's philosophy, the beliefs and truths, the hopes and aspirations, the lifetime and power of Mankind. Perhaps you might agree with me that earthworm language would soon run into trouble with describing what Mankind is all about. Does this mean they should not have the discussion at all? Or, does it mean it is best that the earthworms realise all they can do is hint at the truth, because there is no way of using their language to describe this reality? They may even agree there is no way they can take literally any of the words they use.

Well, the difference between earthworms and Mankind is tiny compared with the difference between Mankind and God. For some reason, we are arrogant and egotistical enough to believe we can use words to describe God, and what is written or said can be taken literally. The wonderful books and scriptures we have, including The Bible, cannot be taken literally because we do not have the words or concepts to adequately describe the Truth of God's reality. We can only catch a glimpse of the Truth. We can only extrapolate from analogy. We can only look at the signposts and say, yes, I get a sense of what the Truth is, what God is. But that is all. The books and scriptures, including the Bible, may be inspired by God, but they have been physically committed to paper, and translated where necessary, by men and by women. We are fallible and we have Egos, and both of these facts act as filters to what the real Truth is. Also, we need to remember the audience for whom the words were written, and for whom the original teachings were given. What is meaningful to us in the twenty-first century would have been totally meaningless to people living 1,000, 2,000, or 4,000 years ago.

The authors, translators, and scribes have done the best they could; I am sure of that. I am equally sure nothing that is written can be taken literally when it is describing God and his Truth. Nevertheless, we must try, just as many philosophers and writers have done before us, to make some sense of what that Truth is. Please accept the total inadequacy of words and concepts, and try to get a sense of the Truth. Allow any preconceptions to rest for a while as you open to what may be a perception of the Truth that is very different from that to which you have been accustomed.

Since we will start this integrative discussion with our various perceptions of God, perhaps we should revisit the question: Does God exist? We need to agree on this point as a priority.

CHAPTER 18

Does God Exist?

We have discussed the question of God's existence at length in Part One and the appendices. If you already believe, or have been convinced by the discussion so far that God does exist, there is little further to debate here, and you can move on to the next chapter. If you are an atheist, I would like to ask you what the basis of your atheism is. Just give that some thought for a moment.

For Atheists and Other Non-Believers

If you are an atheist because that is the way you were brought up, or through a neglect or reluctance to explore the larger issues, then you are no different from many a church-, synagogue-, mosque-, or temple-goer. You believe what you believe because you have not given it any serious thought, and it is easier to believe what you have been told than to challenge it. So, here is an opportunity to discover something a little different.

If you are an atheist after seeing what religion has offered the world and have rejected what you see, may I suggest you read this book very carefully and reconsider your position. Many atheists may well reject the Almighty God in Heaven who presides over His sinning subjects and decides who is heading for Heaven and who for Hell, eternally. If that was all there was on offer, I would be an atheist too. Spirituality is so much more than that, and presumably, if you have read this far, you can now see another possibility of Truth: moving towards an understanding of what life is all about and where you fit into it. If you are a convinced and shutdown atheist who will not budge from your beliefs, then, like any other zealot or fundamentalist, you are unlikely to be reading these present words anyway.

While I assert there is a God and atheists may assert there is not, I wonder at this point whether it is semantics at fault. **The God Franchise** encompasses evolution as part of God's Plan, and an aspect of God can be seen in the very life force that animates the whole of the universe. When you allow for the possibility of a life force that animates you and is your inner quiet self when you are totally at peace, you may realise this is the essence of God-Consciousness. When you allow your Ego and mind to stop clamouring to control your very being, there, in that quiet place, you may just get a glimpse, a sense, of God within you.

Even if you are tempted to call it something else, let me assure you that what you call that presence of being is exactly what I call God. Think of God as **Being** rather than as **a Being**. Then we may not be too far apart.

If your position is that it is unreasonable to believe in God, or that there is no way of knowing whether God exists, or that so much harm has been done in the name of God through religion, then I will give you a free pass.

However, if you are still unable to accept that God exists, please reread Part One, *Does God Really Exist?* and the associated appendices. For the rest of us, let's move on...

CHAPTER 19

Is God One or Many?

T he God Franchise asserts that God is one. Most religions agree that God is one, although some seem to have more than one God. Let us look into this a little more closely.

Hinduism has thousands of gods. Some accounts say 330 million or even six billion deities! To the average monotheist this seems to be ridiculous. However, what is overlooked is these gods or deities are all seen to be aspects of the Supreme One, Brahman (in soft polytheism). And Brahman is the eternal, infinite, immutable, omnipresent, transcendent God of monotheism. Even when any of these many gods and deities is treated as a separate being from Brahman, (as in hard polytheism), it is still realised that Brahman is the Supreme Being. And, as we can now understand, the Supreme One is experiencing Himself through each of these gods and deities anyway.

Apart from the sheer number of deities, what is the difference between this Hindu view of God and, say, the Triune Godhead, the Holy Trinity of Christians? In the Bible, God the Father appears to be separate from God the Son, and also separate from God the Holy Spirit (Holy Ghost), and yet Christianity is a monotheist religion. As Kevin Connor writes:

> "The Scriptures give us the revelation of the eternal Godhead, who has revealed Himself as one God, existing in three Persons, even the Father, the Son and the Holy Spirit; distinguishable but indivisible in essence; co-eternal, co-existent, co-equal in nature, attributes, power and glory. There is but one eternal Godhead, who is one undivided and indivisible essence; and

in this one essence there are three eternal distinctions, the Father, the Son and the Holy Spirit."[101]

Islam has only one God, Allah, and Judaism has one God who is addressed by many titles. The name of God is YHWH (the Tetragrammaton) which is traditionally not pronounced. Some Jewish people will write the word God as G_d in the same spirit. The Bible says God told Moses that His name was I AM and also said I AM THAT I AM.[102] The word YHWH has a complex etymology and appears to mean *He who is* or *He who exists*. I AM is just as appropriate. The name may also be written as *Jehovah* or *Yahweh*.

Sikhism is monotheistic as a development from Hinduism and Islam. Baha'i developed from Islam and is monotheistic. A basic Baha'i belief is that all religions come from the same source, so there is considerable respect for all religions.

It is interesting to read in *The Compact Guide to World Religions*, a Christian publication, that Zoroastrianism is seen as dualistic with *"two opposing Gods"*[103] and Christianity is seen as monotheistic and their doctrine asserts that *"God is one in essence (or being, or substance) and three in person"*.[104] The truth about Zoroastrianism is they have one God, Ahura Mazda (*Wise Lord*), and according to Zoroaster, Spenta Mainyu (*the Good Spirit*) and Angra Mainyu (*the Evil Spirit*) both issue from Ahura Mazda. Far from existing as independent beings, these two spirits are found together within Ahura Mazda.[105] Zoroastrianism is, in fact, monotheistic, and these *"two opposing Gods"* are similar to the Holy Trinity of the Christians. One could also mention the prominence given by Christianity to Satan, who of course is the equivalent of the *Evil Spirit* of Zoroaster.

What about Buddhism? The Buddha is said to have dismissed

101 Conner, K., *The Foundations of Christian Doctrine*, City Christian Publishing, Portland, OR, 1980, Pg. 41. (used with permission www.CityChristianPublishing.com)
102 *Exodus* 3:14
103 Halverson, D. (Ed.), *The Compact Guide to World Religions*, Bethany House, Minneapolis, 1996, Pg. 15.
104 Halverson, Pg. 115
105 Refer to Hopfe, L., and Woodward, M., (Eds.), *Religions of the World*, 8th Ed., Prentice Hall, Upper Saddle River, NJ, 2001, Pg. 223-226, for a detailed explanation of this.

ideas of a Creator God as irrelevant. It was not that he was atheistic, but rather that he saw focussing on such matters did not aid release from *samsara* (the cycle of birth and death) and *dukkha* (suffering). Full attention should be placed on attaining *nirvana*. Nirvana *"is cessation of existence, as we know existence; the attainment of Being (as distinct from becoming); union with Ultimate Reality. The Buddha speaks of it as 'unborn, unoriginated, uncreated, unformed', contrasting it with the born, originated, created and formed phenomenal world."*[106]

The Ultimate Reality spoken of here is easily the same as the unborn, unoriginated, uncreated, unformed, transcendent God-Consciousness beyond the created universe. Buddhism simply does not accept that there is *ultimate* reality in the physical world.

There are also many smaller religions, some of them folk-religions, that believe in multiple gods. These gods are often the result of looking at nature, and then deifying the natural forces at play. There is no need for us to look at these specifically for our purposes. Pantheists see the whole of the universe, including nature, as God. **The God Franchise** sees God-Consciousness as both transcendent (distinct and separate from His Creation) and immanent (present throughout the universe).

Within the World Religions, there would appear to be a common acceptance of a monotheistic God, even if that God is not the personal Judeo-Christian-Islamic God. We will discuss the question of God being a Personal God in the next chapter, so we can take that aspect out of the picture for the moment. So, in almost all religions, we find there is ultimately one God.

Even in the Ultimate Reality of Buddhism and the Tao of Taoism there is a common acceptance that there exists a greater reality than ourselves that is a part of our lives, either directly or indirectly, either now or at some future time in nirvana. In both cases, they do not like to even give It a Name, so Ultimate Reality and Tao will have to suffice for our purposes. Neither Buddhists not Taoists are atheists — rather, they feel that the Truth is beyond what we can talk about. It is this Reality that I have called God-Consciousness.

---

106 Humphreys, C., *A Popular Dictionary of Buddhism*, Arco, London, 1962, Pg. 138. (Copyright © The Buddhist Society, with acknowledgment to The Society of Authors as their Literary Representative.)

To clarify:

Christianity	God
Islam	Allah
Judaism	YHWH
Hinduism	Brahman
Zoroastrianism	Ahura Mazda
Buddhism	Ultimate Reality
Taoism	Tao ("the eternally nameless")
The God Franchise	God-Consciousness

Why are we disagreeing? There is one supreme state of being and Its Holy Name is God-Allah-YHWH-Brahman-Ahura Mazda-Ultimate Reality-Tao-God Consciousness.

But what of the atheists? Atheists appear to be fixated on proving that God does not exist. They are fascinated by the fact that people might believe in God, and they are fascinated by the great harm that has been done in the world in the name of religion. When you look into this more deeply, you will find the vast majority of anti-theistic feeling is towards the Personal God of Judaism, Christianity, and Islam. Dare I say that many of their points are valid? The case has been well and truly made, and yet the theists *know* that there is a God and that the atheists cannot be right. This is an impasse.

We have also just seen that the vast majority of us believe in One Supreme Being whom we have called God-Allah-YHWH-Brahman-Ahura Mazda-Ultimate Reality-Tao-God Consciousness, or *God-Consciousness* for short. The only way to find the middle ground is for us to accept that *perhaps* the Judeo-Christian-Islamic God is simply not the most accurate concept of God. This statement flies in the face of over half of the world's population who are nominally Jewish, Christian, or Muslim. It does, however, cover the other nearly half of the world's population who don't believe in the Judeo-Christian-Islamic God.

As I have already declared, the God I believe in is God-Consciousness, and *that* God may well meet the needs of both those who believe in a Personal God and those who don't. It may even include the needs of the atheist. This is the next question we need to discuss: Is God a Personal God?

CHAPTER 20

Is God a Personal God?

According to estimates,[107] just over half the world's population sees God as a Personal God. Since *"God created man in his own image, in the image of God created he him,"*[108] it follows that God must be a Person. The Bible gives God many attributes and these include emotions and the ability to give us moral standards to uphold. He is able to judge us, His subjects, and on the Judgement Day, He will decide individually whether we can go to Heaven (Paradise) or whether we go to Hell for eternity. He has the power to forgive us our sins, however, if we show allegiance to Him before we are judged.

God cares for us and is good to us. For this, we must show our gratitude and praise and worship Him. We can pray to God and He will hear our prayers, and if we are worthy, He will answer those prayers. God is knowable through the scriptures, and through direct communion with Him. God longs for us to turn to Him so that He can love us and grant us salvation. Fellowship with God can be seen as the purpose of life, thus giving our life meaning.

Dean Halverson writes, *"Holiness indicates God is personal, rather than an impersonal oneness or an impersonal energy, because only persons are able to*

---

107 There are many references on the Internet to about 2 billion Christians (29% of world population of 7 billion) and 1.6 billion Muslims (23%). There are other much smaller religions that also believe in a Personal God, so the total is over 52%.

108 *Genesis* 1:27

make moral distinctions."[109] God may be seen as absolutely holy. (Holy means *endowed or invested with extreme purity or sublimity. Sublime means of high moral, aesthetic, intellectual or spiritual value; noble; exalted; inspiring deep veneration, awe ... .*)[110] The Bible says, *"Be ye holy; for I am holy."*[111] We need to be holy before God will accept us.

However, many people cannot accept God as being limited in the ways just described. God is far greater than this description of a Personal God allows. It almost makes God petty and vain. It makes God a dictator. A Personal God invokes fear and control, and the hope that He cannot see into the darker recesses of our being. The notion of a Personal God also empowers His so-called representatives on Earth to wield power over His subjects — something many of us find particularly repugnant.

I like the way the Kabbalah (Qabalah, Cabala), the mystical system of Israel and Judaism, looks at God. The Kabbalist's Tree of Life has also been used by the Western Esoteric Tradition, and the Kabbalah has gained resurgence in popularity in recent times. Beyond the 10 Sephiroth (plural of Sephirah) and the 22 Paths between them as laid out in the Tree of Life, there are three layers of Godhead: Ain, Ain Soph, and Ain Soph Aur. While all 32 Paths (10 + 22) have names of God (from the Old Testament) associated with them, these three layers beyond the Paths indicate the totally unknowable aspects of God, the Unmanifest. They are termed the three Veils of Negative Existence: Ain (Negativity), Ain Soph (The Limitless) and Ain Soph Aur (The Limitless Light). Kether, the highest of the 10 Sephiroth, the I AM of the Bible, comes out of Ain Soph Aur. Realise that the use of the word *Negative* is not the opposite of positive in a comparative way. It is an indication that whatever it is, it is unknown to us, as it is Unmanifest.

Thus, the starting point for Man's finite understanding is Kether, the first Sephirah, and what is beyond is *That*, which is Unknown. Note, It is not necessarily Unknowable, it is just Unknown at this stage of our evolution. So, Kether is the most transcendent aspect of God

109 Halverson, D. (Ed.), *The Compact Guide to World Religions*, Bethany House, Minneapolis, 1996, Pg. 18.
110 *Collins English Dictionary*
111 *1 Peter* 1:16

we can conceive, and the Kabbalah still allows for three layers of God beyond that. While all this is incomprehensible to us, I see this as an indication of Truth and Reality. It also indicates taking the Bible and other books and scriptures literally is quite simply limiting God.

Much of what I have said in this chapter is quite vague and uses words that may not mean a lot to us. The Kabbalah is very interesting, but without study, it all sounds very strange. What I want to convey is God, the true God, at the back of everything that exists, cannot readily be known by Man. He is the Unmanifest, the Unknown, the Ultimate Reality. The real reason for this is we, in the manifest world, do not have the words or the concepts to describe or know God. Whatever we say is less than what God is. We are like those earthworms trying to describe the wonders of Mankind and Mankind's achievements.

This does not mean God does not know us. Just as we know a huge amount about earthworms, probably everything there is to know about earthworms, so God knows absolutely everything about us. So, if we pray to Him, or praise Him, and worship Him, He is fully aware of that and what it means. If we are in a relationship with God, then that is a real relationship from both our own perspective and God's. If you are looking for the peace of knowing God loves you as a Father would, and that you can take your troubles to Him at any time, then you have it.

Nevertheless, this does not make God a Personal God in the sense that He is a person. A person is a manifestation, and God is beyond manifestation, in Himself. He is God-Consciousness. We have to allow God to be far greater than a person is. We have to allow Him to be omnipotent, omnipresent, omniscient, immutable, and eternal — a state that is not a personal state as we experience personal.

Now, this is the interesting bit; as we have said, God-Consciousness made the universe, including you and me, out of His very substance — out of Consciousness. As Dion Fortune puts it, *"The universe is really a thought-form projected from the mind of God."*[112] Therefore, God-Consciousness is in you and in me, and **is** you and **is** me. This means that God **is** the ultimate Personal God. He is in and is every person on

---

112 Fortune, D., *The Mystical Qabalah*, Ernest Benn, London, 1935, Pg. 17.

this planet, and is in and is every living creature on this planet, and is in and is everything in His Creation, and is in and is everything in the universe.

If you wish to treat God as a Personal God whom you can talk to as a friend and companion, that is fine. If I choose to feel the wonder of His being in everyone and everything around me, then I can. My Personal God is in everyone I meet. Treat everyone you meet face to face **as if it is God whom you are meeting face to face**. For, in fact, it is.

I cannot limit God to being some sort of Super Man living in a place called Heaven with Jesus to His right hand and angels and archangels all around. I am sorry. That is not the God I know and can believe in. He is far, far beyond that in His own essence (Ain, Ain Soph and Ain Soph Aur), and He is so much closer than that, as He is me. He is the food I eat, He is the house I live in, He is my books, He is my friends, He is every person I will ever meet, and He is my life. He is also you.

At a personal level, God-Consciousness is your Higher Self and my Higher Self. This is God manifest in the world today, experiencing the world through you and me, and as you and me. How more Personal a God do you want?

The Christian assertion that a sense of morality and relationship, that forgiveness and holiness, can only belong to a Personal God and, therefore, this proves that God is personal, is flawed in its simplicity. While these qualities may need to be expressed in a personal way, this is done through the very personal Higher Self, which is God-Consciousness in manifestation. Christians believe God is omnipresent (*"For in him we live, and move, and have our being."*[113]), so He is in and is every part of our being. He is more personal in this way than the average Christian ever conceives.

God is also transcendent, and is above and beyond His Creation, another belief that Christians hold. The Truth is that the two concepts have become confused and merged. They just need to be understood as two separate concepts and two separate Truths. They are both true and

---

113 *Acts* 17:28

do not contradict each other.

Holography is very interesting in that a recording is made of the scattered light from an object at the time the image is recorded, and then the projected image provides a 3D hologram of the original. This can be viewed from different angles as if the object was physically being viewed from that position in this moment. The point I want to make about holograms is that if you break the image into small pieces, each of the pieces still contains the full image and it can still be viewed in detail (although quality suffers).

DNA is rather like that too. The DNA code for the whole body is held in each cell of the body. Even though each cell has developed to play a particular role in a particular organ or structure of the body, the whole person is still represented through the DNA in each cell of the body.

God can perhaps be seen in this way too. Although He may be seen as transcendent, and so, outside His Creation, He is also present within each of His Creations — every person, every animal, every plant, every rock, and of course within every cell of every living thing, and in every atom of every molecule of every physical manifestation in the universe. This is what *omnipresence* means.

So, while I have said I do not accept the Personal God of Judaism, Christianity, and Islam, I can accept the Personal God who is within me as my Higher Self, who is closer than breathing, who comforts me every step of the way, and who inspires me as I write this book.

Think about it. Or don't think, and just absorb the Truth pointed to by this signpost.

CHAPTER 21

Are God and His Creation One and the Same?

The previous chapter may lead some people to believe I am saying that God and His Creation are one and the same. Am I saying that? Well, the answer is yes and no, so I had better explain.

Pantheists and some others would have us believe God is in his Creation and not outside it at all. Mother Earth effectively becomes the Goddess. You can understand this thinking when you look at the beauty, complexity, and wonder of the created universe, and if you have no contact with God or concept of God outside that Creation. At least you are part right in that; yes, God is very much in and of His Creation, including you and me.

However, I also say no; God is also definitely outside His Creation. Remember our diagram in Chapter 9? Our part of Creation, the universe as we know it, is represented as a space-time bubble inside the Eternal Now of God-Consciousness.

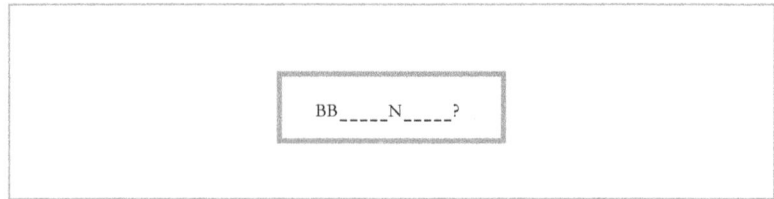

(Where BB = The Big Bang, N = Now, and ? = The end of our universe at some future time)

So pantheists are correct in their assertions if they are only looking at the inner rectangle. However, with this they are only looking at part of the story; there is also the transcendent side of God present outside this rectangle in Eternity. One of God's qualities is that He is omnipresent, which means He is present in everything and is everywhere. The only way He could do this and be this is by being in His Creation. So God is both transcendent (distinct and separate from His Creation) and immanent (present throughout the universe).

This ability to be both transcendent and immanent simultaneously is a similar concept to the Christian concept of God the Father and God the Son (and God the Holy Spirit) being separate yet One. One can even see God the Father being the transcendent aspect, the Creator, while God the Son is the immanent aspect, the Creation. And just as God created the Creation out of His own essence, so God the Son was born of the Virgin Mary (that is, fathered directly by God). The analogy is in the creation (birth) as a first cause rather than in the way Mankind creates things or produces a son.

To complete this analogy, God the Holy Spirit can be seen as the spirit or soul of each one of us — this is our Higher Self. This is the part of us that is God-Consciousness in manifestation, in experience. By contrast, our Lesser Self is manmade Ego and it is that Ego who sins, if we are to use that terminology. Our Higher Self, as we have already said, is the Personal God Christians have a personal relationship with, and is God the Holy Spirit.

The above is rather a powerful concept, so I would like to repeat it in a different way. Christians see the monotheistic God as *"one in essence (or being, or substance) and three in person."*[114] So we could say:

God

=

God the Father

God the Son

God the Holy Spirit

---

114 Halverson, D. (Ed.), *The Compact Guide to World Religions*, Bethany House, Minneapolis, 1996, Pg. 115.

To this we can add the concepts described above:

God	God-Consciousness
=	=
God the Father	**The transcendent aspect of God** (Ain, Ain Soph, and Ain Soph Aur)
God the Son (Jesus born of the Virgin Mary)	**The immanent aspect of God** (The Creation, created by God the Father out of His own substance — Consciousness as first mover, first cause, first generator[115])
God the Holy Spirit	**The individual human spirits or souls** (Our individual Higher Self)

So, God is separate from and is His Creation at the same time. There is absolutely nothing that exists that is not God-Consciousness. This is the essence of reality, and is totally in keeping with the Christian concept of God.

---

115   See St Thomas Aquinas in Appendix 4.

CHAPTER 22

Are There Many Paths or Only One?

Most religions and spiritual paths are tolerant towards others, and recognise there are many paths to the summit of the mountain, the goal of our existence, whatever that is seen as being. Nevertheless, there are fundamentalists in many religions who are intolerant of other faiths and believe their own approach is the only acceptable one. Likewise, there are different sects or denominations within a religion that believe their version of the religion is the only acceptable interpretation of that religion.

In my research, it has become apparent that most of the religions are saying very similar things anyway, and the apparent differences in faith are due to culture and tradition. So, why should one be better than another? We should choose what suits us best, and as we have said, God-Consciousness is experiencing these different faiths through us all anyway.

The Crusades of the Middle Ages were holy wars between Christians and Muslims, each trying to instil or maintain their faith as the only valid one. However, those times are past, and in the last few centuries it is mainly the Christians who have put much effort into missionary work. The Christian world of today is Christian only because of the intensive work done by its missionaries. Christianity is the widest spread religion with about two billion adherents. Islam is a close second.

The Christian view is that every person is born a sinner and, therefore, needs to be saved, and that such salvation is only available through acceptance of Jesus Christ as their Personal Saviour. This raises a question in my mind. Using figures I have gleaned off the Internet, it would appear that less than 10 percent of people who have ever lived have called themselves Christian. Naturally, many of those who classify themselves as Christian may not have accepted Jesus Christ as their Personal Saviour. It would appear from this that God, who is omnibenevolent, omnipotent, omnipresent, and omniscient, has not reached over 90 percent of people with His exclusive salvation scheme. This indicates to me the Christian Path cannot be the only path, and salvation, redemption, or union with God cannot be restricted to less than 10 percent of the world's people. It is just not logical (or fair).

The God Franchise suggests a much more equitable view of life and of God. Naturally, Christianity is a valid path, and if it is really working for you, then this is what counts. If it is not working for you, be aware there are other opportunities for you to attain your spiritual heritage. As you will discover in Part Four, this spiritual heritage is a lot closer to you than you might suppose.

Islam, Judaism, Hinduism, Buddhism, Sikhism, and all the other *isms* are also totally valid paths. So are the so-called New Age religions. Whatever works to help you tune into your Higher Self and help you remove the veils covering that shining reality is a valid spiritual path. May you choose the path that truly works for you!

CHAPTER 23

What Happens After We Die?

There are essentially five possibilities of what eventually happens to the human spirit or soul after death and after any possible waiting period (e.g. purgatory):

+ **Annihilation**: Your mind, body, and soul are totally annihilated and you cease to exist.

+ **Heaven/Paradise**: You remain in Heaven (Paradise) for eternity and stay as an individual in a conscious state of eternal bliss in the presence of God.

+ **Hell**: You end up as an individual in Hell for eternity, separated from God, with no escape from everlasting torture and torment.

+ **Reincarnation**: You reincarnate into a new body and life, which may be human or some other living form. Some people believe that a person can only reincarnate as another human being. The term transmigration of souls is also used.

+ **Supreme Oneness**: You lose your individuality and merge with the Supreme One, with God-Consciousness outside form.

These are huge differences in belief. Naturally, most of us would like to think we continue as ourselves, and preferably in some sort of heaven or paradise. If we believe in Heaven (Paradise) as a preferable destination, we are also aware there may be a Hell, and we will end up there if we are not worthy of Heaven (Paradise). This is the carrot and stick approach to encouraging people to do the right thing.

While dreams of Heaven or Paradise are great, would any of these five be a problem for you? Frankly, the only one that would be a problem is Hell, as that means conscious awareness of eternal torture. If you are in Heaven (Paradise), you will be blissfully happy all the time; if you are annihilated or you merge with God-Consciousness, you will have no awareness of self or sense any loss at all; and finally, if you reincarnate, you are back in a life form. It is within your control to improve your life in each successive lifetime by earning good karma.

A fear of going to Hell is what keeps many people on the straight and narrow path. However, if God is omnibenevolent, it is impossible for Him to even conceive of sending anyone to an experience of eternal (that is forever and unceasing) conscious torment and torture, with no hope of escape or redemption. It is illogical and it is untenable.

I have neither the direct experience nor the space here to debate what does in truth happen to us after death. However, I can say without fear of being wrong, that whatever lies ahead of us after death will either be the continuation of positive life experience in some form or another, or it will be a formless non-experience that will not be of any consequence to us at a personal level. Hell is not an option.

It seems to me that speculation on this subject, and using what might happen to us after death as a carrot or reward for what we do now, or even as a threat of punishment, is a fruitless exercise. It is more important that we look at our experience in the Now — the present — and leave the period after our deaths as something to experience (or not-experience) when it happens (which it definitely will!).

Lastly, may I venture that the idea of continuation as an individual as opposed to being subsumed into the Formless and losing all individuality, is a question of Ego. It is your Ego that wants this continuation and recognition. Your Higher Self, who is God-Consciousness anyway, is not dependent on such trivia.

CHAPTER 24

Is Religion Necessary?

Personally, I see a big difference between spirituality and the mainstream religions. Spirituality is what it is all about, and if a person is a genuine seeker and is finding answers for personal growth and understanding, all is well. Many people find such spirituality within organised religion and that is perfect for them. However, there are many people who are brought up in a religion they do not understand or believe, one they cannot accept as having answers for them, and they are left in a spiritual wilderness. Many fear leaving the religion they have been taught is the true religion – they are literally held by fear. Others turn to secularism and avoid all thoughts of spiritual matters, and some, who are perhaps more indignant about the role of religion, become atheists.

Nevertheless, religion does have its place. I am very grateful for the ten years or so up to the age of twenty that I spent in a Christian Sunday School learning about God and the Bible, and most importantly, having an opportunity to ask the many questions that came up. It was something I looked forward to every Sunday, and I wish there was more interest in attending Sunday School or similar study groups among the young people of today. Drawing young people in with the lure of (Christian) rock music and emotional or social events and meetings only goes so far, unless the teachings and ability to ask questions and receive considered and authoritative answers are also readily available. The spiritual aspect of Man is far deeper than the emotional aspect.

Religion allows the man in the street to discover something of the

Truth, and if the interest is instilled, he can then explore and discover more about spirituality when he is ready. Spirituality is about life, and everything is spiritual. We just have to use secular and physical terms and concepts for things in everyday life to differentiate the mundane from the higher truths. However, everything we do and think, and everything that exists, is spiritual in the final analysis. It is not something that we can save and then bring out for Sundays, the Sabbath, or Holy Days.

It can be said that one of the main things that separates us from the animals is that we have religion. We need to find meaning in our lives. Also, and this is not very helpful, we try to escape from what is here now. While animals accept their situation and get on with it, humans are looking to the afterlife, to Heaven, Nirvana, or Paradise as their goal. Religion colludes with this aspiration, giving people the precepts to achieve that, and to avoid the other place.

Historically, religions have much to account for. There have been many wars and battles fought in the name of God. There have been many riches acquired and crimes and atrocities committed in the name of God. Frankly, God's patience must have been stretched more by those who professed to love and worship Him than by the godless masses. Despite this, we are not here to debate the past, but to reach an understanding in the present.

The God Franchise accepts that religion is a part of what is here now, even if it is not perfect. It has its place and it is a real part of today's world. The only hope is the views expressed here will help to open some people's eyes to a greater Truth, one that is not always available through the restraints imposed by organised religion. There is nothing to stop you from continuing your worship within an organised religious environment if you wish, and in so doing, add to the understanding and openness that is there. In fact, that would be a great service to your community, your church (etc.), and to Mankind.

The spread of many new ideas and a developing interest in spiritual matters over the past few decades is wonderful to see. Do not be afraid to embrace these new ideas. See what sits well with you. Open your mind to Truth and allow whatever is revealed to you to enter — this is personal revelation from God-Consciousness.

CHAPTER 25

What is Special About Humanity?

A s the evolutionists will tell us, we are just a very clever form of animal. We are mammals, primates, hominids, and *Homo sapiens*. Our closest living relatives are the chimpanzee and bonobo (the pygmy chimpanzee). Our DNA is closer to that of a chimpanzee than mouse DNA is to rat DNA — it is between 96 and 98.6 percent the same, depending on the source of the data. Work continues on the comparison of human DNA with the DNA of our closest relatives so we can see exactly what makes us different in genetic terms.

It is true that many animals have intelligence, communication, emotions, and self-will; so, what makes humans special? Certainly we have more complex language and music; we have art, philosophy, and religion. We have the intelligence to develop technology. We have a conscience and know right from wrong, (we discuss morality in the next chapter). We, perhaps, think more rationally and think ahead to the outcomes of our actions, and so control our natural instincts and reactions. We are self-aware. We have imaginations, and consider the past and the future in depth. We seek to improve ourselves and our lot in life. We make choices. We use writing and other symbols in our communication. We can think in abstract terms.

I believe it is fair to treat humanity as special; after all, you and I are members of humanity. We do have something to offer to the development of the universe, and we do offer God-Consciousness a considerable amount of interesting experience. Nevertheless, it would be presumptuous of us to say that humanity is the pinnacle of creation.

We have no idea what other types of existence there may be. There could be other universes; there could be advanced intelligent life on other planets within this universe; and there could be angelic regions on a whole different plane. Does any of this musing have any significance? No! What matters is that we are human and that we are blessed with the opportunity to experience life here and now. God-Consciousness has chosen to experience life through this form (amongst others) and who are we to belittle that?

CHAPTER 26

Does Our Morality Come from God?

Morality, ethics, and conscience are big subjects, and these values are often raised by the church as a proof there is a God, as they do not fit with the theory of evolution. So, one argument for the existence of God is *The Argument from Morality*. This states that most people have a moral ethic, and the original source of that morality is more likely to be God. So God must exist. Many Christians are particularly strong on this point as they say God has set the moral standard, and we have all fallen short of it through sin.

The God Franchise takes the view that God-Consciousness is our Higher Self, and our Higher Self is what drives our moral code, our ethics, and our conscience. In that sense, our morality does come from God. However, God-Consciousness has not set this up as a set of fixed rules we must obey. Rather, it just means our innate nature is moral, is good.

Some people think morality comes from religion or from God on High, if I can put it that way. They sometimes even consider atheists to be totally without morals, integrity, conscience, or worthiness. As I will show shortly, this is just not true – we are moral anyway. Morality was here before religion and before any concept of God was formed. Morality is the starting point for both theists and atheists.

In his book, *Morality Without God?*,[116] Walter Sinnott-Armstrong

---

116 Sinnott-Armstrong, W., *Morality Without God?* Oxford University Press, New York, 2009, Pg. 14. (By permission of Oxford University Press, Inc.) This chapter on Morality owes much to this book, although I take full responsibility for the statements made here.

discusses the claims that theists make about atheists with regard to morality. He discovered that, contrary to those claims, history and personal experience shows that not all atheists are immoral, just as all theists are not necessarily moral. However, there are differences of opinion on what is the moral stance on particular issues. Prejudice and bigotry are more likely to be present amongst religious people than secular ones. This is often because the perpetrators feel scriptures justify their beliefs. Scriptures can be interpreted in different ways and, therefore, can be misused, even unwittingly. Homosexuals, Jewish people, black people, and even women are discriminated against based on perceived biblical or scriptural grounds.

Research studies have found no grounds to suggest that secular societies are more immoral, untrustworthy, or crime-ridden than religious ones. There are good people and bad in both types of society. Even when it comes to charity, while religious people do appear to give more than secular people do, this can perhaps be explained by the encouragement given by their churches (synagogues, temples, mosques) for them to give. Also, there will be some people who are trying to buy their way into Heaven. Secular people are quite open to giving money or time to their favourite charitable causes. There is also no reason to suspect that secular societies are bound to become corrupt and depraved. My own experience is that people generally are good and kind, whether they are religious or not.

The vast majority of people (if not all people) throughout the world have a *good* and *moral* state of mind most of the time. That is the starting point from childhood. That is where a person prefers to be when he or she is relaxed. Of course, that state is interrupted for many people when their fundamental needs are not met (water, food, shelter, clothing, etc.), or when their Ego tries to assert itself in some way. The Ego is driven more frequently and more destructively by people who have experienced pain and suffering at the hands of others, and this can lead to an increase in anger, aggression, fear, and other negative emotions and attitudes. It can lead to thoughts and actions that can be seen as immoral. Rather than fundamental evil that is coming to the surface, it is fundamental good being overwhelmed by ignorance and misunderstanding. It is seeing the Lesser Self as being all there is, and the Higher Self being swamped and lost in the veils of mental and egoistic darkness.

Regarding objective morality, a normal result of evolution is a moral feeling in individuals. From the time you are born, you seek to be accepted by others, and you soon discover if you are nice and pleasant, people like you more. Also you find people who are *nice* are the ones you are drawn to. I experience people as generally moral, pleasant, and positive in their essence. Even the staunchest gang member or darkest criminal has a moral code with regard to their families. They love them and do what they can for them. There is also *honour amongst thieves.*

From this feeling of community between families and groups of people, comes the corollary that you would like other people to treat you well and, therefore, you need to treat them well. We know from experience that if we are immoral in our dealings with others, they won't want anything to do with us, and society would break down if morality and conscience suddenly disappeared. We all share a sense of fairness or fair play.

Nevertheless, this does not determine what morality is. Morality is the sense of what is right and what is wrong. Theists believe that God determines what is moral, and they follow the commandments and instructions laid out in the scriptures. In other words, you do what you are told to do. Atheists and others who do not follow the scriptural teachings closely go with what they feel is right or wrong in terms of their own conscience. It comes down to not hurting someone else. You know this because you don't want to be hurt yourself. You seek happiness and pleasure, and it is logical to a human being that other humans would also enjoy happiness and pleasure. As Sinnott-Armstrong writes: *"What really makes certain acts immoral is not what I or anyone wants but, instead, that such acts cause harm to other people for no good enough reason."*[117]

You don't murder, rape, steal, lie, cheat, or harm someone else because you would be taking from them something you would not want to have taken from you. This does not mean everyone is moral all the time. We all can make mistakes, and might also be encouraged to break

---

117   Sinnott-Armstrong, Pg. 64 (By permission of Oxford University Press, Inc.)

this moral code when we have problems in our lives we don't know how to handle. While we might know right from wrong, we sometimes believe we can make exceptions to the rule. We do this through a lack of understanding of how things work in reality. We discuss our primary problem in the next chapter.

For now, the point is that *morality* is not determined by God's setting of the rules we have to follow. Rather, we have free will, and we know that morality is the best policy. Having said that, let's not forget that each one of us has a Higher Self, who is God-Consciousness, and this is our conscience with which we maintain our moral sense. It is not God outside us telling us what to do; it is our own Higher Self (or God **inside** us) nudging us in the direction of morality because it makes sense.

People have different views of what is moral. There is much debate and acrimony surrounding subjects like abortion, euthanasia, homosexuality, green issues, the place of religion in government and schools, stem cell research, and so on. Who is right? Each side thinks they are. This does not mean that one side is moral and the other is not. Whatever our specific view is on morality, we each have moral rights and we each have moral obligations.

Among the main reasons theists might be motivated to be moral is through the threat of an eternity of Hell or the promise of an eternity of Heaven or Paradise. If you look at this closely, this does not make better people since there is no need for a moral sense here. If a person is convinced they are going to Hell due to a specific act in their past, they may reason that now they can do whatever they wish to do, as it will be their only opportunity, and anyway, the punishment cannot get any worse. This is why a serial killer can just keep going, as there is no practical incremental punishment. And if they can be redeemed in time by turning to the salvation offered by Jesus, they might as well leave this until they are sitting on death row. No, a person is best judged as moral or not by their natural inclination, rather than by whether there is any stick or carrot in place to make them act morally.

In concluding his argument for the independence of morality from God and religion, Sinnott-Armstrong makes this very interesting point:

"[The Bible] cannot serve as a reliable guide to morality. If we follow all of the Bible literally, then we will be led astray into immorality because of passages like those I cited[118]. *On the other hand, if we pick and choose which Bible passages to follow, then we need not be led into immorality, and we might even be led toward morality, but we will need to use our prior moral views to guide our choice among the various passages. Either way, the Bible cannot provide a solid foundation for morality or for knowledge of morality.* **To the contrary, you need morality as a user's guide to the Bible."**[119] [My emphasis].

Before we leave the subject of morality, I would like to mention that Muslims, Confucianists, most followers of Judaism, and most New Agers believe that humanity is essentially good and moral in nature. Hindus and Buddhists see our true selves as extended from and one with the Supreme Being, and that we are personally responsible for our own karma, yet essentially, we are living in a state of illusion and ignorance. With the sole exception of Christianity, the other religions, as well as atheists, believe there is good and bad in humanity, and that this can be resolved through one's own efforts, education, and appropriate upbringing. Further, the Law of Karma plays a role in balancing this picture for many people.

Christianity (or rather certain denominations within Christianity) is the only religion that believes Man is a born sinner and needs redemption. Christians are the only ones who believe it is not for us to make our own effort to be moral, but rather that we must rely on God's forgiveness after we have accepted Jesus Christ as our Personal Saviour. This belief, and the propagation of it, is a very powerful way for the Church to control its adherents. It also does a great disservice to the spiritual awakening of many devout Christians.

---

118 See *Exodus* 21:17 and 20-21, *Leviticus* 20:10 and 20:13, *Deuteronomy* 13:6-10, *Joshua* 10:40 and 11:20, *Mark* 10:11-12, *Luke* 14:26, *1 Corinthians* 14:34-35, *Ephesians* 5:22-24, *Revelation* 21:8. There are many more examples.

119 Sinnott-Armstrong, Pg. 145 (By permission of Oxford University Press, Inc.)

CHAPTER 27

So, What is Our Primary Problem?

It is funny, but I used to think I was the only one who had problems. Everyone else seemed to get on okay in life. They seemed to be having fun and doing things with their lives. It was only me who was unsure what to do, who couldn't get things started and didn't do much except schoolwork. How self-centred was that? Of course, you were probably feeling the same way at that stage of your life too (and maybe are still feeling that way!).

Apart from those lucky few who appear to have perfect lives, or who are enlightened, we all seem to have issues in our lives. There is always something more or something different we want. We seem to feel pain, we seem to get upset or stressed, we seem to have other people impacting on our lives, and we always seem to be short of money or opportunities or time.

I say *we*, but who is really having the problem? Just think about this: Who am I? Who is having these issues in my life?

We discussed the Higher Self and the Lesser Self back in Chapter 12. There we said that the Higher Self was God-Consciousness individualised in form as *me*. The Lesser Self was created by us through the formation of an Ego and through our embracing free will. In doing this, we have embraced the limitations and pain that are associated with the Ego and free will and passed from generation to generation (since Adam and Eve if you like). We concluded that the Ego is the source of all our problems.

Let us take a look at what religion says our primary problem is. Once again, I won't label the religions (although some might be obvious), so you may associate with whichever approach you feel is correct:

+ We were all born in sin due to the Original Sin of Adam and Eve. We are sinners and we require the salvation of Jesus Christ our Saviour. Jesus died as atonement[120] for our sins, so by accepting Him as our Personal Saviour, we can hope for a place in Heaven when we die. *"Ultimately, sin is going our own way in defiance of God. Sin separates us from knowing and serving God."*[121] We are *"spiritually separated from God because of our sin and rebellion against Him."*[122]

+ Sinning is a much more personal thing and is not a basic characteristic of humanity. The term *sinner* largely applies to decadent and evil people rather than the average person who might occasionally do something wrong.

+ We are ignorant of our true nature, which is Oneness with God. We, therefore, do wrong through ignorance and error of judgement. We acquire karma in each lifetime, and this is carried through to the next life on Earth through reincarnation.

+ Due to our desires and karma, we live in a world of suffering and reincarnation. By ceasing all desires through knowledge, good works, and devotion — all made possible through our own efforts — we are freed from the cycle of reincarnation and reach Nirvana, the blessed state of bliss and union with Ultimate Reality (which we have called God-Consciousness).

+ We contravene God's Laws and, accordingly, will be punished in Hell. Our only deliverance is by admitting the error of our ways, requesting God's mercy, and becoming obedient to the Law of God. We can then expect a place in Paradise (Heaven).

---

120 Atonement is *"the reconciliation of man with God through the life, sufferings, and sacrificial death of Christ."* (*Collins English Dictionary*)

121 Halverson, D. (Ed.), *The Compact Guide to World Religions*, Bethany House, Minneapolis, 1996, Pg. 136.

122 Halverson, Pg. 167

+ By going our own way and contravening what the gods (or God) expect of us, we anger the gods (God) who will punish us. The only way out of this is to appease the gods (God) through offerings and sacrifices.

+ (Non-religion/atheism) Our biggest issues are superstition, dogma, and irrational thinking. The solution is in rational thinking and living life realistically. After that, we die and cease to exist anyway.

This list makes interesting reading. Whether the problem was passed down through the generations, or we picked it up from our family, our teachers, our friends, and our peers, we all seem to be in a state of suffering, sin, wrongdoing, and pain. If we believe in God, we all look to God to free us from that at some future time, be it through our own efforts or through His Grace.

We touch on sin again in Part Four. For now, I would like to repeat that all these issues are due to our abuse of free will and the importance we give to our Egos. Those who believe we are sinners are emphasising our Lesser Self. They are giving it validity and blaming the problem on Adam and Eve. Sure, we are feeling separation from God — the more we focus on our Egos or Lesser Self, the more the veils are over our eyes and the less we can relate to our Higher Self, our direct link to God-Consciousness.

It is the same with succumbing to desire, feeding karma, and contravening God's Laws — we allow our Ego to take precedence. We all have the same problem, whatever we call it and however we think it arises.

Our primary problem is focussing on our Ego, our Lesser Self.

CHAPTER 28

Why is it the Ego's Fault?

We have identified the Ego or Lesser Self as the primary problem we have to face as humans, and this has grown out of our having free will. Normally, one associates one's individuality with Ego. How can one be a separate individual if one does not have an Ego? Let's take a look at how some of the major religions view this.

The fundamental Buddhist teachings are the Four Noble Truths and the Eight-Fold Path. The Four Noble Truths[123] are:

1. *There can be no existence without suffering.*
2. *The cause of suffering is egoistic Desire.*
3. *The elimination of Desire brings the cessation of suffering.*
4. *The Way to the elimination of Desire is the Noble Eightfold Path.*

The Noble Eightfold Path is *"the Buddhist scheme of moral and spiritual self-development leading to Enlightenment. The eight constituent parts are: Right View, Right Mental Attitude or Motive, Right Speech, Right Action, Right Pursuits, including means of Livelihood, Right Effort, Right Mindfulness, and Right Contemplation."*[124]

---

123 Humphreys, C., *A Popular Dictionary of Buddhism*, Arco, London, 1962, Pg. 79. (Copyright © The Buddhist Society, with acknowledgment to The Society of Authors as their Literary Representative.)
124 Humphreys, Pg. 139

The Buddha places the source of suffering firmly on the Ego, and homes in on Desire as the biggest issue. The Hindu is also aware of suffering and sees that we are ignorant of our true self (*atman*).

> *"We have forgotten that we are extended from Brahman* [God-Consciousness] *and that we have mistakenly attached ourselves to the desires of our separate selves, or egos, and thereby to the consequences of its actions. Because of the ego's attachments to its desires and individualistic existence, we have become subject to the law of karma."* [125]

Once again, it is the Ego that raises its head. From a Christian viewpoint, we can see it is the Lesser Self, the Ego, who is the sinner, the one born in Original Sin if you like. The Higher Self is God-Consciousness, is the soul or spirit, and is *atman*.

As we said earlier, it does not really matter in the greater scheme of things whether the soul is immortal or not. It is the Ego that wants to continue as an individual in Heaven or Paradise. The Ego wants to feel special because it has been chosen to sit in the presence of God, and because it is better than all those who did not make it into this exalted company. If your individual soul is not immortal and you cease to exist, you will not feel a thing, and it is not for you to complain about that either. This is God's universe not yours. If the soul is immortal and you go to Heaven (Paradise, Nirvana), that is great. You can enjoy it and be pleased that you made it. If your soul reincarnates, then you still have individual life, and what is more, through the Law of Karma, you have control over whether or not you improve each life experience. Finally, if your soul is immortal and you end up in Hell, condemned to eternal suffering, unceasing torture, and everlasting separation from God — forget it. It is not going to happen. A God who created everything that exists and who is omnipresent cannot suddenly be separated from you, and He is not going to seek to experience eternal suffering and torture. He is also omniscient, so He is not stupid. Give the God you love some credit, and realise your Ego is the Adversary, the Deceiver, the Enemy, the Tempter, and the Satan you fear.

---

125 Halverson, D. (Ed.), *The Compact Guide to World Religions*, Bethany House, Minneapolis, 1996, Pg. 89.

The suffering we experience in our life on Earth is similar in concept to pain in the body. Pain is there for a reason. It is to tell you there is something wrong, something has damaged or is going to damage the body and, therefore, you need to take some remedial action. So, when we suffer, it is our inbuilt response to encourage us to modify our behaviour. We need to control the Ego in order to reduce or eliminate suffering — it is that simple.

The other thing that causes suffering is resistance to what is here now. "What is here now" is a brief way of saying, "what our physical, mental, and emotional reality is in this moment." If we accept what is here in this moment, and just for this moment stay with what is here, suffering disappears. Instead, it becomes experience. Apart from resistance to what is here now, suffering is caused by fear and worry about the future (and the future usually turns out to be very different to what you expected or feared) and regret and anger about the past (and you cannot change the past). Who resists? Who fears and worries? Who regrets and is angry? It is the Ego every time.

Another Christian form of suffering is the feeling of alienation from God through sin and rebellion. Who is alienated from God? It is the Ego. The Higher Self *is* God-Consciousness, so we cannot be alienated from God unless we are completely alienated from ourselves. Remember that God is closer *"than breathing, and nearer than hands and feet."*[126]

So let's come back to the question of losing your individuality if you lose your Ego. Don't forget that one's individuality resides in the Self, and therefore, the Higher Self (God-Consciousness) is just as capable of maintaining that individuality for day-to-day living on this Earth. If we could accept that our individuality is safe in the Higher Self and the Higher Self is God-Consciousness, we would not be troubled by suffering, and we could allow Nirvana, Paradise, or Heaven to be an important (but imaginary) part of our lives right now.

The (Christian) desire to maintain individuality after death and to live in eternal direct communion with God is a desire of the Ego. We need to drop all desires, including this one. In comparing Christianity with Buddhism, the Christian says,

---

126 Alfred, Lord Tennyson (1809–1892) in a short poem The Higher Pantheism.

"Because in Christianity God is personal, we can find permanence in Him without the undesirable consequence of having to deny our value and existence as persons. The result of salvation is not the individual disappearing in the Void, but being joined in an interpersonal relationship with God."[127]

The *"undesirable consequence"* is an indication of the desire one still holds. Who values *"our value and existence as persons"*? If it is the Ego, that Ego and our desire are the source of all pain and suffering. If it is God who values our individuality then you can be sure your individuality will remain. This is God's universe. If God does not value our existence as persons after our death, then who are we to complain? The outcome, whatever it is, is the right one in God's terms.

Finally, who needs *"an interpersonal relationship with God"* after death (and salvation) if not just the Ego? I, personally, am sure that whatever God has in store for me, be it continuation of my individuality so I can give Him further experience of life, or a resting back in the Void like a splash rests back in the Ocean, I am happy.

---

127 Halverson, Pg. 65

CHAPTER 29

So, Do We Need to Strive for Anything?

This is a very interesting question. There are a number of different beliefs in this regard, and you will probably subscribe to one or more of the following views:

+ You treat everyone as you would like to be treated yourself, so you make the effort to do good works and avoid bad ones. You are honest and upright. You act morally as a matter of principle.

+ There is no need for personal effort, since if you genuinely accept Jesus Christ as your Personal Saviour, God will forgive you your sins and grant you salvation. *"God has provided the means for reconciliation and forgiveness through Jesus Christ, as we confess our sins and place our trust in Him."*[128]

+ You involve yourself in spiritual development, and meditate, pray, and attend church and/or seminars so that you can improve yourself and become more spiritual.

+ Rather than add spiritual knowledge and put in effort to improve yourself, you strip away all false beliefs, forgive yourself, and allow your Inner Light, your True Self (Higher Self) to shine through.

+ You seek to gain psychic powers, learn occult secrets, perform ritual magic using candles and symbols, and generally increase

---

128 Halverson, D. (Ed.), *The Compact Guide to World Religions*, Bethany House, Minneapolis, 1996, Pg. 62.

your personal powers. (We are speaking of white magic and positive outcomes here, rather than black magic.)

+ You look to other beings to advise and guide you, be they angels, spirits that have already passed over, or advanced beings from other planets or galaxies. You also have a personal guardian angel.

+ You live in the present Now and allow the future to take care of itself. In this moment you do things consciously and remain aware of and responsible for the consequences of your actions.

Essentially, there are two types of motivation for everything we do throughout our lives. One is to get what we want and experience what we want to experience in this lifetime, and the other is to prepare our way for the afterlife or the next life.

For this lifetime, you may be motivated to be successful — to gain power and/or knowledge and/or money. Some are motivated to be happy and have fun. Some look for peace and love. Some merely want to get through the day so they can have fun at night. Some people are working just to get to the next weekend or next holiday. Some want to do things for others, be it their family or their favourite cause or charity. Some want just to survive, and others really don't want to even survive. The usual motivation is being happy in this lifetime, and thus doing whatever you think will make you happy. Of course, you apply your own definition of what happiness is to you.

The other motivation relates to the afterlife or next life. If you don't believe in an afterlife or reincarnation, this motivation does not apply, unless you are secretly hedging your bets. Many people believe this life is short, temporary, and one-off only, so put considerable effort into being prepared for the next life. Their beliefs hinge on making sure they are in the best possible position to make it into Heaven/Paradise/Nirvana, as that is what is eternal. Then, there are those who are motivated to avoid going to Hell, as that would mean eternal suffering and separation from God. They do good purely because they fear going to Hell — and for no other reason.

If you believe in reincarnation and karma, you will be motivated to attain good karma in this lifetime so your lot is better in the next life.

Ultimately, you aim to get off the cycle of rebirth and enter Heaven/ Paradise/Nirvana. Your motivation in this life is to improve your karma ratings through maximising good karma and minimising bad karma.

If you believe in annihilation or that you are destined to merge with the Ultimate Reality of God-Consciousness, you may look for more outcomes to give you satisfaction in this lifetime on Earth, as there won't be an afterlife to anticipate. Also, if you believe you are pretty good in this life, the afterlife might not motivate you as you take it for granted that you will be good enough to be accepted when the time comes.

The question regarding the need for personal effort can be viewed in two opposing ways. Some believe that Enlightenment/Heaven/ Paradise is attained by one's own efforts (e.g. Hinduism, Buddhism, Islam, and Judaism) and others insist it is granted by God's Grace and Forgiveness (e.g. Christianity). The former approach flows from humanity to God, whereas the latter approach flows from God to humanity.

The Christian approach is based on the scripture in Ephesians *"For by grace are ye saved through faith; and not of yourselves: it is the gift of God: Not of works, lest any man should boast."*[129] In other words, you are saved through faith in God and through the gift of His Grace, and not through your own efforts and works as these lead to personal pride. I have some trouble with this. You could live a life of complete debauchery and crime, and without any consideration for others. Then, in the hours or days before your death, you could (sincerely) accept Jesus Christ as your Personal Saviour, throw yourself at the mercy of God, admit all your sins, and ask for His Grace and forgiveness. No, I don't accept that this is what is expected of Christians. I believe that Christians should (if I may say that!) adhere to the precept of *"Love thy neighbour as thyself"* just like the rest of us. They will surely be rewarded in Heaven if that is the way it turns out.

In essence, if you believe in any need to prepare for an afterlife, then you must put in the effort in this moment, because it is what is in

---

129 *Ephesians* 2:8-9

your heart in this moment that judges you. If, in each moment, you are honest with yourself and strive to do the best you can (which frankly we all do anyway), the end result will be a happy one. To clarify, even those who do unspeakable evil, are still doing the best they can, with the resources and awareness they have at that time. Undoubtedly, they are in huge pain and suffering, and in the fullness of time, whether in this life or another life, their Higher Self will reveal itself and the veils of suffering, Ego, and ignorance will slip from their eyes and they will be whole. God-Consciousness is the Being, the Truth, the Life, and the All of every one of us, whether saint or sinner. It is our Lesser Self, our Ego, that causes the pain and suffering we so dearly wish to avoid. That is our only mission from a purely individual and selfish point of view — to stop the pain and suffering we feel.

Do we need to strive for anything? The answer is clear — yes and no.

CHAPTER 30

Are We There Yet?

We have reached the end of Part Three. In Part One, I posed some questions, and along the way I have raised some controversial issues or deferred discussion until later. Now that we have discussed **The God Franchise** in detail and have seen how beliefs differ in the different religions yet can largely be harmonised or viewed from a different perspective, perhaps I should summarise the essence of what we have covered. Following that, we can move on to Part Four where we discuss daily living as a God Franchisee.

1. **God is expected to:**

   Be conscious. Yes, God is conscious. In fact He is Consciousness itself. In essence all that exists is God-Consciousness. Even His Creation is Consciousness. As the scientists have seen, when you delve deeply into matter it dissolves into space. There is very little matter in matter, and what matter exists is derived from Consciousness. It is a denser form of the essence of God, which is Consciousness. We have used the term God-Consciousness as a reminder of what God really is.

   Be eternal. Yes, God is eternal. Everything that we know in the universe has a cause. It needs motivation. Something cannot come from nothing. The Prime Cause in the universe is God-Consciousness. Since there needs to be a cause for everything, there can be no time when a Prime Cause, or the very first cause, did not exist. Therefore, God must have existed forever. The conundrum of *Which came first, the chicken or the egg?* can only have one answer. God either created the chicken or the egg to start things off. Now I am not saying that in the sense of the Book of Genesis, but in terms of the theory of evolution. The process had to start somewhere — neither chickens nor eggs are eternal.

Be omnipotent (all-powerful). Yes, God is omnipotent. This does not mean He can do the logically impossible, such as create a square circle. It just means if it can be done, God-Consciousness can do it. There can be nothing more powerful than God-Consciousness because nothing exists or can exist that is not God-Consciousness. So, while you may be able to dream up some way in which God is not omnipotent, either you are asking for something which is intrinsically impossible and, therefore, nonsense, or you are dreaming up something that is unreal and does not and cannot exist.

Be omnipresent (present everywhere). Yes, God is omnipresent. God-Consciousness is the essence of everything and, therefore, wherever there is something, there is God-Consciousness. There can be no place that exists where there is something that is not God-Consciousness. This also implies He is immaterial in His essence, even if He is also present in all matter. God-Consciousness is present in every atom that exists — in every sub-atomic particle.

Be omniscient (all-knowing). Yes, God is omniscient. God-Consciousness is in everything and is everywhere, so He knows whatever there is to know. He does not know what cannot be known at this time. For instance, 100 years ago, God did not know what a DVD player was. This is because even the greatest minds in the world had not conceived of a DVD player or anything remotely resembling that creation. Due to free will, we are free to create our own futures. We are God-Consciousness in essence, and in order to enable free will to operate, God-Consciousness has chosen not to view the future within our universe. From a perspective outside time, God-Consciousness knows all there is to know, but within time, He experiences things as they happen in general terms. The ability of clairvoyants and fortune tellers to see the future does not contradict this statement, allowing of course that the seeing of the future is genuine and is not either trickery or the intuitive assessment of potentials, and that God-Consciousness is prepared in that instance to allow that future to be glimpsed. It is like God peaking beneath the blindfold if He has reason or purpose to do so.

Be the creator of the universe. Yes, God is Creator. God is the Prime Cause of everything, He is the only thing that is eternal, and therefore, He must be the ultimate Creator. Also, everything is made out of the essence of God-Consciousness. This is not to say what the mechanism is that He has chosen to use. For instance, He may have created the Archangels and Angels first and instructed them to create the universe we see. Of course, the Archangels and Angels are made of the substance of God-Consciousness too, so whatever we conjecture still comes back to the same thing. We can definitely accept that the Big Bang and evolution is part of the mechanism, as the evidence is there for us to see. However, the Prime Cause behind that, the answers which science does not have, is a lot more than *"the God of the gaps."*[130] It is the only rational answer.

Have a purpose for His creation. Yes, God has a purpose for His Creation. Firstly, we can be sure that God-Consciousness is not going to do things without a reason. Secondly, His main purpose appears to be to have experiences. Without a Creation of some description, God-Consciousness would be like a very bored dreamer who had nothing to dream about. Experience and interest require something to experience and be interested in. Since God-Consciousness is all there is, the idea of the

---

130 Dawkins, R., *The God Delusion*, Bantam Press, London, 2006, Pg. 151. (Copyright © 2006 by Richard Dawkins. UK and Commonwealth: Published by Bantam Press. Reprinted by permission of The Random House Group Limited. Rest of the world: Used by permission of Houghton Mifflin Harcourt Publishing Company. All rights reserved.)

Creation being there specifically to praise God is nonsense. God-Consciousness does not need to praise Himself to be fulfilled. Nevertheless, praise that is heartfelt appreciation of our lives and our experience (God-Consciousness' life and experience) does not go amiss. It is just appreciation and recognition. However, it is not **the purpose** of God's Creation. The purpose of God's Creation is to experience.

Be absolutely good (omnibenevolent). Yes, God is omnibenevolent. Since God-Consciousness has created the universe out of His own essence, why would He create anything He did not see as good? Having said that, in God's terms, there is neither good nor bad, there is just experience. God can be seen as omnibenevolent because He has not gone out of His way to create evil, pain, suffering, catastrophes, and the other aspects of evil cited as part of the Problem of Evil (see 4. below). We, with our free will and Egos, have created these ourselves!

Be immutable (unchanging through time). Yes, God is immutable. God-Consciousness is and always will be God-Consciousness. God-Consciousness is outside time, is all-encompassing, and so is unchanging. Yes, within Himself He has created our universe as a source of experience. This experience does not change God-Consciousness in essence as He has no need to change. Experience is experience and that is all it is.

2. **God is a Personal God if you want Him to be, and is not if you prefer not**. Since He is the essence of every single person, He is a Personal God. God is not a separate Person sitting in Heaven judging us, His subjects, from afar. No, He is right here, alongside us, experiencing everything as we experience it. How more personal do you want to get? If you choose to go it alone and cut yourself adrift, you will have no Personal God. Nevertheless, God-Consciousness is right there experiencing life as a person who has cut himself off from his essential being. This is what free will is all about. Apart from His experience as individual people, and all other individual separate experiences He has

within the universe, God-Consciousness is also transcendent, being outside time and outside the universe.

3. **You can pray to God, praise Him, and ask for His intervention or forgiveness or acceptance or fair judgement.** While there is no Personal God in the traditional Judeo-Christian-Islamic sense, there is God-Consciousness within you. This is your Personal God. You can pray to this God-Consciousness within you, praise Him, and ask for His intervention or forgiveness or acceptance or fair judgement. The experience will be your Lesser Self talking to your Higher Self. It will be your Ego talking to your true essence. And because your Higher Self is God-Consciousness itself, It can hear your prayers, feel your praise and adoration, intervene for you in your life, forgive you, guide you, heal you, accept you, and be fair in judgement of you. This is not playing with words — this is real.

4. **The Problem of Evil is no longer a problem.** The source of all evil, pain, suffering, catastrophes, and the other aspects is free will, or rather, the misuse of free will by the Ego. If God had preordained everything, there would be no aspects of evil, and there would be no free will. Everything would be rosy, except there would be nothing that God-Consciousness could experience that He had not planned Himself. By adding free will to the mix, what God-Consciousness gets to experience is a life of free will, of interaction of Egos, of highs and lows, of knowing and ignorance, and in the end, of Good and Evil. This is the true meaning of the Tree of the Knowledge of Good and Evil sitting in the midst of the Garden of Eden. We need to accept that the Law of Karma and the Law of Manifestation is fair to us all, and that we attract into our lives and experience what we have drawn to us. Evil is not a problem — it is a fact of life while we are in a state of comparative unconsciousness. When we come to truly realise our identity as God-Consciousness, all evil will dissipate.

5. **There are many inconsistent teachings, both from different religions and from within specific religions.** These

inconsistencies have come about through the Egos of teachers and priests, of writers and documenters, and of scribes and editors, getting in the way of the Truth. Also, the teachings have often been changed for political reasons, whether doctrinal or secular. Nevertheless, there is also much consistency in the essence of the teachings from different sources. They can be seen as different paths up the same mountain. They may differ to suit the people they are directed towards. Each one of us can benefit from finding the teaching that rings true to us, and then adopting that as a path to follow. It would indeed be wonderful to move towards a teaching that was more all-embracing and closer to the one Truth that must underpin the universe, yet there can still be local flavourings to suit the people who choose to live by that teaching.

6. **Has God really been conspicuous by His hiddenness?** God-Consciousness is in everything and is everywhere — how can He be hidden? He is your inner soul, whether you believe it or not. He sits on the sidelines of your daily searches for Him and smiles, the glint of love and joy in His eyes. He will reveal Himself when you allow Him to do so. In the meantime, He greets you as your pet dog at the gate, the rainbow in the sky, the music in your ears, the bacteria in your petri dish, the stars in your telescope, and the mud in a landslide.

7. **Free will is our gift from God, and we will never lose it until we no longer need it**. The fact that God is omniscient does not contradict the concept of free will. At the simplest level, if you choose to do B out of a choice of 26 options coded A to Z, you have chosen option B with free will. If God, by looking into the future, sees you have chosen option B, He knows you have made that free will choice without compromising either His omniscience or your free will. Despite its appeal, free will has also filled the world with Ego, evil, pain, and suffering. There may come a time in the future when we no longer need or desire free will.

8. **Won't God need to be complex in order to have created the universe, and still keep it running at an individual level, answering prayers and supporting each conscious being?** Complexity is not what was needed, although I am sure that having omniscience and omnipotence was very helpful when designing and creating the universe. Regarding keeping the universe running, that is simply handled by His being the essence of and the reality of the whole universe at an individual level. He answers prayers and supports each of us by being each of us. In addition to these points, I would even say that God-Consciousness Himself is not complex; i.e., *"made up of various interconnected parts; composite; ...intricate or involved."*[131] God-Consciousness is omnipotent, omniscient, omnipresent, eternal, and all His other qualities, and is, therefore, essentially simple (in His transcendent state) due to the vast implications of those qualities. The complexities within His Creation are handled in a differentiated way. For example, as the consciousness of 7 billion people, He is conscious through each of us and so needs to be no more complex than is our individual consciousness seen separately.

9. **Scientists have proved the Big Bang theory and the theory of evolution (and natural selection) to us**, but they have no answer to the origin of life,[132] the origin of the eukaryotic (complex) cell and the development of consciousness. Rather than discard the valuable information science has discovered for us, let us embrace it. This knowledge will grow. We know the origin of life and the development of consciousness in the universe are directly from God-Consciousness, as we have seen all life and all consciousness *is* God-Consciousness incarnate. Science may one day come to accept this fact, and the answers to many other questions about the universe will also be revealed. May neither the scientists nor the theologians throw the baby out with the bathwater!

---

131 *Collins English Dictionary*
132 Abiogenesis, or the spontaneous generation of life from non-living matter, has long been postulated but has not yet been proved or achieved in the laboratory.

10. **The existence of God ought to be verifiable by science**. Maybe this will be possible one day, although the God the scientists will find is not the Judeo-Christian-Islamic God they are currently proving does not exist. Many of their current proofs are quite acceptable as they stand. However, the God they will find is God-Consciousness. The scientists are currently looking for the lost penny where the light is under the lamppost, rather than looking for it in the place it was lost.

11. **Can Man know God or is the gulf between us too wide?** In reality, there is no gulf as we have discussed. One day, Man will wake up to his Higher Self, and meet God there face to face.

12. **The world is the best possible world, and an omnipotent, omniscient, and absolutely good God has created the best possible world**. Leaving aside the Problem of Evil, one has to marvel at the beauty, the diversity, the intelligence, the wonder, and the uniqueness of the universe. Sure, at times I think it would be handy if humans had six limbs like insects do, or that rain was a function of night-time so we didn't have to put up with rainy days, but on balance, I think God-Consciousness has done a pretty good job.

Then, looking at the Problem of Evil, as we have already said, this has come about directly as a result of the misuse of free will. In a sense, Man rather than God has created Evil, although it is true that God-Consciousness is in everything, and therefore, is in all aspects of people's Lesser Selves as well as in things judged to be Evil. This is all experience to God-Consciousness and cannot be classified in absolute terms as good or bad.

There have been very different experiences of the world over the centuries and each of these have been the best possible world at that stage of evolution. Each was a different experience to God-Consciousness, and it is not for us to judge what living in those times was like. People in two or three centuries' time looking back at the history of the late twentieth and early twenty-first centuries will certainly find us very barbaric and ignorant. Likewise, the apparent disadvantage of those born blind or with other disabilities, or born into abject poverty is a subjective assessment. Great things can be achieved from that place as many who have lived there, or have been connected with such people, will affirm.

13. **God's purpose for His Creation is to experience Himself.** Our purpose is to naturally be party to that, and in the fullness of time, come to the self-realisation of our own true Being. Individually, we may have other purposes as well that relate to the evolution of both the universe and ourselves. This is the inbuilt force which directs us ever onwards and upwards.

We have discussed the essence of **The God Franchise**. Now, let's look at it from a practical perspective. How does **The God Franchise** affect you and your life? Part Four, *Daily Living as a God Franchisee*, discusses the direct effect that **The God Franchise** has on our everyday lives.

PART FOUR

Daily Living as a
God Franchisee

CHAPTER 31

What it All Means

Now that we have clarity on what a God Franchisee is, let's discuss what this means in the real world — in the practical world of work and play, learning and trivia, life and death.

So what is a God Franchisee? It is you, of course. It is you as you are today. No special conditions apply, other than that you are a human being. Having said that, animals and other living creatures and plants are also a part of God-Consciousness, but their role is not identical to that of Man. Likewise, there may be living entities on other planets in the universe, there may be angels and archangels, and there may be entities we have never dreamt of who are also God Franchisees, but let's not cloud the issue. Part Four is really about you and me, and all men and women.

The fact you now realise you are a God Franchisee does not mean you necessarily have to change a thing. Whatever you do right now you can just keep on doing. And everything you don't do now, well, there is just no need for you to do it. God is satisfied with experiencing whatever it is you experience. There are 7 billion people experiencing things, so what you experience is absolutely fine. There are 6,999,999,999 other human experiences happening too, so God has plenty to experience.

There are some rules to experiencing though, and you might be interested in understanding a bit more about those. God-Consciousness in essence is *happy* to experience anything, be it *good* or *bad*, be it *pleasant* or *painful*. To God, it is all just experience. However, God's Laws apply at all times. We discussed these in Chapter 15 and found that all Laws are in operation and are non-negotiable. The Ten Commandments (and their corollaries) are the only rules we have that we can choose to break; and then, the Universal Laws apply anyway. The Ten Commandments are moral guidelines rather than laws.

The Law of Cause and Effect, often depicted as the Law of Karma, ensures whatever you do will have an appropriate effect back on you. So, if you do good, you get good back, and if you do bad things, you get bad things back. While it may not always be obvious what the relationship is between different events in your life, you can be sure the connection is there, and you **will** reap what you sow.

Likewise, the Law of Manifestation is a powerful (and little understood) Law; it ensures whatever you focus on is attracted towards you, be it for good or bad. This too is not always obvious to us, but let me assure you, it all balances out over time. If you look at it honestly, you will find your life is panning out much as you deeply believed it would. This is not about hope or wishful thinking; this is about deep down reality where your consciousness and Ego reside. If you look at all the beliefs and attitudes you have, the things you treat as important, and what you believe life is all about, you will find your life is totally in keeping with that. You may not be happy with your life as it is, but it is what you have drawn to you. We cover how you can change your life — should you wish to do so — in more detail shortly.

The net result of these two Laws, and the other Universal Laws we have discussed (and of course the further ones we have not discussed), is your experience in life. Some of the things you experience you will enjoy and class as *good*; other things you experience you will not enjoy and will class these as *bad*. Nevertheless, they are all experience, and God-Consciousness will *happily* accept the experience.

Moving into Part Four, we discuss what it is like to be a God Franchisee and how we can live our lives in such a way that we experience more of what we would like to experience, and less of what we would rather not experience. We will see God's Laws in action, and learn how to live life wisely. Of course, we don't even have to do that; we have the free will to do what we individually choose to do. Sometimes, it is a good idea to make decisions consciously and be aware we can choose how to live our lives, rather than live in a world that seems to be pushing us around. And then, we also have the free will to choose to experience things *randomly*, although you and I both know there is nothing random about it.

This is your life and your experience. God-Consciousness will be happy with however you choose to experience it.

CHAPTER 32

Taking Wise Action

L iving as a God Franchisee, how do I know what to do? How do I take right and wise action? This is not too hard to answer, and will not be difficult to practise once you get used to thinking this way. By being aware of what you are doing and thinking, that is, by living in the Now, you will soon be automatically making right and wise decisions.

Okay, let's reel that back a bit. You are already living as a God Franchisee — everybody is. You can't avoid it, as this is the way the universe works. What you can choose to do is improve the quality of your decisions and actions so you live a happier life. Some people might see this as a more spiritual way of living, but that is not necessarily true. Everything we do can be viewed from a spiritual aspect because everything we do is being experienced by God-Consciousness. However, we do know some actions cause us pain and some cause us joy. We have preferences in every aspect of our life, and that is what makes each of us individual and different. So, why not do what you enjoy doing, and experience the effects and implications of the causes you set in motion as ones you are happy to experience? Why not? There is no rule that says life has to be difficult, or that you can't enjoy yourself.

While I don't want to be prescriptive, there are three simple tests you can put to every thought and every action you consider taking. If it passes the test, then you can proceed in the knowledge this is wise action. If it fails the test, then you can choose to drop the idea, or modify it so it passes the test. Of course, you can also choose to disregard the tests altogether, although this may result in your taking action you might later consider to have been unwise.

Test 1: Is it going to hurt anyone, including myself? This is a good starting point, and is in line with the hippy philosophy from the '60s of *"Do whatever you want to do, just so long as you don't hurt anybody."* This is also in line with the Wiccan Rede: *"An it harm none, do what ye will."* Now, before you get excited about hippies and Wicca, just think about this philosophy. It gives you free will, which is your birthright from God-Consciousness. It also says don't hurt anybody, and that *anybody* includes yourself. They are just experiences you wish to have and you are not imposing yourself on anyone else or interfering with their personal choices and their free will. It is in keeping with the Christian (and Jewish) precept *"Do unto others as you would have them do unto you."*

So, for example, if you want to have a sexual experience, you are not going to rape someone or act as a paedophile because this hurts somebody else. However, if you are unattached and find a willing and consensual sexual partner, then you are not hurting anybody else. If you are already involved in another relationship, how does this affect your other partner? Are you hurting them? What about yourself? If you practise safe sex, you are not hurting yourself or the other person either. If you don't, you could hurt yourself and/or the other person. Naturally, as you progress through the experience, you may have some other decisions to make, and each of these need to remain faithful to the question: **Is it going to hurt anyone, including myself?**

Test 2: What is my motivation and is it moral? Motivation is all-important. Understanding why you are doing or planning to do something is enlightening. Not only are you acting in a responsible way, but you are also learning more about yourself as you come to know your motivations. You look at the purity of your motivation as well as of the action itself.

Morality is concerned with what is right or wrong, and good or bad behaviour; it is often connected with what is acceptable as conventional standards of conduct. What standards of morality are we talking about here? Frankly, you need to trust your own sense of morality. You have a conscience because you have a Higher Self. If you get in touch with that Higher Self, then you will know instinctively whether a thing is right or wrong.

You also may have moral standards that were taught to you in childhood by your parents, your school, and your church. You need to consider these too as you determine what you believe is moral. In the end, it is your decision as to what is moral and ethical in any situation, and of course, you will already be taking into account Test 1 (*Is it going to hurt anyone, including myself?*). I have a strong belief that most people have a very good idea of what is wrong when they think about it. If you are not sure, just note down what is good about the idea and what is bad about it, and how it affects other people and yourself. This will give you clarity as it objectifies your decision.

Going back to our previous example, you may have found yourself a consensual and safe sexual partner, and you may be unmarried with no current relationship, so therefore, the proposed experience is not going to hurt anyone, including yourself. But is it moral?

You may have been brought up to believe it is immoral to have sex outside marriage. You may believe you need to have an emotional relationship with the person before you have a sexual encounter with them. You may believe sex is just a bit of fun between consenting adults and need have no greater significance than that. This is where your own conscience comes in. What is right for you?

It is important for you to be an honest judge of this as you are the one who is going to have to live with the consequences. Also, it is important to ensure your partner in this experience has a similar sense of morality about it. It is not so much that you are responsible for that person, but it is important they don't have differing expectations to yours due to poor communication. So, if the other person believes an on-going relationship is on the cards, whereas you are looking at a one-night stand, there may be some moral issues to resolve before continuing.

If you do not satisfy this moral issue for yourself, you are going to feel guilty. Guilt is all about not satisfying moral issues before you embark on some particular action. Sure there are other sources of guilt, but this is a big one, and one you can avoid by considering the question: **Is it moral and what is my motivation?**

Test 3: Is it real? This question brings you back to being present. Being present in the Now is vitally important to your happiness, or at least to the reduction of your suffering and pain. If we were all real about everything, and we all knew the Truth (whatever that is), the day-to-day experience of everyone would be perfect, with no sign of suffering or pain. We would live in Heaven on Earth, and we would all take wise action at all times because there would be no point in doing anything different. Why do something when there is loss rather than gain?

The first step towards this utopia is being real now. In my opinion, fantasy, or being unreal, is one of the biggest problems the world is facing, and I see little evidence it is being taken seriously. It will be one day, but in the meantime, you can still be real in your own life.

Only twenty-five years ago, fantasy was a small part of people's lives. Sure, reading a novel is going into a fantasy world, but you were aware it was just a story even if it did affect you emotionally. The same applied to the movies or the theatre. You went in, saw a film or play, and came out. You may have been inspired, or emotionally involved, or even frightened, but there was a limit to the effect it had on you. You were also totally aware that what you had experienced was unreal and was performed by characters or actors.

The rapid advance of computers, computer games, the Internet, mobile phones, music videos, iPods, iPads, iTunes, iGoodness-knows-what, Facebook, Twitter, Internet dating, phone-sex, virtual reality, the innumerable television channels, and fantastic special effects (FX) in movies, have all added to the unreality that people experience in the so-called developed world. In particular, young people are constantly bombarded with sensual experiences that are synthetic and backed by loud music, fast moving images, and sounds. They are texting, tweeting, and Facebooking as if this was the only way to communicate. Kids develop Attention-Deficit Hyperactivity Disorder (ADHD), Obsessive–compulsive disorder (OCD) and other psychological and behavioural problems more frequently and from an earlier age than they did previously. While doctors look at heredity, food intolerances, biological causes, and psychological explanations, I believe the environmental factors of a high-speed world must be having a huge detrimental effect on the mental health of children, their parents, and their teachers. Some kids and grownups are able to cope, but some just can't.

Then, of course, there are recreational drugs. These range from alcohol to marijuana to many kinds of synthetic pills. The use of drugs amongst young people has increased over the last few decades, and these too lead into a fantasy world of altered reality, enhanced senses and confidence, as well as hallucination. Binge drinking of alcohol has almost become a national sport. The proportion of car accidents where drugs and/or alcohol is involved remains high in spite of efforts made by authorities to cut them back. While not all users are dicing with death, they certainly are dicing with their minds and their beings.

Money is readily available for all these new enticements through credit and credit cards. Those who can't get credit and are envious of those who are able to purchase these enticements are easily sidetracked into crime in order to acquire them.

The point is, a large part of this sped-up, electronic, chemical, and moneyed world is fantasy! It is not like the real world of just twenty-five years ago. Then, one played real games with a real ball in a real garden. One sat in a real classroom with a real teacher taking you through real lessons using a real book and a real blackboard and chalk. You learnt to really write, to really read, and to really do arithmetic. One had a real job and earned real money (cash) which one spent on real things like food, clothes, and shelter.

Please don't misunderstand me. It is not that I don't appreciate technological development. I have owned eight computers over twenty-five years. I think the Internet is great and use it all the time. I have a mobile phone and I can text. I have a Facebook account. I have four websites, have had others, and no doubt will be getting more. I also like drinking wine, and I have credit cards and mortgages. This is not the issue.

The issue is perspective. It is about putting life into perspective and doing things that are real in the real world. Each of the technologies I have mentioned may be used in a positive, life-affirming, real way. For instance, I could play a video game with my grandson, bonding and having a great deal of fun. However, spending hours and hours every day playing computer games, surfing the Internet, or keeping up to date on your Facebook account, are an abdication from reality. I realise that all these things are conducted in the present in the modern real world. But where is the mind? What is the individual's concept of the real world away from electronics or drugs? What perspective is one getting of reality when one walks or travels with an iPod constantly pulsing into one's ears, and with texts needing to be constantly read and sent?

Of course we need recourse to entertainment and relaxation, but just check what it is you are buying into. For instance, some computer games, particularly ones played over a period of days, weeks, months, or longer, can become totally absorbing and addictive. Second Life® offers an Internet-based virtual world where you can live out all your aspirations as if in the real world — except it is not the real world. Other computer games are particularly violent and would make great indoctrination and training material for soldiers, mercenaries, and serial killers (and they do). The mind cannot distinguish between fantasy and reality in terms of its emotional response and the training it gets to react and respond. Playing violent computer games can easily spill over into the real world, as the reactions to similar stimuli become the same — with potentially serious and permanent results in the real world.

So, Test 3 (**Is it Real?**) is an important test to make of any action you are considering. Does what you want to do relate to reality and to life? Is it adding to you as a person? Are you going to be present in the physical world, or are you going to be lost in the world of the mind and fantasy? Remember too, that now is the only time that is real, so is this thought or action predominantly about now? Often we can drift into thoughts about the past or about the future that achieve nothing in the now, and therefore, are not real.

Returning to our example about a proposed sexual encounter, if this is about experiencing something in the real world, the test is passed. However, if it is just a titillating fantasy of what might happen or what you would like to happen, then one can easily recognise it as unreal.

This reality check completes your three tests. If your thought or proposed action passes all three tests, you know this is a wise action. If it fails, you can choose to either drop the idea, or review it and make changes so that you can retest it and turn it into a wise action. Have fun with this. Serious fun. It will soon become intuitive, and you will instinctively know how to act wisely at all times.

Being a God Franchisee, however, does not imply you have to take *wise* action. You have free will to take whatever action or non-action you wish to take. God-Consciousness will live with that experience or non-experience quite happily.

CHAPTER 33

Secondary Gains

L et's say you have got yourself organised now. Everything you do, all your actions, are measured up against the three wise action tests. You are doing things that don't hurt anybody, your motivations are pure, and you are living in the real world. Nevertheless, you feel life is not working out for you. You may be in a job that does not pay well, you may be chronically ill, or you may be in a relationship that is not quite what you would have hoped for. Despite all your right actions, everything is still not right. You are somehow not manifesting the life you feel you ought to have.

Consider this: perhaps your life is being sabotaged by secondary gains. Secondary gains are wonderfully tricky things, and it is very helpful to be aware of them. A secondary gain is the indirect social, interpersonal, or monetary gain one might get from having a *disability* or living in an apparently unfavourable situation. For example, if you are ill, secondary gains from that might include the following:

+ An increase in attention from others
+ Relief from doing a share of household chores
+ Avoidance of unpleasant situations or responsibilities
+ Monetary gain from social welfare benefits
+ Sympathy and/or love.

Being unemployed has the great secondary gains of your being able to watch TV all day, indulge in your favourite hobby, visit friends, sit in the sun, and so on. Secondary gains can be an aspect in any situation you want to change or claim you want to change.

So take any issue you currently have, whether a health issue, an emotional issue, a spiritual issue, a money issue, or any other personal issue. Write down on a sheet of paper all the benefits you gain from having this particular issue in your life. What are the secondary gains you enjoy because this issue is in your experience? These will be all the hidden bonuses you might receive, such as in the examples above. Take this seriously and make every attempt to find them all. You will be surprised what is lurking there in the background. Great isn't it?

Once you have completed this exercise (and of course you can always add to the list as you need to), investigate each secondary gain individually and ask,

+ Do I really enjoy this secondary gain? (The answer is often YES)
+ If I were to resolve my personal issue, would I lose this benefit?
+ How do I feel about that?
+ If I still want this benefit, is there another way of gaining it not linked to my personal issue — so it's no longer a secondary gain?
+ Do I want to accept my personal issue as being okay rather than lose the benefit of the secondary gain?

Then write down your decision with regard to this secondary gain. The answer will be either be you are genuinely able to forgo that benefit, or there is some other way to achieve it which is overt (above board) so it is no longer a secondary gain.

Now, move on to the next secondary gain and review that in the same way. Work through the whole list of secondary gains until you have the answer on each one. Be honest with yourself. When this exercise is complete, you have enough information to make a very informed decision on which benefits (secondary gains) to do without, which benefits you can still get in a more wholesome way, and whether to continue to have this personal issue.

It might be worth checking to see if you are holding onto some secondary gains that are contrary to or interfering with many aspects of your life. Secondary gains could be preventing things from manifesting in your life in many different ways, so it is very worthwhile to spend some time and seek them out. You will find that if the personal issue is no longer supported by secondary gains, it will heal and/or disappear completely in a surprisingly short time.

As you become more aware of secondary gains, you will begin to spot them as soon as they rear their heads. You can smile at them and then let them go as you take true, wise action.

You might ask, what do secondary gains have to do with **The God Franchise**? The point is that, with your free will, you have the power (and the right) to choose whatever life experiences you wish to experience. Secondary gains are tricks the Ego plays to derail the choices you would prefer to make. This chapter, along with many others in Part Four, makes you aware of one of the strategies the Ego, or misidentification of your True Self, uses. Being aware of these strategies and being present to who you are and what you are doing, enables you to live your life in a more conscious and directed way — if you like, in a more spiritual way.

Nevertheless, it is always your total free choice as to whether you want to bother with this or not.

CHAPTER 34

Applying the Law of Manifestation

We have covered wise action and watching out for secondary gains, so let's take a look now at the Law that manifests everything in your life. It manifests the good stuff and the bad stuff, and it doesn't seem to mind which. How can we harness this Law so we get more of the good stuff and less of the bad stuff? How can we master this Law so our lives flow with abundance, health, love, and joy?

This Law, the Law of Manifestation, has been popularised in recent years as the Law of Attraction. As we mentioned earlier, the Law of Manifestation is one of God's Laws; it is as constant and powerful as the Law of Gravity. In fact, its operation is very similar to that of the Law of Gravity.

The Law of Gravity tells us every physical object in the universe attracts every other physical object in the universe. This is what keeps the universe together. Gravity is always an attractive force — it never repels. It has an infinite range and it cannot be modified or protected against, so we can see that all the objects around you exert a gravitational pull on you. Naturally, Earth is the largest body in your vicinity, and that is why you are drawn most noticeably to Earth. We see the effect of the gravitational pull of the Moon on water thus causing the tides, and naturally, the gravitational pull of the Sun stops Earth flying off into space. The position of everything on Earth and everything in the universe is the net effect of all the gravitational pulls of each object on every other object.

The Law of Manifestation works in the same way. What comes into your life as objects, people, or experience is the net effect of all the different and perhaps conflicting thoughts, beliefs, and attitudes you have. Added into the mix can be peer and ancestral (family) thoughts, beliefs, and attitudes, as well as those of your country, race, and so on. Effectively, you buy into group thoughts, beliefs, and attitudes as if they were a part of your DNA, and I suspect they are in your DNA. If you are unaware of this connection, as most people are, you can easily believe you have no control over what happens to you. If bad things happen, you blame Fate, the Universe, God, or your fellow Man. You see yourself as a victim in a hostile world.

The fact is, you have virtually total control over your life because you are a God Franchisee. I say *virtually* to allow for the possibility of some other forces at play, but frankly, I do not know of any. As I see it, your life will play out in keeping with your overall thoughts, beliefs, and attitudes at the very deepest of levels. Often you may not be aware of the subtle fundamental beliefs you hold, but they have a powerful effect on your life nevertheless.

Journey or NLP Practitioners,[133] as well as Cognitive Behavioural Therapists (CBTs), have tools and techniques to help clients uncover beliefs they have absorbed and vows they have made — often in childhood or during their teenage years. These beliefs and vows are now buried deep in the cells of their bodies. The practitioners remove these beliefs/vows and replace them with more wholesome beliefs/ vows. Doing this has an enormous impact on clients' lives and makes these techniques very powerful. There are probably other modalities of healing that use similar methods to get rid of unwholesome beliefs and vows as successfully.

In 2006, the world was given the film and the book *The Secret*[134] by Australian Rhonda Byrne, causing a sensation. Despite the title of the book, the Law of Manifestation was not a secret and has been written

---

133 The Journey™ was developed by Brandon Bays. Accredited Practitioners take clients through a Journey Process to help them resolve emotional, spiritual, and/or physical issues in their lives. NLP (Neuro-Linguistic Programming) offers alternative tools to resolve personal issues. Some of the techniques used by The Journey are based on NLP. Use the Internet to find a practitioner in your local area.

134 Byrne, R., *The Secret*, Atria Books, New York, and Beyond Words, Hillsboro, Oregon, 2006.

about many times.[135] Nevertheless, the book was marketed well, and the result was the whole profile of the Law of Manifestation, or Law of Attraction as it has become better known, was raised.

The Law of Manifestation has also been given different names at different times:

+ The Law of Manifestation
+ The Law of Attraction
+ The Law of Abundance
+ The Law of Conscious Creation
+ The Law of Intention

These names are all variations on a theme, and they all operate according to the principles that we are calling the Law of Manifestation here. The Law of Manifestation has been defined as follows:

+ Like attracts like
+ Like creates like
+ *"That which is like unto itself is drawn"*[136]
+ *"As you seek, you attract and are attracted to that which will fulfil your search."*[137]

In essence, whatever you absolutely believe — that is not contradicted by a stronger law or force — will manifest in your life without fail. The Law of Manifestation is guaranteed to work because it is Law. It is God's Law. You prove it in your life every day. Let me hasten to add that this is not a glib, vague promise that if you wish for something and believe you'll get it, you will get it whatever it is. It is not the brief employment of wishful thinking to make you millions overnight. It is, rather, a very deep, practical, immutable, spiritual law that ensures what is truly in your consciousness is what will manifest in your life as concrete reality.

There is a necessary time lapse between the time you focus on a

---

135 See separate section under Bibliography for a small selection of books on the Law of Manifestation.

136 Hicks, E. & Hicks, J., *Ask and It is Given – Learning to Manifest Your Desires*, Hay House Inc., Carlsbad, CA, 2004, Pg. 25.

137 McArthur, B., Your Life – *Why It Is the Way It Is and What You Can Do About It*, A.R.E. Press, Virginia Beach, 1993, Pg. 58.

particular desire and when it manifests, although the process is slowly at work throughout that timeframe. This prevents you from making rash requests you might later regret. The popular stories of magic lamps and genies clarify the dangers of this. Even the saying, *"Be careful what you ask for: you might just get it,"* is another warning to take the Law of Manifestation seriously. If the desire has not yet manifested, you can always change your mind about it. In fact, this happens naturally as people flit from one desire to the next without clarity or focus.

Despite the awareness of and great interest in the Law of Manifestation, many people still do not have it working for them. The problem is people have yet to understand how it actually works. It is very subtle, and it is very specific. If you are currently in a place of lack, loneliness, depression, fear, loss, or sadness, it can also seem to be very difficult to change your consciousness in such a way that you can get The Law of Manifestation to work for you.

Let's take some time to go through the principles and the various steps of the Law of Manifestation. Different books will tell you different things, and emphasise different aspects, but the overall thrust is the same. The following is a good place to start.

The Essential Principles of the Law of Manifestation

The Law of Manifestation works for you every moment of every day. It is God's Law, and is as fundamental to the operation of the universe as is the Law of Gravity. It brings experiences into your life whether they are what you want or what you don't want, and whether they are beneficial or detrimental to you and your wellbeing. Why is this? Why would God do this to you?

The purpose of life from the perspective of God-Consciousness is to experience. Nothing more, nothing less. All experience is equal, as God-Consciousness does not judge experience as being good or bad. Man judges experiences and things as good or bad, not God. God-Consciousness has given you individual free will to make whatever choices you wish in life. This is your God Franchise. You can manifest the life you wish to manifest.

As a God Franchisee you can, like God, create whatever it is you want to experience. God-Consciousness is your very essence and being, and is expressed most clearly in your Higher Self. However, through your free will, you have become an individual Ego who appears to be separate from God. This is fine — it is all part of God-Consciousness' experience. Nevertheless, you still have the power to create. This appears to be a God-given right, if you like, although of course it is God-Consciousness creating through Himself anyway, since He is your very being and you are a God Franchisee.

The mechanism that allows you to create your life and experiences is the Law of Manifestation. Whatever you absolutely believe (that is not contradicted by a stronger law or force) will become manifest in your life without fail. The key then is to be clear as to what you *absolutely believe*. Just as with the Law of Gravity, the Law of Manifestation works from the net position of everything you think, believe, and hold as an attitude. Perhaps we could call this the *Fundamental You*, and in practical terms, this is the sum total of all your beliefs, all your values, and all your attitudes, vows, promises, and rules. The thoughts you have that are truly important are those you believe are true. Likewise, the attitudes you display are based on what you truly believe. The vows and promises you have made at various times are based on what you believed at that time, and these are now locked into your consciousness. Also, the rules you have set to live by are directly based on your beliefs. So, for ease of discussion now, and for any practical work you might do, it is your **beliefs** that are the key.

We can say that the Fundamental You, with all your core beliefs, is the source of everything you experience in your life. This Fundamental You is who is really running the show. It is what you truly believe within yourself, the place you are really coming from, that counts. What you say, do, pretend to be, what role you play, what body you wear, and all the other accessory parts of you are beside the point whenever they differ from what the Fundamental You believes. Of course, if you say, do, pretend to be, play roles, and use your body in ways that endorse and are congruent with (corresponding to) the Fundamental You, then you are encouraging the Law of Manifestation, and in so doing, speed up the manifestation of that which is congruent with your beliefs and expectations.

This means that if you inwardly believe you are worthy of receiving wealth into your life, then you will attract wealth to you. If, conversely, you fundamentally believe you are not worthy of wealth, in fact that poverty is your lot, you will attract more poverty. The Law of Manifestation works perfectly to match harmonious experiences in life with the Fundamental You. Whether you like them or want them is absolutely beside the point. What you put out as the subtle frequency of the Fundamental You is what creates the manifestation in your life. We could call it a *Creation Frequency.*

Your beliefs act as a template for producing your subjective experience. What could be simpler than that? It is true, however, most people have not realised this simple fact, and so do not make the effort to change the template in order to experience what they wish to experience and avoid what they prefer not to experience.

Whatever you conceive in your Mind, supported by your fundamental beliefs, determines the template for your experience.

If you create a template for wealth, you will experience wealth in your life.

If you create a template for ill health, you will experience ill health in your life.

If you create a template for friendship, you will experience friendship in your life.

If you create a template for poverty, you will experience poverty in your life.

If you create a template for happiness, you will experience happiness in your life.

If you create a template for intelligence, you will experience intelligence in your life.

If you create a template for love, you will experience love in your life.

If you create a template for hate, you will experience hate in your life.

If you create a template for strength, you will experience strength in your life.

If you create a template for ugliness, you will experience ugliness in your life.

If you create a template for abundance, you will experience abundance in your life.

Do you get the idea?

So *"by their fruits ye shall know them"*[138] is true. You do get your *"just deserts"*[139] in life. The only way to make changes in your external world is to make the changes internally.

We will discuss beliefs in greater detail in the next chapter, while here we will delve more deeply into the details of the Law of Manifestation.

The Seven Steps of the Law of Manifestation

We can choose to allow the universe to throw at us whatever it wishes. This is what many people unconsciously do, although what they don't realise is they are personally attracting these things into their lives. Alternatively, we can be proactive and decide consciously what it is we want to experience, and then go out and get it through the self-same Law of Manifestation. Whether we are conscious of it or not, every one of us is a God Franchisee and, therefore, we are able, thanks to our free will, to create the life experience we want to have.

When consciously using the Law of Manifestation to create the experiences you want, you can use the seven steps detailed below. **The God Franchise** gives you the power to do what you will. However, there is one proviso to this. It does not morally give you the right to affect, for good or ill, any other person or being in the universe. This is because every other person has an identical God Franchise, and no one has any right to affect you, for good or for ill, either. I say *morally*

---

138 *Matthew 7:20*

139 Spelling is correct as the meaning is *things deserved* and the phrase has nothing to do with arid deserts or delicious desserts. See http://www.phrases.org.uk/meanings/just-deserts.html (authored by Gary Martin).

because, in practice, if you wish to affect others you can, although there is a corresponding price to pay for this. This is usually called karma.

The interaction between people, the very dance of life, is the outward expression of how each of us God Franchisees manifests our experiences, either consciously or unconsciously, through the Law of Manifestation. And God-Consciousness is here, in each one of us, enjoying the experience.

There are a number of different ways you can use the Law of Manifestation, and different writers have come up with different steps and methodologies. While each will work, it is reasonable to expect that some methodologies are more effective than others. We will touch on some of the options, and then go into more detail with our preferred approach to the Law of Manifestation.

The recent popularisation of the Law of Attraction is through *The Secret*. There are three main steps to the Law of Attraction according to Rhonda Byrne:

Step 1: Ask
Step 2: Believe
Step 3: Receive.

In *Ask and It Is Given*,[140] Esther and Jerry Hicks offer the following steps:

Step 1: You ask (This is your work)
Step 2: The answer is given (This is not your work)
Step 3: Receive or allow (This is your work).

In *The Attractor Factor*,[141] Joe Vitale gives us five steps:

Step 1: Notice what you focus on that you don't want in your life
Step 2: Decide what you do want and activate it
Step 3: Clear inhibiting beliefs
Step 4: Feel that the thing you want is already complete
Step 5: Let go. Want the outcome without needing it.

---

140 Hicks, E. & Hicks, J., *Ask and It is Given – Learning to Manifest Your Desires*, Hay House Inc., Carlsbad, CA, 2004.
141 Vitale, J., *The Attractor Factor*, John Wiley & Sons, Hoboken, New Jersey, 2005.

I recommend the following seven steps when working with the Law of Manifestation consciously:

Step 1: Appreciate, be grateful, and give

Step 2: Decide specifically what it is you want

Step 3: Check inside how you feel; remove all doubts

Step 4: Declare your intention

Step 5: Feel your belief

Step 6: Stay in tune and do nothing

Step 7: Receive gratefully.

While this may seem longwinded, what we are doing is going through the process of applying the Law of Manifestation in great detail. Once you have had several experiences of creating and attracting what you want in your life, you will find you are able to play much more lightly with the process, and many of the steps will be instinctive. Getting started is often the hardest part. We like the concept. It is great to read about. We can imagine the expected results to be wonderful. But it is that stage of specifically putting in effort to achieve what looks so good that is so daunting.

We may also find that the difficulty with getting started on something new is that everything is unknown. It means stepping outside our comfort zones. With self-improvement, it means I am going to have to change. *Tomorrow I won't be the person I am today. Will I like the new me? Will I recognise the new me? Will I survive the trauma and pain of change? Can I afford the disruption to my life? No! Let me stay as I am!*

So, we first have the challenge of even contemplating change. However, if anything about the Law of Manifestation excites you, then you have two choices. One is to find an exciting novel, read some other exciting words, and eavesdrop on somebody else's (imaginary) life. The other is to bring that excitement you feel into reality in your own life — and that means change. That means using the Law of Manifestation to create exactly what it is you want in your life rather than attracting your life experiences by default.

Step 1: Appreciate, Be Grateful, and Give

It may seem strange to start using the Law of Manifestation by appreciating, being grateful, and giving. *After all, I want something don't I? I need it, and what is there to appreciate or be grateful for just yet? And giving? Why would I want to give when I am the one who needs to receive something?*

Let's take it slowly. It doesn't work quite like that. As you will see when we discuss the Universal Laws in detail (Chapter 40), there is a Law of Balance. This Law ensures there is equilibrium between what you give and what you receive. Is it not better to give appreciation, gratitude, and help to others first so that you create an imbalance in your favour which can then be filled through your desired manifestation? Is it not normal to give of your time at work before you can expect to be paid? This is also tied in with the Law of Cause and Effect — the cause pre-empts the effect.

In addition to that, by giving appreciation, gratitude, and help to others, you are in an appropriate state of mind. You demonstrate to the universe that you are allowing the energies to flow, or even causing them to flow. You have tuned into an energetic flow that will also help your manifestation flow to you. This is the first step of manifesting anything. You are literally paving the way.

There is a subtle difference between appreciation and gratitude.

Appreciation is a general feeling of being blessed, and acknowledging having numerous things and people in your life that you enjoy and value having.

Gratitude is specifically acknowledging something or some benefit you have just been given or promised.

To help you to attract what you consciously desire using the Law of Manifestation, it is essential to be constantly appreciative of what you already have, and feel grateful for what is coming to you. As you feel appreciative of the abundance you already have in your life, this fact will automatically attract even more abundance.

Joe Vitale tells the story of a friend who healed himself from double pneumonia in 24 hours by repeating to himself hourly one particular sentence, playing the sentence back to himself on a tape, and looking at signs he had written and put up throughout his home. Vitale quotes his friend's sentence: *"Thank you, God, for all the blessings I have and for all the blessings I am receiving."*[142] This is truly using the power of appreciation and gratitude.

The same principle applies to *giving*. If you are of a nature that always wants to receive, it means you consider yourself as lacking and needing. By giving to others in any way you can, even if it be the widow's mite,[143] you are tuning into and trusting your abundance through the Law of Manifestation.

Note that all three of these — appreciation, gratitude, and giving — are best practised on a daily basis as evidence of your normal regard for the abundance you experience in your life. In this way, when you have a specific desire, you will be able to receive with ease.

Appreciation Exercise

As a daily exercise, think of all the things, people, and qualities you have in your life right now — those you truly appreciate. Use the words "I appreciate ..." and just name someone or something you wish to acknowledge. Then repeat "I appreciate ..." and name the next one you wish to acknowledge. And so on.

As you do this exercise, really feel the emotion of appreciation inside you. Really feel how *lucky*, how blessed you are for having each of these things, people, and qualities in your life right now. Express yourself from your inner being — allow it to come from that place of complete and utter appreciation.

Gratitude Exercise

Whenever you are offered anything by anybody, no matter how small, accept it and acknowledge it with gratitude. The only reason to turn something down is if you genuinely do not want it. If you are offered a piece of cake and you are not hungry, or if it is obviously a type of cake you do not wish to eat, then turn it down politely, and still show

---

142   Vitale, Pg. 134
143   *Mark* 12: 41-44

gratitude for the offer. If someone offers you a seat on the bus, take it with gratitude. However, if you see an older person, or someone who looks tired or frail, you might then offer the seat to them.

The idea here is that you remain in a receiving state of mind, allowing what the Law of Manifestation provides in your life. If you turn things away, you may just turn away something you have asked for or need. What God-Consciousness offers you may sometimes appear to be different to what you asked for. I would say appearances can be deceptive.

Giving Exercise

Whenever somebody asks you for help in some way, consider giving of your time, your advice, or even money. Likewise, if you notice a need somewhere, volunteer to help in whatever way you are able. If you do this with right motivation and with love, and without seeking any specific reciprocation, you will allow abundance to flow to you in many ways.

It is important not to force your generosity of time, advice, or money onto someone who either does not want it or who does not appreciate it, as you could easily be doing them (and yourself) a disservice. By being aware of your motivation and of the recipient's true need, you will be guided to act in an appropriate way, or guided not to act at all.

The bottom line is **Count Your Blessings!**

Step 2: Decide Specifically What It Is You Want

So now that you have embarked on using the Law of Manifestation consciously, the next step is to decide what it is you want in your life. This is easier said than done, I know. However, it is true that if you don't know what you want, how are you going to attract it into your life? And if you did get it, how would you recognise it?

There are a number of areas in your life, and it is good to review these from time to time to see how you feel about each of them, and how your life is panning out. Some people just let life happen to them, and then complain when things aren't always smooth. As we know, the Law of Manifestation constantly brings into our lives whatever it is we are focussed on, and those people who allow life to happen to them, are attracting exactly what they *happen* to have as a Creation Frequency.

By deciding what you want in your life, you take control of your life, and ensure you get more of what you want, and less of what you don't want. Here are some of the areas of your life to consider — you can add any other areas of focus important to you:

+ Relationships with others, including family and friends
+ Your personal relationship with your lover, partner, or spouse
+ Money, home, and possessions
+ Career
+ Recreation, travel, and fun
+ Health, fitness, sports and exercise
+ Spiritual matters
+ Personal power
+ Your interest in world affairs and the planet
+ Art and creativity
+ Knowledge, learning, and information.

Remember you are a God Franchisee! What would God want? Or, what would God want for you, if you prefer that approach? Perhaps now is the time to brainstorm as God, with no limits to your imagination, no limits to what is possible, no right or wrong. You can always fine-tune what comes up later, but for the moment, play God. Take on your true role as a God Franchisee.

When you work through the following exercise, remember that anything is possible. Be expansive. The physical world is malleable and, in reality, nothing is set in concrete. Beliefs you might have had about the physical world are probably not correct, so create a new world for yourself. Think big and shoot for the stars. Decide what you really want. There is also no shortage or limitation in the world. People see shortage or limitation around them, but that is their belief. There is no limit to money, and the faster it circulates between people, the more there appears to be. Keep the energy flowing.

And while I don't want to put a dampener on your desires, it's important to remember you do need to truly believe that what you ask for is reasonably possible. So, if you are staring at a heap of unpaid bills, and you decide you want one million dollars by tomorrow morning, it might just stretch your sense of credulity. However, if your goal is to achieve one million dollars over the next year or the next five years, this may well seem absolutely possible to you. What matters is what you really believe is possible.

Another small reminder — check to see if you are being greedy, and if your motivation is pure. It is absolutely fine to want the best physical comforts a person could imagine; however, desiring something you don't need just because you can is tantamount to greed. Likewise, desiring something just so you can outdo your neighbour is not exactly a pure motivation. Here, desire is driving you rather than the other way round. Just check inside to see how you feel, and you will immediately know if there is a problem with your desire. If necessary, ask yourself, "For what purpose do I want this?"

It may also help for you to focus on the *experience* you desire rather than the money to pay for it. This is far more powerful, and you may be able to experience it without money coming directly into the equation. However, if you have a good reason to focus on the money, that is fine too.

So the bottom line is, there is no need to feel inhibited or limited. You can have what you really desire. And there is no need to have everything all at once, because as a God Franchisee, the same opportunity to create will be here for you again tomorrow. Decide what you really want right now. If you have desires in different areas of your life, you can work on those aspects one at a time — there is no need to wait for one manifestation to appear before working on another.

Choice Exercise

Decide on the subject you want to work with. Alternatively, review all the available subjects to see which ones you want to start with. As you review these subjects, acknowledge and feel appreciation for what you already have (Per Step 1). In that sense of appreciation you may find additional aspects you would like to add to what you already have, or changes you might like to make.

I apologise at the outset for asking you to write all this down in a lot of detail, but it does help focus the mind and stop fuzzy thinking.

It also means you can work with your manifestation exercises over a period of time. Yes, it is also more concrete to write them down!

So write down any areas where you would like to experience or have something extra or different. You can use either positive or negative words for the moment. Just write down whatever comes to you. Include as much detail as you can — be specific about what it is you want — even paint a verbal picture.

Come to a point of completion, where you feel you have a list of specifically what you would like to work with.

Refining Your Choices Exercise

Now that you have identified some things (*desires*) you would like to experience or have in your life, write each desire onto one of two separate pages, a MANIFEST page and a DON'T WANT page. You may consolidate some of the things on your original list from the previous exercise if you find they are very similar or go together well.

Then, for each desire write down what you want or like about the desire on the MANIFEST page, and on the DON'T WANT page write all the things you don't want or don't like about the desire. You can even start the sentences with "I desire ...", "I like ...", "I don't want ..." and "I don't like ..." Be aware of other ways of expressing your positive and negative statements. Statements such as "I like working short hours" may be a negative if long hours are really needed for a business, or to provide your income expectations.

When complete, take all statements on the DON'T WANT page, and convert them into positive statements you can now add to the MANIFEST page. The idea is you don't really want a negative page, and you need to express all your desires in positive terms.

Next, check all your positive entries. Make sure they are worded to perfectly reflect what you really do want. Positive statements are worded so they avoid words like *no, don't, can't, not* and so on. So, if you have written "I don't want to feel sick anymore," your new version will be, "I desire perfect health and fitness in my life at all times." Likewise, if you have written, "I want to stop never (or not) having enough money," change this to "I desire an abundance of money readily available for my requirements."

Once you have rephrased the statements into positive terms, cross them off the DON'T WANT page. Discard the negative list when complete; if any statement should remain, keep the page and we will take another look at it in the next step.

Step 3: Check Inside How You Feel; Remove All Doubts

You now have an idea on paper of what you would like to experience in one or more areas of your life. This step helps you develop a clear intent for what it is you want. This is absolutely essential. The more focussed your intention is, the sooner the Law of Manifestation can bring it into manifestation. Now that you know specifically what it is you desire, you need to check inside to see how it genuinely sits with you.

Checking Exercise

Sit quietly and read each line on your MANIFEST page, and for each one be aware how it feels inside. What you are looking for is an excitement, a warmth, a real happiness that this is coming into your life. Any line with a real positive buzz about it is great.

However, if you feel a sense of misgiving, aversion, fear or any other negative reaction to the statement, you need to review the statement. Likewise, if you ask yourself why you don't already have this in your life, and the reason is a negative one, you need to investigate that reason:

+ Change the statement so it feels better for you, or
+ Identify what the feeling is and ask yourself what belief is tied up with this, or
+ Ask yourself if you have ever made a vow in this regard and identify it, or
+ Identify what it will cost you (in money, time, focus, lost opportunities to do other things, etc.) to fulfil this statement, or
+ Identify what it is you are avoiding, or want to avoid, or
+ Decide not to continue with this statement, or perhaps even with the specific desire at all.

If you do find any incongruent beliefs or vows, you need to change them if you wish to continue with this statement or desire. To do that you may need some professional help, such as a Journey or NLP Practitioner, or a Cognitive Behavioural Therapist (CBT) to take you through a Belief Change process. This is important because this belief/ vow is affecting what you want to do in life, and probably extends to many other aspects or desires in your life. I cover beliefs in more detail in the next chapter.

Once you have completed the MANIFEST list, go through any items left on the DON'T WANT list in the same way as above, adding to your MANIFEST list as necessary. Then discard the completed DON'T WANT list.

Checking how you feel inside is a vitally important step, since your emotions are the best indicators you have of what you are holding as beliefs deep inside the Fundamental You. If you have any incongruent beliefs that contradict what you wish to attract, you are not going to achieve the outcome you desire.

For example, let's say you are an artist, quite a good one at that, and there is great support from your family and friends for you to turn professional and earn your living as an artist. However, if you hold the belief that your art is a gift from God, and that people should be able to enjoy art without having to pay for it, and that commercialism is the enemy of the true artist, and therefore money in the art world is evil, how are you going to attract enough money to live by?

By identifying beliefs like this, you can then either decide not to follow that desire to become a professional artist, or you can get rid of the disempowering beliefs and enable that desire to come to rapid and fruitful manifestation. If you believe what happens to you, or how successful you are, depends on any factors in the outside world, you need to resolve this belief too. Thus, if you believe the economy, the goodwill of others, or the government is a key factor in whether you succeed, you have a belief that indicates you are not the creator of your own life experience.

Other sorts of beliefs are quite subtle, yet are still part of the Fundamental You. You need to uncover these beliefs and replace any negative ones with positive beliefs. Dangerous beliefs include:

Money is dirty
Some people are filthy rich
Money doesn't grow on trees
I don't deserve it
I'm not lovable
I'm not good enough
I'm not smart enough
I'm not attractive enough
I'm not tall enough
I'm not ...
You don't know me like I know myself
There's no point wishing or hoping
I always get disappointed
People don't really like me
And so on ...

Replace all negative beliefs with positive ones that make sense to you and that you can believe. For example:

I genuinely deserve and am open to receiving all the Universe (God, God-Consciousness, Life) has to offer me
Money comes to me in helpful ways
I am loving towards, and am loved in return by, everyone I reach out to
I am master of my own destiny and can attract whatever I wish into my life.

Be aware of all the beliefs you have picked up from your parents, from your teachers, from your friends, from advertising, from song lyrics, from movies, from television, and from all the other influences that are around you each and every day. Filter what you take on board.

Listen to what you say to others. Listen to what you say to yourself. Root out all the negative beliefs in case they take residence or are already resident in the Fundamental You. Choose beliefs that really serve you.

Remove all sources of doubt. Check for all the doubts and reasons your mind comes up with about how your desire might not materialise. If you have a partner who might negatively influence your beliefs in any way, you will need to sort that out as well. Having doubts or negative beliefs coming from somebody you normally trust or listen to, can be very destructive unless you either resolve them or make yourself totally impenetrable to them.

Step 4: Declare Your Intention

Declaring your intention to God-Consciousness (your Higher Self) is a very powerful step, so powerful, in fact, that when you are fully experienced in working with the Law of Manifestation in a conscious way, this may be the only one of the seven steps you need to take. The other steps will remain, but you will go through them automatically and intuitively. You will know as soon as you have declared your intention, you will have set the Law in motion. The word *intention* is used much as the word *prayer* is used in a more religious context. Whether we pray to God for a specific blessing we would like in our life, or we declare our intention to the universe, this is the same thing. Any perceived difference is semantics.

The next step is to write out, in specific terms, exactly what it is you want based on what you have decided as you worked through the previous steps. Some people may rebel against all this writing, but let me repeat: the reason I like writing is that it is specific and cannot be fudged or forgotten. You will need to think about the specific words you use, and you will have the ability to change what you have written and tweak it until it is exactly as you want it.

Intention Exercise

Write down your intention in only positive terms. Write your intention as one that is true for you now. If you say, "I want …," it rather reminds you of its absence in your life right now. If you were to write, "I now have a new four-bedroom home in my favourite suburb," both your conscious mind and your unconscious mind are going to say, "Whoa! That's not true!" So, how about writing, "I now choose to have a new four-bedroom home in my favourite suburb."[144] Isn't that great?

---

144 See Anthony, R., *Beyond Positive Thinking: A No-Nonsense Formula for Getting the Results You Want*, Morgan James, Virginia, 2004.

Now, add the words, "— this or something better" to your intention. Also add the words "— and with good to all concerned" and/ or "— in perfect ways." The first statement allows for the possibility there may be an even better manifestation available to you than what you have conceived. The second statement ensures only good comes from the manifestation, and you are not causing loss to someone else through it. If there are two of you competing for the same thing, it does not mean you cannot succeed because the other person thereby loses; it means there is a solution that is equitable and perfect for both of you.

As you did in Step 3, just check how this intention feels to you.

Attach this intention to your back-up detail MANIFEST sheets. This lays out the specifics of what you want and includes the specifications, if you like, of your new job, your new partner, your new house, or whatever it is. If the desire you are working on is simpler than that, and the whole thing is encapsulated in your intention statement, there is no need to attach the sheet.

Write the intention on a small card so you can keep it with you at all times. This is an optional step some people like to use to keep their focus clear.

When you are ready, sit in a meditative state, and then read each of your intentions clearly and declare them specifically to God-Consciousness (your Higher Self). Repeat this three times if you wish to. The important thing is to have absolute clarity about your intention. You need to really feel your intention, feel the excitement of it coming into manifestation. Remember, you are creating your Creation Frequency here.

If you would prefer to treat this last step as a prayer to God, this will work just as well, if not better for you.

Know that this is the single most important step in this approach to the Law of Manifestation. In the past, we may often have had a fairly clear idea of what we wanted, and even pictured it or held it in a dreamlike state in our mind as a desire or even an obsession. Yet we may not have spoken that desire openly to God-Consciousness. We need to ask in order to receive. We need to ask specifically in words.

However hard this is for you, however much it goes against the grain, you need to *ask* in order to receive. You have free will, and unless you ask, you are not making your intention clear. You are a God Franchisee and have the right to ask, in fact, the duty to ask so that you can better fulfil God's purpose and your own, to manifest and experience all your life's potential.

Step 5: Feel Your Belief

Belief is a funny thing, so I need to be very clear about what I mean — and what I don't mean. Even the words *Feel Your Belief* need careful attention to ensure you have grasped exactly what I mean by this.

Firstly, belief has nothing to do with the blind faith of religious assertions. It has nothing to do with hoping it is true, or believing it is true with a slight tinge of uncertainty. It is *knowing* absolutely that the Law of Manifestation works and that it will work in this particular instance. Of course, this becomes easier to do as you gain experience in using the Law of Manifestation consciously. Nevertheless, it is worth working towards in the early days.

Regarding feeling that belief, what I mean here is you need to really feel what it will be like to achieve the result you have asked for. You will feel the excitement of the experience and the anticipation of it, and you will be smiling and ready for it. So imagine the scene of success, allow all your senses to come into play, and then experience what it *feels* like to achieve that desired result.

The good news is that you can trick the mind to some extent! Really work on feeling the excitement, perhaps by remembering other times when you felt similar excitement about something coming. Then, when you feel it, transfer that across to the new situation and your current desire. You can add anticipation and expectancy in the same way, and you can smile. You can also daydream about what it will be like when you have manifested your desire.

The mind is a tool for you to use, and it cannot differentiate between objective reality and make-believe unless you specifically tell it the difference. So, if you daydream and experience your desired outcome as if it has already manifested, with no thoughts of doubt, you will create the same vibration as the thing you desire. The Law of

Manifestation uses these vibrations to draw your manifestation to you just like a magnet or gravity. This is your Creation Frequency.

As you really feel the success of your intention, breathe deeply into it. Give the intention the *breath of life* just as God did to Man. *"And the Lord God formed man of the dust of the ground, and breathed into his nostrils the breath of life; and man became a living soul."*[145] In this way, using your God Franchise, breathe life into your intention, your creation.

Joe Vitale describes a wonderful process called scripting.[146] Here, you take a sheet of paper and write out a script as if it was for a movie. You write the scene you desire as if it had just happened. You describe how it feels for this to have happened, and describe the whole imaginary scene in detail as if that is how it played out. How you feel about it — the joy, the gratitude, the wonder of it — all this is vital as it enables you to experience how you will feel when your desire is manifested in your life in reality. The emotional practice run should be as real for you as it will be when the manifestation itself occurs.

Step 6: Stay in Tune and Do Nothing

When you have your vibration, your Creation Frequency, in place and you are tuned into what it is you want, it is easier to recognise all the signs your desired outcome is on its way. You may not receive the manifestation in exactly the way you anticipate it, so when something else comes from left field, you need to be ready to recognise it. It may, for instance, be the opportunity to meet the person who is going to help you with the manifestation. It may be further information that comes your way to help you with it.

You need to stay in tune and be vigilant and expectant, without focussing on the exact form it will take. Stay open. You can miss opportunities if you do not remain vigilant.

It is possible to undermine yourself through careless thought, so you need to stay in tune and beware of self-sabotage and doubts. Stay in

---

145 *Genesis* 2:7
146 Vitale, Pg. 139

the vibration for your expected[147] outcome by feeling now how you will feel when your desire is manifested. Then when anything related to it comes along, its vibration will enable you to recognise and embrace it.

If any doubts arise, identify them immediately and handle them as you did in Step 3. Doubts are anathemas to your Law of Manifestation work, as they change your Creation Frequency. The word *anathema* means *curse*!

Other than staying in tune, all you need to do is...

Do Nothing

This may seem a little strange, and yes, the time for action does come. By staying tuned and doing nothing you are in the right space to be inspired to take the necessary action when the time is right. You don't need to fuss and worry over what to do next. Just hold the space, and when the time is right, you will know what you need to do. The Law of Manifestation will draw that which you desire to you — you don't need to chase it. And then, when manifestation is imminent, or an important step in the process is reached, you will know what you need to do. You will follow your intuition.

You may feel there is something you can do to help. You may implement it, and then find out later your desire would have manifested anyway, whether or not you had undertaken the extra step. If your desire is pure (that is, untainted by doubt, or negative motivations), and you have turned it completely over to God-Consciousness, then you are guaranteed to get a manifested result.

Let go of any feeling of need. Yes, just let go of the need for this thing or experience in your life. The problem with wanting too much is that there is an element of neediness in there, and neediness implies lack. If you put out a vibration of lack, what are you going to attract? More lack! Having a feeling of need or wanting too much also implies

---

147 I have used the word *expect* and its variations a little loosely in this book. There is a subtle way in which you can expect something with the feeling of it being a right, almost a challenge to God-Consciousness to provide you with exactly what you want. This is Ego speaking. Counting your chickens before they hatch can only lead to disappointment. The real answer is to believe strongly and trust the perfect manifestation will come into your life, and accept it may be in a form different from what you might have expected.

a lack of trust, perhaps even a doubt.

Just allow whatever will come your way to come your way. You have let God-Consciousness know what it is you would like, and now it is His job to deliver. This is true deliberate creation. Also, let go of any need to know how it will manifest. Needing to know how the mechanism is going to work, or trying to guess what that mechanism is, implies a limitation. You may not be able to see any way your intention can be manifested, and where does that put your belief system? **This step of the manifestation process is not your responsibility.**

Step 7: Receive Gratefully

Now to the final step. You manifest your desire. Your creation is now complete. What has come into your life as an experience, an object, or a person may be exactly what you were expecting or it may be different. In Step 4, you added the words *"This or something better."* This means that what you have manifested may be better for you than what you wanted. Also, it is difficult for you to really evaluate the full benefits of what has come into your life. There is frankly nothing you need to do except accept this manifestation as just what you need at this time.

Accept what you have manifested as being absolutely perfect, because it is. Be absolutely and utterly grateful. Just as you felt in the emotional run-through in Step 5, feel the joy, the gratitude, and the wonder. This is the real thing now, and you have everything to feel grateful for.

You will also notice that we started the manifestation process in Step 1 with gratitude, and we also end with gratitude in Step 7. Appreciation for what you already have, gratitude for what you are currently manifesting, and an attitude of giving rather than taking are fundamental qualities to express when consciously working with the Law of Manifestation.

As you will have realised during this discussion on conscious manifestation, a vital factor in the process is what we are holding in consciousness as our beliefs. So a deeper discussion on beliefs is called for, and this we cover in the next chapter.

CHAPTER 35

It is All About Beliefs

Henry Ford (1863-1947) said, *"If you think you can do a thing or think you can't do a thing, you're right."* The single most important aspect of the Law of Manifestation, and for that matter of how you experience your whole life, is the set of beliefs you hold. This is the active part, you could say, of the Fundamental You. Your beliefs drive everything, and you experience everything in terms of your beliefs.

How cool is that? Or how scary is that, how immobilising is that, how fantastic is that, how beautiful is that, or how … is that? Your experience and acceptance of this concept (or fact) is, frankly, determined by your beliefs! As we have said, the Fundamental You, with your core beliefs, is the source of everything you experience in your life. It is, therefore, essential that you align your core beliefs with what it is you really want to experience.

Your core beliefs are fundamental to the way you view your life and the world around you. You may well agree that some of those beliefs are ones you have picked up from other people, particularly your parents, as you grew up. Some beliefs have been formed by your own life experience, or the life experience of those around you. But, right now, these are your core beliefs and you have ownership of them.

So, just for this moment, hold onto the beliefs and feelings you are aware of right now, and realise this: These core beliefs are like a key signature frequency that you produce — we have called it your Creation Frequency. Because every one of us, no matter where we are in the world, has different core beliefs (in overall, all-inclusive terms), each of us is absolutely unique. This means that our Creation Frequency is unique too. If you don't accept or believe in this concept of frequencies, by all means use a different concept. Treat *frequency* as an analogy for what really is the attracting force between who and what you are on the one hand, and the things or experiences you desire on the other hand.

Talking of analogies, let's use the analogy of old-fashioned (analogue) radio stations by way of example. Each radio station (in a particular area) is broadcasting at a unique frequency. This means if we have a radio, we can pick up one station at a time. So, from the hundreds of radio stations (on FM, MW, or SW frequencies) we could pick up right here where we are, we will only pick up the one we tune into. Sometimes, radio stations are crowded closely together, but if our radio is sensitive enough, it can home in on one particular station. If that station is a classical music station on 99.0 FM, then we would not expect to hear the rap music that is being broadcast on 98.0 FM. In fact, if we are tuned into 99.0 FM, we will get only what is being broadcast on that station (say classical music).

Similarly, the exact frequency you are tuned into through your core beliefs — your unique key signature frequency — is exactly what will vibrate throughout the universe, and so attract manifestations that resonate with it. The word *resonate* means one thing is vibrating in harmony at the same frequency as another. Because the Law of Manifestation is "Like attracts Like", it follows that whatever you really and absolutely believe in essence, at the core of your being, is what will be attracted into your life.

To put it another way, the inner state of your being determines or creates the life you experience, provides you with everything you have, and maintains everything you lack. Therefore, if you believe that life is a happy, joyous experience, you will attract more happiness and joy into your life. This will prove to you that "life is a happy joyous experience." It is self-fulfilling. By the same token though, if you believe life is hard and painful, you will attract even more experiences of hardship and pain into your life. And once again, this will prove your assessment of life is correct.

It is interesting that there is so much argument in the world about who is right and who is wrong. We invariably believe our viewpoint is the correct one, **because we know that from direct experience**. Well, of course we are right. And so are they right — from their experience. Never the twain shall meet, as they say.

The first key to manifesting whatever you would enjoy experiencing in your life is to ensure that your core beliefs are in harmony with the experience or thing you desire. Without that, you have little chance of it coming your way. As you will appreciate, there are a myriad of beliefs you hold, and some may even be incongruent, that is to say, the two beliefs may be contradictory or mutually exclusive. You need to root out the beliefs that are incongruent with what you choose to believe, and emphasise the ones that are harmonious with what you want to experience.

To help you to achieve this, it is vitally important to protect yourself from stray beliefs. In the modern world, we are open to so much more than our ancestors were in terms of beliefs. This is both good and bad. Sure, our minds are opening up to all sorts of possibilities, and creativity and invention have no bounds. This is great, except we also need to watch the negative aspect of this.

For some reason, people like complaining and being negative. Maybe they feel some comfort in not being alone in the world with their problems. Maybe they want to talk themselves into not having to take responsibility for their own lives. All this focus on negative things, be it crime, or fears, or ill health, or money shortage, or naughty kids, just attracts more of the same. You focus on it; you get more of it.

The newspapers are also full of bad news and opinions. Television stations broadcast many crime shows and so-called reality shows that build up beliefs. Our minds are unable to distinguish between what is physical reality and what is make-believe. Video games and computer games are all very well, but essentially they are the same as flight simulators and military war games, they are training the user to be able to carry out the same action in the real world. There is no mystery as to why crime continues to increase, why there are mass shootings at schools, and life so often emulates fiction. What we believe in and what we focus on is what we attract into our lives.

Be vigilant about what you allow yourself to believe. Keep a sensible perspective on what you class as entertainment, and keep aware of what beliefs you pick up. Some people don't read newspapers or watch the news on television. You decide what is right for you and how you are going to take conscious control of what you believe.

Here are some questions you might ask yourself as you start to identify beliefs you hold.

+ Am I worthy of receiving this thing into my life?
+ I can't have this because … How am I using *because* to justify why I can't do and have something? What are my excuses?
+ If that excuse was not available to me, what would I do or have?
+ If all excuses were not available to me, what would I do or have?
+ Has anyone else ever achieved something like this?
+ What limiting beliefs do I have?
+ What am I waiting for?
+ What am I *really* waiting for?
+ Who is in charge of my life?
+ What is fate dealing me?
+ For what purpose do I want to do or have this?
  (To the answer you get, ask: "For what purpose?" You can ask this question a number of times as you get deeper and deeper into what your real purpose and intention are, and what your real beliefs are.)
+ Do I feel greedy?

I am always intrigued by the story of Roger Bannister and the four-minute mile. It was a known fact (belief) that no one could run a mile in four minutes. So, no one did. From 1947, Roger Bannister kept improving his time on running the mile, but after disappointing results at the 1952 Olympic Games, he almost gave up running. However, he settled on the objective of becoming the first person to run a mile in under four minutes. On 6 May 1954, in Oxford England, Roger Bannister ran the mile in 3 min 59.4 sec. The previous mile record had been unbroken for almost nine years, yet Roger Bannister held this new record for only 45 days. Since then, many people have run sub-four minute miles, with the current record being held by the Moroccan, Hicham El Guerrouj, who ran a time of 3 min 43.13 sec in Rome, Italy, on 7 July 1999.

What beliefs are you holding? Can you imagine what beliefs were being held a little over a century ago with regard to such concepts as air travel, radio, television, computers, digital music storage, mobile phones, space travel, and so many other things we take for granted in the modern world? Be a visionary for your own life and dream the impossible!

The key to how things manifest in our lives, how we gain the experiences we live, is belief. We each have our own belief system, which is the essence of who we are. Everything we think, say, or do is based on this fundamental belief system we call *I*. We are not able to act outside this belief system since it would be incomprehensible to do so.

There are essentially three levels to this belief system. At the base of the belief structure, so to speak, is the collective unconscious. This is the home of the fundamental beliefs we share with others, like material laws such as gravity, and in general terms, the objective material world around us. This also is the home of all the beliefs of our generation, our ancestors, our country, and our race.

Then, there is our personal *fundamental belief system*, and this is the most important one from a personal viewpoint. If you believe you are a fundamentally happy person, that is exactly what you are. Likewise, if you believe you are fundamentally an unhappy person, that too is exactly what you are, an unhappy person. When you are born, you come into the world devoid of any preconceptions, although there may be tendencies and/or karma you bring into this life with you, as you can see when you read an astrological chart of the individual. Nevertheless, you very quickly pick up impressions from your environment and your experiences as a child, and these soon establish themselves as your fundamental beliefs. Your parents, your siblings, your early teachers, and your peers are sources of these fundamental beliefs that are extremely difficult to change in later life, although change is not impossible. In some cases, it is essential that you change them, particularly when these beliefs are self-destructive ones.

On top of the pile are the short-term beliefs you hold from day to day. These flit in and out of your life. Often, they can be buoyed up by the underlying fundamental beliefs you hold, but they can also be totally contrary, and even totally illogical. Holding beliefs that are not in harmony with your fundamental beliefs can cause you confusion and uncertainty, but will normally not be too serious. On occasions, you may believe you are unhappy, and everything is going wrong, but if your fundamental belief is one of happiness, the unhappiness will tend to melt away quickly.

Have you ever noticed when you have an argument with your partner or someone else close to you, how their mood can suddenly change? The phone rings, and they get a call from a friend, and in a flash the argument with you is totally forgotten; they become a new person again, and fall back on their natural character and fundamental belief system.

It is important to keep tabs on your beliefs and recognise when they are not working for you. As they are beliefs, you can, of course, choose to believe whatever you like. You can also choose to change your beliefs. In fact, gaining control over your belief system is the key to enjoying any experience in your life. Whether good or bad, seemingly caused by you, or seemingly not caused by you, there is some part of you that has helped to create it.

Tied in with your beliefs and feeding into them are your attitudes, vows, promises, values, and rules. It could be interesting to write down all the things you believe. Step 3 of the Law of Manifestation discusses this, and certainly you can challenge yourself and discover some of the things you believe. If you discover conflicting beliefs you cannot resolve, it could be worth seeking professional help from a Journey or NLP Practitioner, Cognitive Behavioural Therapist (CBT) or similar. They will help you delve into your beliefs, clear unhelpful ones, and replace them with more helpful and positive beliefs. You will feel like, and will be, a different person.

You might ask, who is doing the believing? Who is this Fundamental You? The deeper the Truths you know, the clearer it is that this wisdom or knowledge is fundamental to the Higher Self. The more unhelpful, negative, and egotistic the belief is, the more you will see that it is Ego-based, a belief of the Lesser Self. It is, therefore, an illusion in reality; however, it remains very powerful in the form of a belief as it directs your life.

CHAPTER 36

Your Environment

The environment in which you live has a huge impact on your beliefs and, therefore, your life. If you are born into a poor family in India, Brazil, or Sudan, what chances do you have to employ the Law of Manifestation? Is all that I have said here just applicable to the wealthy West because they are the ones who are reading this book? Not at all. The Law of Manifestation is as universal as the Law of Gravity. Does the Law of Gravity work for a Zimbabwean subsistence farmer the same way it does for me in New Zealand, or you, wherever you are in the world? You know that it does. So does the Law of Manifestation.

Firstly, we are all brought up by our parents, our peers, and our teachers (formal or extended family) to believe what they believe. Beliefs are passed down from generation to generation. One belief I picked up (and have cleared) is that a son can, on average, only do 10 percent better than his father does. In India, if you are living on US$1 or $2 per day, a 10 percent increase is not going to go very far. Nevertheless, people who are determined to break free from their lowly heritage do succeed time and time again. There are many rags-to-riches stories, and these are supported by the Law of Manifestation. This is not a question of luck. It is a question of having the right attitude and the right beliefs about what is possible.

Opportunities and pointers are given to us frequently. If we are ready to see them, we will. If we are ready to act on them, we will. If we are not, and are caught up in the woe-is-me belief system of the local environment, then we will not even see or conceive of the opportunity. In India, for example, the strong belief in karma means that it is one's lot to be poor, so it is just accepted. I am not saying that acceptance of one's situation is wrong, as many of us do it throughout the world, whatever our level of financial and social resources. I am saying none of us can point to the Law of Manifestation as not working or not being relevant in that situation — or in our own situation.

You are now and always will be a God Franchisee. God-Consciousness is ready to experience whatever it is you choose to experience, whether consciously or unconsciously. So, while your environment has a huge impact on you and your beliefs right now, if you are planning to change your life, you should set aside your environment and your starting position for the moment. You should accept that anything is possible, and decide, despite everything that appears to be true right now, THIS is what I want to experience. As you define what THIS is, you can work through the steps of the Laws of Manifestation, as described in Chapter 34, and **you can make it manifest in your life. It is the Law. It is God's Law.**

Bless you.

CHAPTER 37

Loss and Destruction

I t is interesting that we all look to creation and getting more, be it things or experiences or friends. We don't think so much about getting rid of things or experiences or friends. Loss and destruction are just as much a part of the universe as creation is. We just don't like it, and sometimes it can be very painful.

Energy must flow. If it gets blocked, it stagnates. The East is very aware of energy or life-force, and it is called by a number of names: *prana* (India), *chi* or *qi* (China), and *ki* (Japan and Korea). Their healing practices emphasise the clearing of blockages, as does *feng shui* the Chinese system of ensuring the beneficial flow of *chi* in your environment.

The main purpose that God-Consciousness has for His universe is experience. We have focussed on the Creation aspects of this as, initially, a universe had to be created. Also, we have been discussing **The God Franchise**, which shows that it is our birthright, even our duty, to create further. However, destruction and loss of the old must occur in order to make room for the new.

As you will see in Chapter 40, *Working with Universal Law*, I discuss the Law of Balance which states the need to sacrifice something in order to attract something else into your life. I give some examples: you sacrifice 40 hours of your time a week to receive a weekly wage, and you sacrifice your single days and ways to get a wife or husband. These are simple forms of loss and destruction, but it goes a lot deeper than this. You might destroy an old house in order to build a new one on the same site. You might uproot and destroy some old plants in your garden in order to lay out the bed afresh. You might remove old wallpaper to redecorate. These things are obvious.

However, when we want to create a new energy in our lives, are we prepared to get rid of the old and make space for the new in our lives? Do we throw out clothes we no longer wear, books we no longer read and beliefs that no longer serve us? These things not only take up physical space, they block the flow of energy. They make it difficult for the new to flow. If we hold onto the memories or the love we have for an old house, how are we able to free up the energies to allow it to sell to a new owner? We just trap ourselves in the past.

Sometimes, it is even necessary to *discard* old friends, acquaintances, workmates, even partners and family. If the energy is blocked, and we wish to create new energy in our lives, we have to be ruthless. It is interesting that when this occurs we are unblocking the energy for the other person too. If they are aware and open to their own growth and change, they will benefit from your action of separation as well. If they are closed and self-pitying, they may be grasping and unwilling to let you go; many times, this fact alone is confirmation that your act of separation was necessary.

Whether you are releasing yourself from an object, a house, a person, or anything else, it is worthwhile to consider the use of an energetic tie cut. To do this, just close your eyes and bring the object or person into your mind. Imagine that there is an energetic tie between you and the other — you may well be able to visualise it as a golden band or even just get a sense of it. Now, see yourself (or a guardian angel, a mentor, a spiritual being, or whomever you choose) cutting that tie with a pair of golden scissors. See the energy from those energetic ties being cut, with the energy from your end coming back to you and the energy from the other end going back to the other person or object. Feel the release, and if the other is a person, look into their eyes and see the release that they are feeling too. Feel the completion and completeness of this in your body, and give a word of thanks, a bless you, or whatever seems to be appropriate in that moment. You may then open your eyes when you are ready.

This little process is very powerful and you will find it very helpful when you are trying to move on from someone or something. Any blocked energy is released in this way and you will be free to move on with your life.

The source of the 94 elements that make up matter on Earth was the self-destruction of a star through the process of becoming a supernova. Initially, a star generates its heat and light through the fusion of hydrogen into helium. As the hydrogen is converted, gravity causes the star to fall in on itself, which has the effect of increasing the temperature so that helium can create the next atoms up the periodic table. In this way, carbon, nitrogen, oxygen, sodium, calcium, and iron are created, amongst others. Once the core of the star is formed of iron and reaches a threshold size, gravity causes it to implode. This causes the supernova to shine intensely and explode. The intense heat generated allows the other elements to form, right up to number 94, plutonium.

As the supernova completely blows apart, the elements are sprayed outwards into space, where they can collect over millions of years into planets. So, in essence, if it were not for the destruction of a star billions of years ago, we would not have the 94 elements on Earth that form the building blocks of every form of matter we know today.

Loss and destruction are an essential part of life. Death is an essential part of life. It is the classic cycle of spring, summer, autumn (fall), and winter. There is new life and new growth in spring, finding fruition in summer. Then autumn and winter bring death to leaves, plants, and animals. Their bodies fall to the ground where they decay back into their original elements, fertilising the ground to support new life. Bacteria and small insects help the process; they receive their nourishment through the decaying process, and their own bodies will in time return to the elements.

As they say, *"Earth to earth, ashes to ashes, dust to dust."*[148]

This may be a short chapter, but it is vital that you remain aware of the need for loss and destruction in your life. It is part of the cycle

---

148 From the funeral service in the *Book of Common Prayer* used by the Church of England, and some other Christian denominations.

of life, as from the ashes will rise, phoenix-like, the energy, intention, and life for something new to be born — something even greater and more beneficial to your life than what was lost. Grief and mourning for what is now past and gone should only be given enough time to allow gratitude for and acknowledgement of what you had. Then, let the old, and the grief for the passing of the old, slip away.

You can then bravely face the new day and the new experiences that can now come into your life.

CHAPTER 38

Sin and Temptation

Now that we have some understanding of how life works and how vitally important our beliefs are (since we create the lives we live, aided at all times by the Law of Manifestation), perhaps we should take a look at the practical aspects of *sin* and what that really means in our daily lives.

Religion expects us to be good and not sin. Yet, arguably, the biggest issue in the world is sin. Organised crime involves groups of people working together to make money from the misery of others as they trade in drugs, weapons, stolen goods, illegal immigration, slavery, prostitution, and so on. There is petty crime on the street where goods are stolen for sale at the local pub or on the Internet. There are protection racketeers and hit men who will murder anyone for a fee. There are white-collar criminals who steal from their companies or involve themselves in financial scams that fleece unsuspecting investors, such as in Ponzi schemes. There are Internet scammers. Whichever way you turn, there are criminals committing crimes.

While we may be disdainful towards such people, how many of us minimise our income tax liabilities in ways we would prefer not to have scrutinised? How many of us buy something that is an incredible bargain at the pub? How many of us have exaggerated an insurance claim? How many of us make excuses that are not quite accurate? How many white lies have we told?

Whatever we do that might be classed as sin, is, in the end, an act perpetrated purely for the expectation of benefitting ourselves. It is our own Ego gaining something, even though we know or suspect some other person is losing. Often that other person loses a lot more than we gain, but that does not matter to us.

Is it good enough to go to a Catholic priest in a confessional and say, "Forgive me, Father, for I have sinned?" Is it good enough to leave it to karma to sort out? Is it good enough to think, *I have to feed my family somehow, and the victim is filthy rich anyway, and of course the insurance will pay?* The answer each time is no.

Remember the Law of Manifestation? This applies all the time. So, if we live by the sword, we will die by the sword.[149] If it is in our consciousness and belief system that crime pays, we will also be the victim of crime or similar personal losses. There is no escape. We are caught within the veils of the Ego, the Lesser Self. We feel separation from God and seek to compensate for that by looking after the (apparent) self, because no one else will.

The God Franchise tells us we are God-Consciousness incarnate. That we are individual expressions of God-Consciousness, each having our own experiences, and that having those experiences is the purpose of life. The experience of being good or being sinful is to God-Consciousness the same thing. Either way, it is experience. However, and this is the catch, God's Law is that we reap what we sow. Thus, we will die by the sword if we live by the sword. We will earn bad karma that, at some stage, we will have to repay. We will suffer pain and unhappiness if we cause pain and unhappiness, and of course, sinning causes pain and unhappiness.

Once we realise and truly understand the options available, the good path, "the straight and narrow,"[150] is the only sensible option. By shunning sin, you start to peel off the layers of illusion that glorify the Ego. By doing this, you reveal your Higher Self, the God-Consciousness within, and start to live from a place of Truth.

While we may come to know sinning is not a sensible option, how do we handle temptation when it comes along? Based on dictionary[151]

---

149 *"For all they that take the sword shall perish with the sword." Matthew* 26:52
150 *"Strait is the gate, and narrow is the way, which leadeth unto life." Matthew* 7:14. Note that *strait* means narrow or constricted although the modern expression has changed the word to *straight*, and the meaning is accepted as *"the proper, honest and moral path of behaviour"* (*Collins English Dictionary*).
151 *Collins English Dictionary*

definitions, the word *temptation* can be understood as *the state of being enticed to do something, especially something morally wrong or unwise.* I prefer to see temptation as the desire to experience something that is in conflict with commitments already made. So, for example, if you are a man and see a lovely young lady to whom you would like to make advances, this is fine if you are single and uncommitted. However, that desire is a *temptation* if you are married, since you have already made a commitment of faithfulness to another. Likewise, if you are committed to going to the gym three times a week, it is a temptation if you desire to skip going one day, unless there is a very strong reason for not going, such as illness or having a plane to catch.

If we become practised in identifying and then rejecting temptation, we will make life a lot easier for ourselves. When we are focussed on what we really want out of life, we will see that temptations are always contrary to that intention and primary desire. Therefore, it makes sense to resist temptation and keep our energies focussed.

Nevertheless, if we find a continuing temptation to experience something contrary to previous commitments, we always have the opportunity to realign our desires and commitments. This is likely to involve other effects or results, and we need to consider these too when coming to a decision.

Sinning is the abuse of our gift of free will. It separates us from God because the veils that descend upon us cover our Higher Self, and so, our glimpse of God-Consciousness within. We feed the Ego and that serves to strengthen its stifling rule over our lives. If we allow this to continue and allow the Ego to gain more power over us, we will collapse into depression, sink into the depths of futility and worthlessness, and in the end we will die. God does not punish us for sinning, nor does He consign us to Hell. We punish ourselves through pain and suffering and the feeling of separation from God-Consciousness.

In contrast, as the veils of Ego are ripped aside, we are able to walk into the Light and Truth of our own Being, our Higher Self, and God-Consciousness Itself.

CHAPTER 39

Judgement and Forgiveness

It is the nature of the Ego to judge others. It makes our own Ego feel superior in some way. All too often we read of horrific deeds in our newspapers or hear about them on the news. Murders, beatings, child molestation, sexual attacks, wartime atrocities, and so on. It is with a mixture of fascination and disgust that we look at pictures of the perpetrators and think, *What an evil person. How could you do that? You are disgusting and shouldn't be alive. I hope they lock you up forever and throw away the key.*

Is this the face of evil and wickedness? Is this the Devil at work? Is this what we have come to? When you look at the picture of that person, put aside the horror of what they have done for the moment. Look at them as a fellow human being and ask, "What kind of person would do a thing like that? What would you need to believe to do a thing like that?"

As the answers come back to you, avoid using the words wicked, evil, or bad. You may find that words like scared, hurt, lost, in pain, angry, unloved, frustrated, confused, and so on come up instead. Really try to understand what may have motivated this person, from a deeper level. Separate the person from what they did. Yes, the deed could be called evil or wicked, but what of the perpetrator? Are they really all bad, or are they just reacting from an inner pain they are feeling as a result of being on the receiving end of just as bad a deed in their own past? Did they, in that moment of the crime, forget the other person and just lash out from their own pain — pain they have been carrying for a long, long time? Did they just make a mistake they immediately regretted deep down?

In coming to a place of forgiveness and understanding, reach out to that person. You are definitely not condoning what they did, and you can feel their pain. You can also pray for a break in this cycle of pain being passed on from one generation to the next. You can pray for a break in the nation's pain from atrocities that the country has had to face over the years, over the decades, and over the centuries. Pray for healing. As you look at the person who did this terrible thing, realise that they too, like you, are an expression of God-Consciousness. You are no different in that. You, perhaps, have been more fortunate in the way you have been treated in life so far, and in the way your community has been treated. Be grateful you are not this person, and you are not in his shoes.

As you contemplate this, you may even find there is a deep yearning in that person for something. It may be a version of a spiritual yearning for *salvation*, some sort of greater good or release from pain. Be broadminded about it; be open to the possibilities; allow a wider and deeper truth. Sure, it has been mishandled. The person did get it tragically wrong. Haven't we all made mistakes we regret later?

"There, but for the grace of God, go I"[152] is an appropriate cliché.

But what of God's Judgement? Realising that each one of us is God-Consciousness, the true Judgement of God is something that happens in every moment of every day. The Day of Judgement is not a future day for which to prepare — now is Judgement Day. It does not matter what excuses you give for what you did, or what reasons or provocations exist, or how things appear to be. No, what matters is what is **really** going on inside you. King Solomon sums it up in these words: *"For as he thinketh in his heart, so is he."*[153]

I would find it rather creepy if I knew God was watching over my shoulder, making notes in His Book so that when Judgement Day came, He would know where to send me — either Heaven or Hell.

---

152 Attributed to John Bradford (c.1510-1555) as *"There but for the grace of God, goes John Bradford,"* when seeing criminals being led to their execution.
153 *Proverbs 23:7*

Knowing as I do, that God is everything and everyone, changes that. There is nowhere to hide, nor is there any need to hide. We have no secrets. God-Consciousness experiences what I experience, and I am not judged because He understands exactly what my motivations are for what I do.

Whether we have judged ourselves or others, or whether we feel judged of God or by others, forgiveness is the only way in which we can free ourselves from the guilt and pain associated with that judgement. Forgiveness is a central part of healing. It is this forgiveness that allows us to break the chains of guilt and so allow ourselves to heal. Without true, complete, and heartfelt forgiveness, there will always remain a tie to the past action and pain, and so, an inability to move on. This is true whether the forgiveness is given by you to another person or to yourself, or if it is received from another person or from God. Whether in person, in your imagination, or in prayer, either give or ask for (and receive) forgiveness. In this way, sins of commission or omission can be laid to rest.

You cannot change the past, but through forgiveness you can free yourself from the binds to the past. In no way is what happened condoned. This is not the point. The point is you regret what happened, and as you cannot change the past, you are clearing the past so you and the other parties can move on in the present and the future. Believe me, the giving and receiving of forgiveness, as appropriate, is very healing, and in many cases is essential for healing.

God-Consciousness forgives us through this same forgiving process. If complete and utter forgiveness is given and/or received, as appropriate to the situation, forgiveness is complete and God (God-Consciousness) is not going to hold anything against you to be brought up at a future Judgement Day.

As Jesus said, *"Go, and sin no more."*[154]

---

154 *John* 8:11

CHAPTER 40

Working with Universal Law

We discussed God's Laws in Part Two, and I put it to you that they can be grouped into three different types:

+ Physical and Mathematical Laws
+ The Commandments
+ Universal Laws

As we said, we cannot break physical and mathematical laws. They are what they are as immutable facts, and we live within those constraints. In fact, we can say we would not be alive unless those constraints were in place. The universe only works as it does because of those physical and mathematical laws.

The Commandments are really precepts that are a guide for our behaviour. As I suggested, if we just follow Jesus' Commandments, we have the Ten Commandments covered. These are:

1. *"Thou shalt love the Lord thy God with all thy heart, and with all thy soul, and with all thy mind."*[155]

2. *"Thou shalt love thy neighbour as thyself,"*[156] or *Do unto others as you would have them do unto you.*

You have choice (free will) in the following of these two rules. However, breaking them is called *sinning*, and we have just discussed the implications of that. So, if you steal, you sin. If you loved your

---

155 *Matthew 22:37*
156 *Matthew 22:39*

neighbour as yourself, you would not steal from him. Therefore, you are transgressing that commandment as well — you sin. Despite this, you are not breaking any Universal Law. The Law of Cause and Effect (karma) will take effect if you steal, and sometime, somehow, you will reap the results of that stealing. The Universal Law acts whether you sin or not, and it is totally without moral implications.

You could say that if you look at the Universal Law of Cause and Effect as having either desirable effects (pleasure) or undesirable ones (pain), then sin would be those actions that cause undesirable effects. In order to avoid sin, keep in mind Jesus' Two Commandments and also the Wiccan Rede, which is *"An it harm none, do what ye will."* So, if you take some action that does not affect anyone else, and does no harm to you, it is not a sin. Thus, something like moderate drinking, gambling, or self-pleasuring cannot be classed as a sin. Likewise, having a consensual sexual relationship with another adult, whether same sex or heterosexual, cannot be a sin, so long as you are not already in another relationship and you are not misleading anyone.

A sin is more likely to occur when you are hurting someone else, although it also can occur if you find you are hurting yourself. The sin that you recognise as such, but have not yet resolved, keeps you in a state of guilt. In that instance, you may find that you would like to consider forgiveness. We discussed this in the previous chapter.

So, now we come to the third group of God's Laws, the Universal Laws, and I would like to discuss these a little further here. While there are many of them, I have distilled the main ones down to the following six Universal Laws:

1. God is[157]
2. The Law of Cause and Effect[158]
3. Like creates like[159]
4. The Law of Increase: Your attitude and intention determine the extent of your result[160]

---

157 McArthur, B., *Your Life: Why It Is the Way It Is and What You Can Do About It - Understanding the Universal Laws,* A.R.E. Press, Virginia Beach, 1993, Pg. 121.
158 McArthur, Pg. 79
159 McArthur, Pg. 13
160 McArthur, Pg. 41

5. The Law of Balance: The universe remains constantly in a state of equilibrium[161]

6. The Law of Self: You are a unique individual, and the fulfilment of your desires is of primary importance. The same is equally true of every other person.[162]

Remember that a Universal Law is *"an unbreakable, unchangeable principle of life that operates inevitably, all the time."*[163] This means you can treat them in the same way as physical and mathematical laws. You wouldn't argue with the Law of Gravity would you? Or that 2 + 2 = 4? This means you don't argue with these six laws either, or any of their corollaries.

Note that these laws apply to every person on this planet, whether rich or poor, young or old, healthy or sick, and whatever beliefs he or she holds, and whatever race, nationality, or religion he or she belongs to. There is no escaping these Universal Laws as they are God's Laws. I would also say they apply equally to all other forms of life on this planet and elsewhere in the universe.

So let's go through these six Universal Laws in some more detail. They are important as they explain much of what *happens* to us in life.

1. God Is

This Law has three corollaries I would like to discuss:

The Universal Laws are *created* by God-Consciousness and are, therefore, as infinite, inevitable, and unchanging as He is. The Laws are in truth the very nature of God-Consciousness. By studying, understanding, and in particular, living positively with the Universal Laws, we study, understand, and live with God-Consciousness. I say *positively* because the Truth is whether we do any of this or not, we still do live with God-Consciousness, and there is no way of existing without the Universal Laws.

Remember that as a God Franchisee, you are a creator; therefore,

---

161 McArthur, Pg. 213
162 McArthur, Pg. 147
163 McArthur, Pg. 5

you can create whatever world you desire by using the Universal Laws. Even if they are misused or abused, the Laws still work. They are totally unbiased, amoral, just, and impartial, and apply to each of us equally. If we misuse them, we end up with what we don't like. We may cast around to blame someone else, even the Universe or God! Nevertheless, we are still totally responsible for our own creations, as we created the specific result we achieved using Universal Laws.

Living **positively** with the Universal Laws will create the Life you really desire.

The universe is ultimately good. Evil (or other bad things) is purely the appearance of an absence of good. As we discussed earlier, the concepts of good and bad/evil are man-made, through the Ego. If we were to remove free will and Ego from the equation, there would be no duality of good and evil, there would only be what is, without judgement. We can, therefore, say the universe is ultimately *Good*, as we don't have an alternative word to describe it.

Good and Evil are similar in nature to Light and Darkness. Darkness does not exist as a thing, and you cannot create Darkness. You can only exclude Light. Darkness is an absence of Light, and nothing more. You cannot bring in Darkness to get rid of the Light. So it is with Good and Evil. Good is the power and the presence. If you take away Good, you experience Evil or Badness, depending of course on the degree of absence of Good. If Good is (apparently) totally missing, then you have the ultimate Evil.

Thus, just like Light is the real entity so to speak, so is Good. Each of the things God created in the six days of Creation, *"God saw that it was good."* Thus, in the natural world there is no Evil or Badness. Nature does not work in those terms. Man has come up with the concept of Evil and Badness, and he has created them with his own free will. Evil is not of God's making, and will be vanquished in our own experience as we come to understand the Universal Laws and make smarter decisions about life.

God-Consciousness is in everything, and is everything; therefore, there cannot truly be an absence of God-Consciousness anywhere. Evil is only an appearance of absence, or we could say, a belief in the absence of Good or God-Consciousness.

God loves His Creation, and Love is an essential force of the universe. Just as Light and Dark and Good and Evil are seen as a presence and an absence of a single quality, Love too can be seen in the identical way. I have always felt the way many books and religions speak of Love is too cloying and unrealistic. However, if you look at Love as being the natural state of things, and realise Hate is just an absence of Love, then those objections disappear. Of course God-Consciousness loves His Creation, and the power of Love pervades everything. The excessive expression of Love, just like Hate, is manmade, and will disappear once the reality of Life and Creation is understood.

Love is the bridge between souls, and is reality. Hate is simply the strong feeling of an apparent lack of love.

2. The Law of Cause and Effect

This is the Law that is usually called the Law of Karma or Karmic Law. The essence of all causative factors, including your own intentions and the current way things are with you, result in the specific effect you will experience. The corollaries that apply to this Law are:

+ Nothing is by chance
+ There are no such things as accidents or bad luck
+ Life is the experience of your choices
+ You are responsible for everything that happens to you.

Whatever happens is the effect of innumerable causes. We don't always specifically identify what those causes are, and so it looks like things can happen by chance. The throwing of dice or the spinning of the Wheel of Fortune is **not** chance. Where they stop is the result of the exact physical forces brought to play on the dice or the Wheel. It is allowed to be chance for gambling purposes because we cannot calculate what those exact forces are and thus predict or affect the result in that way.

Likewise, with the *chance* changes and combinations in DNA that have powered evolution, and still lead to the unique pattern of DNA in the offspring of humans, animals, and plants. There are forces at work in each mutation or combination of genes that cause the specific outcome. Just because we cannot predict or control what happens does not mean that, in reality, chance is at work. It isn't.

Your life plays out in line with whatever forces are within your sphere of existence. Your own thoughts, beliefs, attitudes, vows, promises, values, and rules are particularly strong influences (causes) and these are fed by the people around you, your environment, your history, your ethnic background, and so on. This leaves nothing to chance. There are no such things as accidents or bad luck either. Not even good luck. There are causes, driven by you and (potentially) within your control, which drive it all.

Since you create the causes, directly or indirectly, consciously or sub-consciously, life can be seen as the experience of your choices. You can literally choose what sort of experiences you would like in life, and then go out and create them, and experience them. This is what being a God Franchisee is all about.

Because all the above is true, we are, therefore, totally responsible for everything that happens to us. It is handy to be able to blame our partner or our parents or the government for things that go wrong, or for things we dislike. However, we need to take personal responsibility for every situation. We attract to ourselves the experiences that are in our minds and attitudes, and repel those that are contrary. So we wouldn't be involved in the situation we are in if it was outside our consciousness.

This does not mean, however, you need to feel guilt about everything that happens. Taking responsibility is accepting you were directly involved, and if someone else was also affected by the situation, they too are present and responsible. What happened to them was what had to happen to them according to Universal Law, and what happened to you had to happen to you according to Universal Law. You can correct what you need to in your own consciousness, but a feeling of guilt about it is not going to help you or the others involved at all.

The other side of taking responsibility gives us the freedom to create whatever life we want to create for ourselves. We don't have to feel guilty about that either! Nevertheless, the Law of Karma prevails, and you are effectively rewarded or punished for your deeds. This does not come from some outside agency, not even from God, but from the simple working of God's Laws. The Law of Karma is also part of the next Law we cover, Like Creates Like.

3. Like Creates Like

This is the domain of the Law of Manifestation we discussed in great detail in Chapter 34. In addition, the Law of Karma is associated with the concept of reaping what you sow. The Like Creates Like Law has a number of corollaries, and these corollaries together make up the Law of Manifestation:

+ You reap what you sow
+ You must give in order to receive
+ Your life experience mirrors your self
+ Like attracts like
+ As you believe, so it will come into reality for you
+ You intensify what you focus on
+ You attract what you expect.

If you were to plant lettuce seeds in the garden, would you expect to reap carrots? Of course not. So the analogy can be drawn with life. You sow specific causes, and reap the resulting effects. You choose what to sow, and therefore, what to reap. So, if you want to have friends, be friendly! If you want to have love, be loving! If you want to work with professionals, be professional! And if you want to be disliked, then go ahead and be disagreeable with others! You first sow and then you reap.

You may wonder what the timeframe is for reaping the harvest of what you sow. This is not something we can precisely define. Sometimes it is immediate, so-called *instant karma*, other times, it might be years later, and in a totally different situation or different relationship. The point is, you will not be overlooked, because this is not at the whim of another person, power, or even of God-Consciousness. It is Universal Law.

The other aspect that may not be immediately clear is that the form of the *Like* you sowed, may not be the same as the form of the *Like* you reap. However, the *spirit* of it will be. Thus, if you steal time from your employer, it may not be time you lose, but money or other possessions you value as much as your employer values your time. It is the spirit of the action that counts.

Since you reap what you sow, if you sow nothing, you reap nothing. If you want to be paid, you first need to do some work. You must give in order to receive. You cannot expect a pay increase unless you have put dedication into the job to earn that pay increase. Apart from this, there is the need to give out the blueprint of what it is you expect to receive. Give out a desire, and expect to receive the manifestation in your life. Doing this attracts the object of your desire so it is able to manifest in your life experience. This is the Law of Manifestation at work.

The convergence of these two concepts of giving out is found in your attitude. If your attitude is that there should be *good to all concerned*, and your desire is strong enough, you will receive your desire. This is whether it is your regular pay cheque, a pay increase, or any desire you have put purposeful effort into. The creative power is a force that emanates from God-Consciousness; it is a giving out. As God Franchisees, we too must *give out* before we can receive.

If you want to see how you are doing in terms of the Law of Manifestation and the Law of Karma, you only need to look around you. Your life experience exactly mirrors what you believe and the attitudes you carry. Your mental image, your attitude, your intention, and your belief will all average out to a certain and specific colouring of causal impulse. We have called this your Creation Frequency. You draw to you circumstances and opportunities that lead to the creation of the effect or result that matches your causal impulse.

By the same token, that same causal impulse will bypass circumstances and opportunities that are counter-productive to your achieving the result that matches your causal impulse. As you believe, so it will come into reality for you. It is, therefore, obvious you do need to take care about what you believe in, as that does become real for you. This is the whole basis of the Law of Manifestation.

Dr. Holliwell in *Working with the Law* discusses what he calls the Law of Non-Resistance.[164] He suggests that resistance to any experience you wish to counteract is not harmonious with Universal Law, and quotes

---

164 Holliwell, R., *Working with the Law*, School of Christian Philosophy, Phoenix, 1964, Pg. 123. (Revised edition 9780875168081 published by DeVorss Publications (www.devorss.com), Camarillo, 2005.)

Jesus' words *"But I say unto you, That ye resist not evil: but whosoever shall smite thee on thy right cheek, turn to him the other also."*[165] The Law of Non-Resistance is not a separate Universal Law, but rather is a corollary to **Like Creates Like**. I have called it: You intensify what you focus on. If you focus on the negative aspect by resisting it, you only give it more traction, and end up intensifying it. You are far better served by looking for the opposite quality and focussing on that. As that intensifies due to your focus, the undesired quality will fade.

The act of expecting something to occur is very powerful. When you genuinely expect something to happen, you attract it to you, and you will experience it. Expectation is a strong form of belief.

The answer to all the above is to remember: **Like creates like**.

4. The Law of Increase: Your Attitude and Intention Determine the Degree of Your Result

As we have already seen, you reap what you sow. The Law of Increase means that when you plant carrot seeds, you get a large crop of carrots, **and** if you let just one carrot go to seed, you get an even greater number of new seeds back as well! This Law of Increase applies to everything you sow in life. It is part of the Law of Manifestation, and while we have covered these principles already, I would like to repeat them in the context of this specific Law of Increase.

There are three aspects to working with it:

+ **Desire:** The first step in getting any experience is to desire it. Of course this may be conscious or sub-conscious, but where we are working positively with the Law, we need to consciously desire the intended result. The desire sets up an invisible link to the object of your desire, which already exists, at least in principle. If you weaken your desire, or change your mind about that desire, this invisible link is broken and the manifestation will not occur.

+ **Intention and Expectation**: The next step is that you intend to and expect to experience the manifestation of your desire.

---

165 *Matthew 5:39*

There is no doubt in your mind with regard to the outcome. The continuous expectation attracts the object of your desire towards you and to manifestation in your life, almost like the force of gravity. Without this strong intention and a continuous feeling of expectation, your desire is no more than wishful thinking.

✦ **Attitude**: A half-hearted effort will give either a half-hearted result or probably no result at all. Likewise, if your attitude for wanting to create, say, a new car, is just to be one up on your neighbour, that attitude will work against you, and you will not achieve the outcome you desired and expected.

Raymond Holliwell states this principle clearly:

> *"Never expect a thing you do not want, and never desire a thing you do not expect. When you expect something you do not want, you attract the undesirable, and when you desire a thing that is not expected, you simply dissipate valuable mental force. On the other hand, when you constantly expect that which you persistently desire, your ability to attract becomes irresistible. Desire connects you with the thing desired and expectation draws it into your life. This is the Law."*[166]

5. The Law of Balance: The Universe Remains Constantly in a State of Equilibrium

In Nature, there is a law of natural balance — the Law of Nature. In fact, you could almost say the universe runs on automatic. If you watch any particular natural activity, you will see there is a continuous sequence of events that cause certain effects, which in turn act as causes for further effects. An example is the sea flowing in and out at the beach. The waves are caused by a specific combination of current, tide, wind, and gravitational pull from the Moon and Earth. These are just forces at play on the body of water that is the sea. Each wave falls **exactly** as the forces determine. However, if you look into each of these forces, they are determined by greater universal Forces — there is no specific willpower involved at all.

---

166 Holliwell, Pg. 63

Watching each wave break, you will see it push the sand along, and roll the seashells and pebbles. The wave will perhaps float in some seaweed, leaves, or twigs. Everything that happens is like a gigantic display of a force or combination of forces acting as a cause, and resulting in an effect. This effect goes on to be the cause of a further effect. If you and every other animate life form do nothing, nature runs like a huge, eternal automatic machine. Everything happens in line with the Laws of Nature.

Let's bring in animals, insects, birds, fish, and all the other creatures of Earth other than Man. None of these creatures has the Ego or free will of Man. They have instincts and learned responses. They do decide when to search for food, when to move this way or that way or when to sleep, so they do have free will and motivation on a small scale. While they influence the natural scene we have just described, they do this from within the Laws of Nature. They are just another factor.

Man, on the other hand, lives outside the Laws of Nature. He can choose to live within them if he wishes, but all too often he works contrary to them. As it says in Genesis, God gave Man the task to *"replenish the earth, and subdue it: and have dominion over the fish of the sea, and over the fowl of the air, and over every living thing that moveth upon the earth."*[167] We have subdued and dominated indeed, but we have not always worked **with** Nature; all too often, we have worked **against** Nature.[168]

The Law of Nature is one of Balance and Equilibrium. When we work with Nature, we reap many rewards. When we work against Nature, we reap difficulties, dangers, and disasters. There is much information available about the ecological disasters that Man has created in the world, as well as the threat of global warming. There is little need to enlarge upon those travesties at this point.

The bottom line is that the Law of Balance keeps the universe

---

167 *Genesis* 1:28

168 I am fascinated by the skill and influence of Cesar Millan, the Dog Whisperer of current TV fame. He says that he learnt as a boy from his grandfather that one should work with nature, not against it. This deeply moving TV show is one that I can recommend. Cesar's website is http://www.cesarsway.com/.

in a state of equilibrium. If Man were kept out of the picture, Nature would take care of itself. We use our free will in both positive and negative ways to achieve the specific effects we desire, and the universe reacts accordingly to maintain the state of equilibrium. This may lead, for instance, to the extremes of climate the world appears to be experiencing at present.

The other side of the Law of Balance is that Man can create an expectation or a potential for a specific effect, and that will act as a cause to resolve the imbalance. This is all part of the Law of Manifestation.

The corollaries that apply to this Law of Balance are:

+ All exchanges between you and others balance.
+ You have to sacrifice one thing in order to receive something else.

If you receive more than you give, the Universal Law ensures you give more in some other way, to maintain equilibrium. Let's say you sell an item to someone and you know you are taking advantage of them for your own monetary benefit. You will find you will lose somewhere else in life, which will even up the score, so to speak. One reason for this is, because you believe in taking advantage of another, you will also believe others will take advantage of you.

In all your dealings with others, in business, in marriage, and in life in general, always give more than is expected. Always add value. The Universal Law will recompense you with additional blessings in order to maintain the equilibrium.

In order to keep the Law of Balance satisfied, whenever you attract something to your experience in life, you have to sacrifice or offer up something else. For instance:

> You sacrifice 40 hours of your time each week to receive a wage
> You sacrifice your single days and ways to get a wife/husband
> You sacrifice free spending to get a family, house and mortgage
> You sacrifice the price of a product or service in order to buy it
> You sacrifice dishonesty to be seen as a person of integrity
> You sacrifice honour to take up thieving and dishonesty
> You sacrifice *ignorance is bliss* to develop your spiritual nature.

If you want to achieve something specific in life, create something new, invent something, develop something, or learn about a favourite subject, or anything else like this that you want to achieve, you have to put in effort, dedication, self-discipline and time. Nothing is achieved from nothing. All the products and services that are available in today's world are the result of individual people putting in effort, dedication, self-discipline, and time. They had to do it, and so do you.

6. The Law of Self

The Law of Self states: **You are a unique individual, and the fulfilment of your desires is of primary importance. The same is equally true of every other person**. This Law means you are responsible only for yourself, and only you are responsible for yourself. It also means you live your life and no one else can live it for you. Likewise, you cannot live or interfere with anyone else's life. To you, your desires and wants and needs, and their fulfilment, are of essential importance. So you need to concentrate on your own fulfilment, and every other person is in exactly the same position as you are, looking after their own needs, wants, and desires and their own fulfilment.

This all sounds very selfish and self-centred. Not really. You are differentiated as an individual, and God-Consciousness created individuals so that He could have the experience of many different individuals. And so you must live your life. This is not to say you cannot give your neighbour a hand; in fact, service towards others may be a very important part of your life. Nevertheless, in serving others, you are doing it only to satisfy the desire in yourself to help others.

If you help others, but abuse yourself in the process, this is **not** what was intended for you to do with your life. The ultimate sacrifice of giving your own life to save somebody else's life seems to imply that you value the other person's life more than your own. This is contrary to Universal Law.

This covers the major Universal Laws. In essence, they boil down to the Law of Manifestation and Law of Karma, while keeping in mind the Law of Self, the recognition of the individual Self through which God-Consciousness experiences His Creation.

CHAPTER 41

Prayer, Intuition, and Inspiration

"Prayer is telephoning to God, and intuition is God telephoning to you."[169]

This is a wonderful statement — I really like it. So what is prayer? To some people it is kneeling at the foot of your bed each night. To others it is talking over with God any problem you might have. It can even be having a clear intention in your mind when you want to achieve something. In effect, whispering a prayer or having a clear intention are identical. Either way you are reaching to something beyond the Ego and saying, "This is what I would like. Please help me to achieve it, as my Ego cannot achieve this on its own."

Many people pray in a way that implies God is a Person. There is nothing wrong with that if that is what is true for you. However, while one traditionally speaks of praying to God, as if he was some Holy Being out there, we know God-Consciousness is within us, and is us. Therefore, when we pray, we are literally talking to our Higher Self. This does not imply that *all* we have is ourselves to rely on. No, our Higher Self is connected to the angels, the archangels, to Jesus, to Buddha, to Mohammed, to Krishna, right through to the Ain, Ain Soph, and Ain Soph Aur of the Kabbalists, the undifferentiated God-Consciousness beyond all knowing. This statement aligns with the concepts that we

169 Shinn, F. Scovel, *The Wisdom of Florence Scovel Shinn*, Simon & Schuster, New York, 1989 (including *The Power of the Spoken Word* (1945)), Pg. 337. (Permission:*The Power of the Spoken Word* by Florence Scovel Shinn| DeVorss Publications | 9780875162607| www.devorss.com)

are all One and that God-Consciousness is omnipresent.

The act of prayer is important because we take that action with our free will and in that way are approaching the footstool of God-Consciousness in whatever form or lack of form it needs to be. We are subjugating the Ego to the Higher Self and to God-Consciousness, as One.

Before we go any further, let's define[170] what it is we are talking about:

> Prayer is *a personal communication or petition addressed to a deity, especially in the form of supplication, adoration, praise, contrition, or thanksgiving.* (Petition is *any formal request to a higher authority or deity; entreaty;* supplication is *a humble entreaty or petition;* adoration is *deep love or esteem; the act of worshipping;* praise is *the extolling of a deity or the rendering of homage and gratitude to a deity;* contrition is *deeply felt remorse; penitence* and thanksgiving is *an expression of thanks to God.*)
>
> Invocation is *a prayer asking God for help, forgiveness, etc., especially as part of a religious service.*

So, prayer can take the form of requesting something (a petition, supplication, or invocation), or as gratitude (thanksgiving) for something already received, or as praise and adoration.

While prayer is a subject vitally important to the religious person, it is of no interest to the secular *non-believer.* I have always felt there is a crossover somewhere between what is achieved through prayer in the religious sense, and what self-help writers and speakers of a more secular nature achieve. How is it that the same results are achieved, while one party is calling on God or Jesus or others for assistance, and the other is ignoring the religious aspect altogether? To my mind, there can only be one answer to this — one method that works identically from both points of view.

Another puzzle I have always had is how **both** sides of any conflict can pray for God's assistance in winning! How does God decide whether to side with this team or that team, this army or that army, this lawyer or that lawyer? After the battle, why does the winning team

---

170 All definitions in this chapter are from *Collins English Dictionary.*

praise God and thank him for helping them to win? How does the losing team feel about God after losing?

Of course, the answer to this conundrum is simple, as I believe are all conundrums about the meaning of life, once you see clearly. You are praying to God-Consciousness within. You are seeking inspiration from your Higher Self. You are seeking God's intercession from **within** rather than from **without**. Once you do this, God-Consciousness assists both teams equally, but it is still left to the individual player to give of his best, and still, the best man on the day wins.

Apart from petitioning for things or blessings, it is very important to give thanks and show appreciation for what you already do have. By appreciating your blessings, you open yourself to receiving even more. However, by ignoring what you have, or not appreciating it, you close off the channel for further blessings. You may remember that gratitude is Step 1 **and** Step 7 in the conscious application of the Law of Manifestation.

Praise is almost an extension of gratitude. By praising God, or praising His Creation, you are attuning yourself to your Higher Self, and acknowledging the beauty, wonder, and sheer brilliance of all that your life is about. You are acknowledging that this is God's universe and that you deeply appreciate what that means to you as an individual. Praise is recognising your kinship with God, with God-Consciousness.

What then is intuition? Intuition is *"knowledge or belief obtained neither by reason nor by perception; instinctive knowledge or belief."* This is God telephoning you. These are the hunches that come from time to time. The more frequently you follow those hunches, the more often you will receive them.

Inspiration is *"stimulation or arousal of the mind, feelings, etc., to special or unusual activity or creativity."* This is similar to intuition and can also be seen as God telephoning you. By keeping open and following the line of inspiration, your creativity will show no bounds.

After prayer, or anytime when you are not sure what the next step is, just stop and listen quietly to your Higher Self. It is then you will hear what God-Consciousness has to say to you. Whether you see this communication coming from outside you or inside you, know that this is intuition or inspiration speaking. What you believe is the source of that inspiration or intuition is not important. It is more important that you are open to it and listen to it.

When you receive a hunch, just check how it feels in the body. If it sits right, you may go ahead happily with whatever the hunch tells you. If it does not feel good, just ask for clarity, and stay open for a new response. When we receive inspiration or an intuition from out of nowhere, we need to listen. Whether it is our Higher Self, a guardian angel, or some other muse, this is God-Consciousness speaking to us and inspiring us to take certain action. Remember, we are the hands and feet of God-Consciousness. He wants experience and it is up to us to provide that experience.

With practice, prayer, inspiration, and intuition will provide a great communication with God-Consciousness, your Higher Self. And remember, prayer is telephoning to God, and intuition is God telephoning to you. Trust in the power of prayer and intuition and you won't go wrong.

CHAPTER 42

God's Grace

We hear of Grace or God's Grace, but what are we really talking about? The word *grace* means *"the free and unmerited favour of God shown towards man; the divine assistance and power given to man in spiritual rebirth and sanctification; the condition of being favoured or sanctified by God; an unmerited gift, favour, etc., granted by God."*[171]

There are two main aspects that come out of these definitions. The first point is the favour received from God is unmerited, that is, Man is blessed by God-Consciousness even though his own actions do not merit such blessings. The mere fact that we exist as God Franchisees and our whole being is God-Consciousness is indeed a huge blessing. We of ourselves, our Egos, can do nothing and, therefore, do not merit God's Grace. The Ego is built from the abuse of free will and has no real significance. It is a veil of illusion covering our Higher Self, our God-Consciousness.

Secondly, Grace is the condition of being favoured or sanctified (made holy) by God. It is the assistance and power given to us in spiritual rebirth, that is, the recognition of our Higher Selves. As we come to understand our true spirituality, God's Grace will flow upon us and we will realise that we are truly blessed. It is not that God-Consciousness is withholding His Grace from anyone at any time. It is rather that if we believe we are the Ego, and cut ourselves off from our Higher Selves, we are cutting ourselves off from God's Grace.

---

171 *Collins English Dictionary*

Our birthright, in fact our very being, is God's Grace. All we (our Egos) have to do is open our hearts and minds and allow that Grace in. This is another way of saying we need to live as an expression of our Higher Selves and allow the Ego to dissolve into the mists of insignificance and irrelevance where it belongs.

Without God's Grace, we would not exist, either individually or collectively. We could even use the word Grace to describe God instead of the words *God* or *God-Consciousness*. Grace is that significant.

CHAPTER 43

Connections and Relationships

As you might guess, when we have a connection or relationship with another person, whether intimate, friendly, or business-like, we experience a connection or relationship with God. Let's return to the two-statement summary of the Ten Commandments expressed by Jesus:

> *"Jesus said unto him, Thou shalt love the Lord thy God with all thy heart, and with all thy soul, and with all thy mind. This is the first and great commandment. And the second is like unto it, Thou shalt love thy neighbour as thyself."*[172]

Once you truly realise you are an aspect of God-Consciousness, you can do nothing else except love God with all your heart, soul, and mind, and love your neighbour as yourself. It is merely one aspect of God loving another aspect of God.

I have used the terms *connection* and *relationship* rather loosely in what follows as what I describe applies to both, and it would be clumsy to mention both terms each time. By *connection*, I mean that you and the other person connect for a short period or number of short periods, whereas with *relationship* we are looking at an on-going series of connections, or a long-term connection with the other person.

---

172 *Matthew 22:37-39*

A Relationship with Yourself

Before you can love your neighbour as yourself, you must love yourself. Before you can be in a positive relationship with others you need to have a positive relationship with yourself. This means connecting with yourself.

We are all individuals. There is a certain someone whom you know as *me*. When you think about it, it is rather curious that you are you. That never changes — you are always you. You may change as you learn and grow, as you take on board the *good* and *bad* experiences you have, but you still remain you. You never become somebody else. Nobody else ever becomes you.

You can never really see yourself as others see you. You don't know what you look like in the real world and how others experience you. Your view of the world is always looking outwards with you at the centre. How you interpret the world is how you choose to do that, using your own filters, beliefs, prejudices, and preferences. This is your individual view and experience of the world, which God-Consciousness experiences through the form known as *you*. You are unique, and no one, except God-Consciousness, will ever know what it is truly like to be you.

Just observe how you feel about yourself as yourself. Are you comfortable with who you are? Are you overly sensitive to how others might view you? Ask yourself, "Does it matter how others view me? And if it does, why? What would it be like just to accept myself as I am?"

Know that any sensitivity you feel about yourself comes from the Ego. In your Higher Self you are the perfect image of God; [173] your True Self is a beautiful, perfect, intelligent, capable, talented, and expressive manifestation of Life and God-Consciousness. It is your Ego, with its fears, its wilfulness, and its self-centredness that tries to make you superior to others and fears you are not. Your Ego wants to be the best, yet secretly fears it is truly not up to it.

Don't give the Ego the power it seeks. Rather, seek to know the

---

173 "So God created man in his own image, in the image of God created he him; male and female created he them." (Genesis 1:27)

true you and connect with your real self instead. You are not the Ego, whatever it tells you to the contrary. You may recognise there are aspects of yourself you wish were different; nevertheless, you still need to come to accept and like yourself — in fact, love yourself — as you are. Only when you can accept and love yourself are you truly ready to have a relationship with others.

Connecting with the World

Once you have connected with yourself, you are in a better place to be able to connect with or have a relationship with others. There are essentially four types of relationship with others: the ordinary, the close, the intimate, and the spiritual relationship. In practice, we connect with very few, if any, people at an intimate or spiritual level. Our main connection is at an ordinary or close level.

We meet people in all aspects of life. We may pass them in the street, buy something from a shop assistant, work alongside them in our job, and to some extent meet them virtually through TV, radio, or nowadays the Internet. If a person takes your attention, there is some sort of interaction, from your side anyway. I use the word *interaction*, yet it is very subjective and whatever your feeling of interaction is, it is still your subjective experience.

Initially, we feel either attracted to or repelled by the other person. There is something we like about them or something we dislike. If we like something about them, we feel comfortable talking to them, we are more open and friendly, and we enjoy the experience. This may be at a very subtle level. It may just be a smile shared with a stranger, but somehow we feel good inside. We feel good about ourselves, and probably feel recognised or accepted. The whole question of being attracted to or repelled by someone is largely experienced by the Ego. It is the Ego that is judgemental and self-protective.

If we have a feeling of dislike, whether strong or slight, we can feel the barriers come up immediately. We may be less inclined to speak to them and be open with them. We want to move away from their presence as soon as possible. We keep our distance both physically and figuratively. Each person has an energetic field around his or her body that determines whether we feel we can be close or must remain distant. We need our space.

There is only a connection with another person when there is an attraction response from them as well. If there is a feeling of dislike, there is no connection. All connections are an important part of life, particularly with those people who are close to us. We have connections at an ordinary level with our partners, our children, our parents, our friends, and so on. Even if we have a close, intimate, or spiritual relationship with someone, there also needs to be an ordinary connection.

So allow yourself to become more aware of your interactions with others. Feel your reactions to other people — all other people. There is no need to judge your reaction. Rather, just observe it. You don't have to like everyone — there are always going to be some people you like (feel attracted to), whether slightly or strongly, and there will always be people you dislike (feel repelled by), whether slightly or strongly. Don't be put off by the words dislike or repelled — this may just be a subtle tendency and does not necessarily mean more than that.

There may be some people for whom you feel both liking and disliking, and it might be interesting to observe what it is you like about them and what it is you dislike. Notice the effect this situation has within you. Stay connected to yourself and you are far more likely to connect positively with others.

Friends and acquaintances come and go in your life. You meet different people all the time, be it at work, at the gym, on the beach, or through other friends. You are naturally drawn to people who are like you in some way, or maybe even how you would like to be. This is the Law of Manifestation at work. You focus on yourself a lot, naturally, so further expressions of your qualities are drawn towards you, and therefore, people with those qualities are attracted to you and you to them. Sometimes these qualities can be negative or harmful ones; for instance, you might be attracted to someone who has similar problems to you. You will be able to commiserate with them and feel you are not alone; or you might even feel superior to them because your problems are better (or worse) than theirs are.

After a number of connections with a particular person, the connections may become a relationship. You will probably find you acquire friends who give you, or your Ego, something in some way. It may not always be positive, but there will be some apparent gain to you. Treat with respect all friends and acquaintances, in fact, everyone with whom you come in contact, and know you are both aspects of God-Consciousness. You do not have to agree with or condone what other people do, and you can support them through being a shining example.

Business relationships, boss-employee relationships, and customer relationships should also rest on the back of the recognition of the God-Consciousness in the other. You may often strike the other person's Ego, even your own Ego, in the day-to-day activities of the business world. By coming from a place of understanding about the other person, and from a place of authenticity in terms of your truth, you will find the path through the Egos, and the demands of the working world will be smoother.

Commerce, trade, construction, education, transport, social services, and so on are an essential part of the modern world. These activities, in some form, have been an essential part of the world since prehistoric Man stepped outside the caves. This is where Egos have grown big, and where opportunities for the use of free will have been abused the most. Being aware of this as you live in the world, although not necessarily of the world, will be a huge personal advantage to you and your true self, your Higher Self, as you connect to the world through your relationships with others.

Close Relationships

The earliest opportunity for a close relationship is the bond formed between a baby and its mother. There is a wonderful closeness, and the baby comes to really know its mother — and the mother, her baby. There usually is a similar strong bond between fathers and their children. This bond is called love. While the love between parents and their children often continues, the sense of closeness can diminish. Just like Adam and Eve in the Garden of Eden, their innocent connection with each other can become self-conscious. As the children start to assert their Egos, they begin to separate themselves from their parents and stand up as separate individuals. They feel the old closeness cannot be maintained as now they are grown up. The lost sense of closeness may be rebuilt later with maturity, but often it is not. However, as many people do experience, a sense of closeness can be very strong between members of a family, including the extended family.

What about close friends? Yes, of course you may have close friends. You might expect the giving and receiving of unconditional love in a close relationship. There may or may not even be a sexual element to your close relationship, or your friend may become an honorary brother or sister.

Close relationships are extremely important as few of us can live in isolation. We need to have others around us, people in whom we can confide (when we wish to), whom we can ask for help when we need it, and who can add companionship, friendship, protection, interest, and love to our lives. Many people will see these close relationships as being the most important influences on their lives.

Intimate Relationships

To most people, an intimate relationship implies sexual intimacy. I would like to take this definition a lot further. Having a sexual relationship does not necessarily imply you are truly intimate — the sexual relationship you have with someone could easily be classed as an ordinary or a close relationship.

As with a close relationship, an important part of connecting intimately is the giving and receiving of unconditional love. However, there is also a willingness by both parties to show up. This means you have nothing to hide. You are prepared to reveal yourself as you are — physically, mentally, emotionally, and spiritually. You lay all your cards on the table. You stand naked in all ways and offer yourself to that dearly beloved. In the same way, the other person reveals themselves physically, mentally, emotionally, and spiritually to you. You accept them completely and utterly as they are, as you love them unconditionally.

When you are together or communicating with each other, you are totally open and honest. You deeply understand each other, and what you each are saying. You support each other. You love each other no matter what. You laugh together. You love together. You live your lives together. Secrets are about special presents and surprises for your loved one, nothing else. You don't have sex — you make love. You come together in a way that meets each other's needs and also expresses the intense love you have for each other. You are as *"one flesh."*[174] You are not physically shy with each other, but accept each other as you appear. You accept the other as you accept yourself. You love the other as you love yourself. This is often described as being soul mates.

With regard to the sexual aspect of the intimate relationship there needs to be true sexual compatibility. What this means is you each have the same expectations with regard to sex, or at least you are totally accepting of the other's sexual needs. Any imbalance can easily lead to a breakdown in the depth of connection you have with your partner, and thus true intimacy can be lost. To be specific, you may agree that neither of you want to have a sexual relationship — this is perfectly fine, and you are, therefore, sexually compatible and can easily have a fully satisfying intimate relationship with each other. An example might be an elderly couple who have moved beyond the need for sex, although some physical contact such as hugs and kisses on the cheek are still very important. Likewise, close friends might move into an intimate relationship without the need for any sexual contact.

The above may sound very idealistic or very demanding, but in fact it is not. An intimate relationship as described is not something you can force or manufacture. It is something that will develop and appear through a mutual recognition of each other. This is why such couples are called soul mates. Certainly, you may still have to do some work towards maintaining the intimate relationship, although this usually involves the ordinary aspects of the relationship. Intimate relationships must be supported by an ordinary relationship. You still have to buy the groceries and clean up your mess.

Further, let me hasten to add here that this ideal intimate relationship does not imply that you lose your individuality or that you are no longer responsible for yourself and your own life. Of course, you must continue to be responsible for experiencing your own life, for developing new skills and evolving, and clearing up your own mess.

---

174 *Genesis 2:24*

You still need your own space and your own time to yourself. You may even spend a lot of time physically apart, though emotionally, mentally, and spiritually you stay connected.

When you choose your partner and/or your partner chooses you, you choose the person with those aspects of humanness, Ego, and human failings that suit you best. The aspect of God-Consciousness you fall in love with is *just another aspect of God*. As such, he or she is a perfect match. What you decide is, God aside, do I like the look of this physical appearance, this personality, this Ego, this set of skills, this voice, this set of manners, and this idea of relationship? Assuming that you take your thoughts beyond the positive aspects, you ask, "Can I live with this set of failings or weaknesses?"

We can surmise that, from God's overall perspective, He is keen to experience any relationship between different aspects of Himself as both of you are aspects of God-Consciousness. The ideal, one could say, is finding a partner who is a true soul mate. With a soul mate, you have a deep affinity for each other and so you are more able to approach the Higher Self in each other. In other ways, the challenges you might still generate in each other are ones that will help you both to grow. Growth can be defined as a widening of your experience that, of course, is what God-Consciousness wants from you and through you anyway.

So, may I ask you to consider where you sit with intimacy? Do you want to be truly intimate with someone? Are you prepared to be that intimate with someone? Having no desire for such an intimate connection is a totally valid option. However, if you do desire an intimate relationship, then be intimate if that is appropriate. Otherwise, consider your alternatives and consider what you need to do for your personal evolution.

I accept that my description of an intimate relationship is quite specific and includes some high expectations. Nevertheless, if you want a truly intimate relationship and are prepared to offer yourself up to it, you will find it is no chore, and instead is effortless and a joy to experience. If you do not have this, your relationship remains an ordinary relationship or a close relationship, but not an intimate one.

Spiritual Relationships

You may have a relationship with someone at a spiritual level with or without also having an intimate relationship. However, you will need to connect with them at an ordinary level first, even if they attract you in some ways and repel you in others. Your dislike of some aspects of their behaviour or presentation may be what stops your relationship from becoming intimate, or intimacy may just be inappropriate for many different reasons.

A spiritual relationship is always driven by the Higher Self. It is the God-Consciousness in you talking to the God-Consciousness in me. It is connection through the deepest understanding of each other. It is true *namaste (the divine in me bows to the divine in you)*, the traditional Hindu greeting, at the deepest level. Even if your connection shows up at an intellectual level, and is on matters that ostensibly are not spiritual matters, this is still a spiritual relationship. It is the deepest of connections and it does not matter what the subject matter is.

Musicians, sportsmen, artists, and dancers all connect at a spiritual level when the Ego is allowed to drop and the mutual interest is experienced together. So, members of a jazz or rock group who are bouncing musical ideas off each other in front of a live audience become as one as they connect at a spiritual level. Dancers become one as they synchronise in the dance. The best artistic or sports expression appears when the Ego subsides and the Higher Self is able to spiritually connect with the Higher Selves of others. The audience also becomes a part of this connection at a spiritual level.

You may also experience this spiritual connection or relationship in *satsang*, which means "in the company of truth." Usually, there is a guru or teacher who sits in satsang with followers or visitors and gives a short spiritual discourse followed by the answering of any questions that might arise. While there is a communication at a mental level, there is usually a deeper connection going on — the real connection being at a spiritual level. Teachings can be received without words being spoken.

Likewise, you may attend a lecture or talk and you realise you have connected at a very deep level with the speaker. I listen to talks, satsang, and meditations given by Eckhart Tolle and feel a real spiritual connection with him. This is often much more than the superficial listening to his words.

You may well be aware of this spiritual connection with others, and if so, there is nothing more I need to say. If you do not feel this connection and would like to, may I suggest that firstly you need to connect with yourself, and secondly, you may need to put yourself in situations where you meet people to connect with at a deep level. My personal preferences are Eckhart Tolle,[175] satsang, or a live music concert (even recorded).

A spiritual connection or relationship with someone is a wonderful experience and one you will want to develop or maintain. While all interactions with others is the God-Consciousness in you meeting the God-Consciousness in the other, somehow, spiritual relationships make this meeting of God face to face so much more immediate.

The Absolute Relationship

Initially, you must connect with yourself; most commonly, you connect with other people at an ordinary or close level; and occasionally (and specially), you will connect with people at an intimate and/or spiritual level. With either an intimate or a spiritual relationship, you feel a deep closeness with another person. This brings you to oneness with that person, and ultimately, that oneness becomes Oneness with God-Consciousness.

The other interesting aspect is that both intimate and spiritual relationships bring a deep connection with your self. There is somehow a deep confirmation of your very being. You have come a full cycle of having to connect with your self in order to connect with others, and when you do connect with others, particularly at an intimate or spiritual level, you connect even more deeply with your self.

Naturally, just as you are receiving the great benefits of connection with your self, so the other person is feeling the affirmation of their own being and is connecting more deeply with his or her self. You are not receiving something from someone else; rather you receive it from your Higher Self. Having a relationship is not to do with looking

---

175   See www.eckharttolletv.com

for something outside your self — it is to do with sharing your very essence.

If you consider the meaning of life, as we do in the next chapter, there are really only two things you need to do. One is to experience life, that is, experience all the good and bad experiences that come into your life. The other thing to do is to connect with others.

We are not islands or truly self-sufficient. We each need other people at some level, probably at all four levels. In fact, the need can really be called desire — we desire connection with another person or other people. There are extreme cases where connection with another person is not possible, or where there may have been previous bad experiences or non-experience. That deep connection can instead be made with animals, such as a dog, cat, or horse, and through them to one's self and to God-Consciousness. Connection can also be made to other aspects of nature, or art or music and so on. Underneath that is the deep longing for connection to one's self and ultimately to God-Consciousness.

As your connection with your self strengthens, your constant task is to keep in touch with your self. This may sound strange, but it is very easy to slip into fantasy, or slip back into the habits and ways of thinking of the past. Use your relationships with others consciously, and you will simultaneously keep connected with your self. This leads to your being present all or most of the time. The whims of the Ego will be seen for what they are, and you will be able to smile at them. In that smile there is recognition of the absolute relationship you experience — the relationship of one aspect of God-Consciousness loving another aspect of God-Consciousness.

CHAPTER 44

So, What is the Purpose of Life?

If there was no such thing as life, if life did not exist, quite frankly it would not matter a jot to us. We would not be here to miss it. If there was no universe at all, not even space, even that would not matter to anyone. There would be absolutely nothing and no one to notice there was nothing. However, you and I both know there is a universe and there is life. We also have every reason to believe the scientists when they tell us Earth has not always been here, and one day it will be destroyed. They also tell us the universe has not always been here, and that it was initiated 14 billion years ago in what is called the Big Bang.

There is only one explanation for this situation, and that explanation is God. God-Consciousness existed before the universe, and it was He who noticed there was absolutely nothing else around. It was God-Consciousness who decided to do something about it, and so designed and created the universe that has evolved into what we see and experience today. He could not make the universe out of anything other than His own Self as there were no other resources around — there was nothing. The universe is, therefore, made from the very substance of God-Consciousness; and this universe includes you and me.

So, what is the purpose of life?
Some people say, "To worship God"
Some people say, "To have a relationship with God"
Some people say, "To be happy"

Some people say, "To live your passion"
Some people say, "To become enlightened"
Some people say, "To clear your karma"
Some people say, "To do God's will"
And some people say, "Life has no purpose at all."

My view is that there is only one main purpose of life, and that is the purpose for which God created the universe. That purpose is to experience. Before He created the universe, God did not have anything to experience, and so, He created the universe in order to experience the wind through His hair, the water through His fins, the beauty of His sunset, and the feeling of being entwined with His lover. God gave Man a God Franchise so we can be co-creators with Him. He gave us free will so we are not pre-programmed automatons.

God-Consciousness also blindfolded Himself so He would not know all the answers beforehand. He broke Himself (at one level) into billions and billions of pieces just like a Giant Jigsaw Puzzle. In this way, He could experience Himself from many, many different vantage points. He experiences Himself as an atom, as an element, as a tree, as a bug, as an albatross, as a lion, as a man, as a woman, as a beggar, and as a king. God-Consciousness is omnipresent in every single thing in the universe and He experiences what it is to be that thing.

Then, another experience that God-Consciousness wants to have is the experience of putting this Gigantic Jigsaw Puzzle back together again. You could say the purpose of life is to put this wonderful jigsaw puzzle back together, for everyone to realise the Truth, and for them to close Pandora's Box of free will and Ego voluntarily. This is the ultimate purpose of life: the voluntary relinquishment of separation from God, of personal Ego and of free will gone bad. This is the climax of evolution. This is the Heaven or Paradise that the religious seek, and this is the *"new heaven and a new earth"*[176] written about by St John the Divine.

So, if we look at the purposes of life other people have identified, we will see they all are covered by this greater purpose of life. Those people who still think life has no purpose have not been following this

---

176 *Revelation* 21:1

book. If once there was nothing except God-Consciousness, and now there is a universe, I cannot imagine that God-Consciousness created it without some sort of purpose in mind, even if it is not the one I am proposing.

While we all have our individual purpose in life, whether or not we know what it is, we also have these more fundamental purposes people generally apply. Yes, one purpose of our lives is to worship God, but this does not mean we have to do so in a church, synagogue, mosque, or temple. It means that in our daily lives we are always aware, at the back of our minds, how wonderful life really is, despite any difficulties and challenges we might have. We can worship God as the *source* of our life, since without Him we would not exist.

Our purpose is also to have a relationship with God. As we have relationships with many different people on various levels, we should make a point of recognising the God-Consciousness in each of these people. We can look into their eyes and see God there. We can be happy and we can live our passion. As we do this, we show our enthusiasm for life and, therefore, our enthusiasm for what we experience.

If we live a life of true clarity about the presence of God-Consciousness, and allow the veils of Ego to fall from our eyes, then we are truly enlightened. As we become enlightened and see the past deeds that lead to the creation of our karma, we will be able to clear all karma.

And, in experiencing life fully and consciously, we are doing God's will.

PART FIVE

Reaching a
Conclusion

CHAPTER 45

What if The God Franchise is True?

We are approaching the end of this particular work now. You may have reached this point convinced, as I am, that **The God Franchise** offers a very credible scenario for the reality we call God. However, you may be a little confused by it, apprehensive of it, or even downright antagonistic towards it. I would, therefore, like to summarise the main points so you can easily contemplate them and see how well they hold together. You might like to sit with them for a few days or weeks, and then reread the book to gain deeper insight into what it means to you to be a God Franchisee.

Let us assume for a moment what I have written here is the Truth; however, I am the first to admit that when talking about God, the universe, and the whole of reality as we are doing, our minds will have some difficulty taking it all in. Most of us are not trained by school, university, or daily life to cope with such matters. Also, the Ego is likely to feel threatened by these subjects that take it way out of its comfort zone. You may, therefore, feel some resistance at that level.

Fortunately, your Higher Self is an individualised aspect of God-Consciousness itself — it is God with a blindfold on. So, at a deeper level, you are on home turf here. At a deeper level, the Higher Self may just allow the blindfold to slip a little, allow some of the veils to flutter to the ground, and so give you a glimpse of Reality. Allow God to telephone you through your intuition and reveal His Truth to you, while you keep the resistant and doubting Ego at bay.

All you need are some pointers to the Truth — and then more

and more will be revealed to you. If you will accept, for this moment, that the pointers provided by **The God Franchise** are as close to the Truth as any you have found so far, may I humbly suggest you take the following insights with you, and try them out on your further reading and contemplation. What if these things were true? What if you did choose to believe what you have learned here? How would that change your life? How would that change how you view other explanations of Life and Truth?

This is the essence of **The God Franchise**:

+ God needs His Creation as much as His Creation needs God. God created the universe, including you and me, as a way of experiencing His own Consciousness.

+ If there was originally nothing, how would anything get started? There would be neither motivation nor raw material. There had to be some starting point, some initiating cause for the universe, and there seems to be no better candidate than Consciousness, better known as God. Giving God the name *God-Consciousness* is, therefore, a constant reminder of His essential nature.

+ God's qualities of being conscious, eternal, omnipotent, omnipresent, omniscient, the creator of the universe, omni-benevolent, immutable, and having a purpose for His creation, are neither unreasonable nor incompatible with each other.

+ God's purpose in creating His Creation is to have experience — to express Himself and to enjoy Himself. He does not judge His experience as good or bad — it is just experience.

+ The Creation can be seen as a Giant Jigsaw Puzzle that God is slowly watching assemble itself into a complete picture for us all to see and enjoy. God-Consciousness is transcendent (outside His Creation) as well as immanent (within it). The immanent aspect of God is individualised into every piece of the jigsaw puzzle, into every atom and sub-atomic particle of Creation. He is also conscious at every level of grouping such as cells, organs, organisms, and so on. God is thus omnipresent and omniscient through this individualisation in form.

✦ God created the universe and everything in it inside His own Consciousness. The world is not out there — it is in here. In a sense, you and I and everything in the universe are merely thoughts in the Mind of God.

✦ God is not a separate entity in His Heaven, some sort of Father-figure with a long white beard who rules over us and loves us. He is not made in the image of Man. You and I are made in the image of God — we are Consciousness. We are also creators. God has given us free will and a creation franchise — we are God Franchisees.

✦ Since God's Consciousness and His Thoughts are one, we are expressions of a part of God's Consciousness. In the highest possible sense, not in an egotistical or separate way, you and I are Consciousness, are God. While I cannot say I am God, it is true that God is me. Therefore, you and I can truly say: *We are One with God.* The goal of so many spiritual seekers, Oneness with God, is true for you and me right here and now. We can also say this makes God the ultimate Personal God.

✦ We create both consciously and unconsciously as the Law of Manifestation operates at all times. One would expect we create positively when working consciously, although this is not always the case. Much of our unconscious creation is negative, as we do not realise the impact of our beliefs and thoughts.

✦ The driving force behind what we manifest in our lives is our beliefs. The net offset of all our individual beliefs (including our values, vows, attitudes, promises, and rules) is what we truly believe. This set of beliefs determines what we could call the *Fundamental You*, and this constantly generates a subtle frequency, the *Creation Frequency*. Our personal and unique Creation Frequency attracts into our lives the people and things that resonate with it.

✦ God gave Man free will to generate variety and add the factor of randomness to His Creation, so Man did not act as an automaton. In this way, God's experience is as broad as possible. Animals have a lesser degree of free will, and plants and minerals would appear to have none at all. It is also feasible there are other entities in the universe with free will, such as archangels and angels, spirits, and extra-terrestrials, although their existence or non-existence is not necessarily of particular importance to us.

+ The sense of separateness and isolation you and I feel, or may have felt in the past, is due to our Ego, which has unconsciously chosen, through the misuse of free will, to cover our being with many layers of veils. The Ego can be seen as the Lesser Self, while the true self, the Higher Self, is an individual aspect, a blindfolded subset of God-Consciousness.

+ Our primary problem is focussing on our Ego, our Lesser Self. We think and act as if we were the Ego. In this, we are very mistaken. The reality of our identity as an individual aspect of God-Consciousness will become clear to us all in the fullness of time. Our Lesser Self will then be seen to be illusion (*maya*).

+ The Ego is fuelled by negative emotions, and they colour the outcome of any creation and the individual's perception of it. Negative emotions also have a huge impact on the person who is feeling them, leading them into a downward spiral of self-inflicted pain, suffering, and resistance to reality.

+ The way things are in the universe right now is exactly how they should be. Everything is in its right place. What we see and experience is the net effect of every cause that is in play. If we want things to change, we must change. As Mahatma Gandhi (1869-1948) said, *"Be the change you want to see in the world."*

+ There are many different religious beliefs, and on the surface, they can appear to be incompatible. Each belief system has its merits; so a belief that can encompass all beliefs is more likely to be closer to the Truth. **The God Franchise** offers a foundation on which to build such a synthesis. The idea that all religions offer different paths up the same mountain is a good one; so, worshipping God in your preferred way is totally sound. We talk here of beliefs, and beliefs comprise of what we have been brought up to believe and what we choose to believe. They still remain, in essence, nothing more than **beliefs** and are **not** reality.

✦ Good and bad/evil are human concepts. The omnibenevolence of God points to the fact that He created everything for a positive purpose. It is Man's Ego and the misuse of free will that have created things and experiences that are considered good or bad/evil. Sinning is the abuse of our gift of free will, and is the cause of much pain and suffering — we unwittingly punish ourselves rather than earn punishment from God.

✦ There is no real reason to question what scientists are telling us. Any errors in data or interpretation will soon be picked up and corrected through peer review and new discoveries. For the purposes of daily living in a wholesome and authentic way, we can be assured that generally accepted scientific discoveries are probably close to the truth. Thus, the theory of evolution and the Big Bang cannot realistically be questioned on philosophical or spiritual grounds. Since God-Consciousness has no time constraints, this method of creation is as good as any other He might have chosen to use, and no doubt is the best.

✦ To give stability to His Creation and to make it feasible, God-Consciousness has put in place a number of inviolable laws, God's Laws. These include the physical laws (such as mathematics and gravity) and Universal Laws (such as the Law of Manifestation and Law of Karma). There are also moral precepts like the Ten Commandments, but these can be broken, although the Universal Laws (such as the Law of Karma) will ensure that the appropriate *price* is paid.

This covers the main platform of **The God Franchise**; by necessity, it is a short summary. May it serve to give you food for contemplation, and may **The God Franchise** have a profound effect on your life.

To conclude our exploration of God and His universe, and to satisfy scientists and those who like their proofs to be specific and simple, let's see how **The God Franchise: A Theory of Everything** stands up to scientific scrutiny. Stephen Hawking provided an excellent definition of a scientific model in his book

The Grand Design. Let's see how **The God Franchise** model measures up to it. Hawking said, *"A model is a good model if it:*

1. *Is elegant*
2. *Contains few arbitrary or adjustable elements*
3. *Agrees with and explains all existing observations*
4. *Makes detailed predictions about future observations that can disprove or falsify the model if they are not borne out."*[177]

Using the above summary of **The God Franchise** as the model, we can say:

1. It is elegant. Solutions to the mysteries of God and the universe that invoke a God who is superhuman-like, raise the hackles of the atheists, and of many other people, including myself. The true *God* is infinitely much more than that. Likewise, the scientists who come up with theories like the multiverse and M-theory with its eleven dimensions are certainly not being elegant.[178] Scientists cannot explain consciousness or how a group of complex molecules at some stage gained life and consciousness, whether this was suddenly or happened over billions of years.[179] It is, therefore, my contention that this model is as elegant and as explanatory as it is possible to devise: that God is Consciousness; God provided the initial cause, and Consciousness provided the raw material for the creation of the universe.

2. There are no arbitrary or adjustable elements. While it is true we may never know everything there is to know about God (I say this lightly), it is also true that, as we open to the Truths available

---

177 Hawking, S. and Mlodinow, L., *The Grand Design*, Bantam Press, London, 2010, Pg. 51. (UK and Commonwealth: Reprinted by permission of The Random House Group Limited. Rest of the world: Copyright © 2010 by Stephen W. Hawking and Leonard Mlodinow. Used by permission of Bantam Books, a division of Random House, Inc.)

178 See Appendix II

179 That this took place over billions of years as scientists contend is meaningless. At one moment in time, there was no life, and in the next moment life appeared. At one moment in time, there was no consciousness, and in the next moment, consciousness appeared. However rudimentary it was, and even if it only had to happen once, it still had to happen at some moment in time. Scientists still cannot explain how either life or consciousness appeared.

to us here and now, we will learn more and more of what it is to be God Franchisees. We will also learn to create the lives we wish to live more consciously than we do now, and in that way, avoid all the unnecessary pain and suffering we currently, unconsciously, draw into our lives.

3. The above model agrees with and explains all existing observations. Naturally, in a book of this nature, one designed to reach a wide readership, I have covered few of the observations that have been made on Earth, or elsewhere in the universe. I contend though that any observations that have been made can be tested at the door of this thesis and will pass the test. This is true scientifically, philosophically, and spiritually.

4. I make three detailed predictions about future observations that can disprove or falsify the model if they are not borne out:

> Innumerable scientific discoveries will continue to be made about the universe, and not one of them will disprove that the root cause and substance of this universe is Consciousness.

> No absolute and irrefutable disproof of any of God's qualities as presented here will ever be devised. God is conscious, eternal, omnipotent, omnipresent, omniscient, the creator of the universe, omnibenevolent, immutable, and has a purpose for His Creation.

> It will be proved beyond doubt that each individual creates his own present and future, whether consciously or unconsciously. So, it will be proved that each individual is a creator — is a God Franchisee.

I will also make four other predictions, although the failure of any of these does not disprove or falsify the model:

> In the shorter term, there is likely to be an increasing schism in society, and it will become clearer a more spiritual outlook has huge benefits, and the materialistic and egoistic path causes increasing problems, difficulties, pain, and suffering. This will be a time of learning for all people.

People will become increasingly enlightened and spiritual. There will be a movement towards personal spirituality and away from the old-school religions. This may take some time, although one can already see the signs of this trend.

A similar trend will be seen in medicine, with a movement towards holistic solutions and away from drugs and allopathic medicine in general, except in critical situations.

Science and spirituality will come together in time as they discover the common ground that is the Truth of God and the universe.

The ultimate questions of life and science are: What is the true nature and origin of the universe, of life, and of consciousness? All other questions pale in significance. Science and philosophers have made huge steps towards answering the details this side of these questions, but the answers to those specific questions themselves have eluded them so far. *The God Franchise* has tackled these questions head on, and offers a thesis that is elegant, simple, and eminently feasible.

It would be wonderful if religionists and theologians took up the real challenge presented by science and moved forward into the modern world. Likewise, it would be equally admirable if scientists were to open their eyes and allow that there are some real aspects of the universe that are currently totally incompatible with their scientific knowledge. I believe this mutual recognition and acceptance will happen in the fullness of time. There can only be one Absolute Truth, and the religious and spiritual amongst us need to work with the scientists amongst us, so together we can approach that Truth and wonder in awe at its meaning, its significance, and its beauty.

My prayer is that *The God Franchise* assists in this endeavour.

CHAPTER 46

Benediction

Ten percent of this book is one hundred percent true, while the other ninety percent consists of pointers to the Truth. Unfortunately, I cannot tell you which ten percent is the true part. Does this help you? Of course it does. This book is not about facts. It is not an intellectual treatise. It is a book to help you free up your concepts. Its aim is to allow you to open into the realm of Truth and Reality through the realisation of your own potential and the infinite possibilities available to you for expressing **The God Franchise** you have been given.

What do I **know** about the nature of God anyway? Absolutely nothing. However, I am certain He is not a superhuman sitting in a place called Heaven, and ruling us from above. I am equally certain that God is our personal essence, and everything that exists anywhere in this universe — and any other universes — is made up of His Essence. All is God-Consciousness in some form or another, and that is all there is to it. I have chosen to call this situation **The God Franchise**.

I like the concept offered by the Kabbalah as I have mentioned a few times. The Tree of Life is headed by Kether, the most transcendent aspect of God we can conceive, the I AM of the Bible. And then beyond that, there are three layers of the totally unknown aspects of God, the Unmanifest. As you absorb this concept when reading about or working with the Kabbalah from a good source, a true sense of peace descends upon you. There is no need to know and no need to understand.

So, this benediction is for the invocation of God-Consciousness in your own being.

May God-Consciousness reveal Itself to your human consciousness as your Higher Self, so you can more easily pull aside the veils in your own life.

May your heart open and receive direct access to the Truth of your own Being.

May you appreciate that your Higher Self, your true Consciousness, is God-Consciousness Itself, and you are truly blessed.

May you come to realise that all that stands between you and Freedom, Heaven, and Absolute Bliss is your insistence on maintaining your Ego and your personal sense of free will. As you surrender to the reality of your Higher Self, the sheer ridiculousness of your previous life, your fears, your prejudices, and the protection of your personality and Ego, will become apparent.

Bless you. Bless you. Bless you.

APPENDICES

THE APPENDICES

In these appendices, I would like to run through some of the various theories or proofs that have been raised by philosophers over the centuries, either for or against the existence of God. Let me clarify that we are not looking at **whether it is reasonable to believe in God**. We are looking at **whether God really exists or not**. Some atheists might argue that if God did exist, He would be so beyond our comprehension it is unreasonable to believe in Him, as the belief has no foundation. That is unacceptable to me. Let's be brave and either prove God exists, or prove He doesn't.

There are five appendices, namely:

These appendices can be read in conjunction with Chapter 2 or separately. Their aim is to discuss the case for and against the existence of God. They flow into one another and can be read sequentially as part of the text of the book.

APPENDIX I

The Atheists' Case

We begin with the atheistic viewpoint of the question: Does God really exist? An atheist is someone who believes there is no God. There is a secondary or wider meaning: that atheists reject the belief in God, but that definition to me is for those people who have not thought about the issue and just choose not to believe. So, in the following, we are looking for proofs of why God does not exist, not why it is unreasonable to believe in God.

Warning: We may have to face some arguments like the one that says God cannot be omnipotent because if He was, He would be able to create a being more powerful than Himself. This is just playing with words and proves or disproves absolutely nothing. Nevertheless, arguments like this exist, on both sides of the fence.

In the past, it was unusual to find people who did not believe in God, as it was just the normal thing to believe in a god or gods of some description. Here are some of the arguments put forward by those who believe there is no God, and I will comment after each one.

1. **The Problem of Evil.** How can a God who is omnipotent, omniscient and omnibenevolent allow the evil we see in the world? Epicurus (341-270 BC) explained it in what became known as the Epicurean paradox:

   + If a perfectly good God exists, then evil does not
   + There is evil in the world
   + Therefore, a perfectly good God does not exist.

This is probably the most difficult question facing those who believe in God, and one that has been tackled by theologians and philosophers through the centuries.

My Comment

Some suggest that if God requires the greater good of our having free will, then we need to have the choice between good and evil. Others see God created a perfectly good world, but Adam and Eve brought in the concept of Sin through their eating of the fruit from the Tree of the Knowledge of Good and Evil in the Garden of Eden.[180] This became the basis of the Christian doctrines called *Original Sin* and *The Fall of Man*.

I concur with these thoughts, although I would put them into rather different terms, which I do in this book. Of course, God could get rid of evil, but since He designed and created everything that has been created, He must be accepting of the way things are right now, and they must be within the realm of His Purpose for His Creation. The reason I say this is clear in the body of *The God Franchise*.

This argument does not prove there is no God. It just clarifies that the concept often held of God is inaccurate.

2.   **The Argument from Inconsistent Revelations.** There are many major religions, and within them are many divisions; and there are many scriptures and other holy books, and each of them has a different, mutually incompatible, and even inconsistent teaching. Only one can be right, so the chances of your picking the wrong one, and therefore, "going to the wrong hell," are very high. You have less than one chance in one hundred of choosing the true religion and so being able to gain entry to Heaven.

Since the proponents of these teachings often claim divine revelation, the inconsistency amongst them all leads one to deduce they all could be wrong, and there is no God.

---

180 *Genesis* 2:16-17, 3:1-24

My Comment

On the face of it, this is very sound logic, and is one of the reasons I have chosen to write this book. If God really does exist, and if He has been inspiring Man with His Truths, then there has to be a way of viewing His teachings that maintains consistency. This book offers such a view.

As an aside, it should be noted that scientists are not very consistent either. Often, there are different camps of belief, and often what has been conclusively proved is overturned by further contrary scientific revelations. So, both sides of the argument may be tarred with the same brush. This is all part of developing thought and understanding. The divine revelations that were appropriate 3,500 years ago were not appropriate 2,000 years ago, and likewise, those from 2,000 years ago are not necessarily appropriate now. Each age and each group of people have the spiritual and scientific revelations they need. The present years of the late twentieth and early twenty-first centuries are indeed exciting times. My expectation is that the times will continue to get even more exciting as the so-called spiritual, religious, secular, and scientific worlds come together to provide one holistic understanding of the Truth.

This argument does not disprove the existence of God. Once again, it just proves a limited view of God is insufficient to describe the reality.

3.   **The Argument from Non-belief (or Divine Hiddenness).** If God is omnipotent and omnibenevolent, He would be able to ensure everyone believed in Him. God has been conspicuous by His hiddenness. He, therefore, does not exist.

My Comment

As before, I am sure God has very good reasons for keeping Himself hidden as He appears to be. Christians, for one, are quite right in asserting that love of God through faith is much more desirable than being forced to love Him. On the other hand, I wonder how much He is keeping Himself hidden. And that, of course, is part of the story of this book.

This does not disprove the existence of God. Just because you and I cannot see or understand electricity does not mean it doesn't exist, and that it is not an important part of daily life.

4. **The Argument from Free Will.** The concept of an omniscient God who can, therefore, see into the past and future, is incompatible with the concept of free will. Because God knows what will happen, all free will is lost.

My Comment

There is no incompatibility in my view. Let's assume we have total free will and there is no God. Today, we decide with total free will to do number 82 of 100 options. If we look back at that tomorrow, we can say with certainty we freely chose option 82 of 100 options. Now, if we add a God who can see the past, the present, and the future, and if He were to focus on tomorrow, He would merely see that we had chosen option 82 out of 100 options with our free will. It is that simple.

This argument does not disprove God. It is merely confused about the meaning of omniscience and the effect of that omniscience.

5. **An Eternal, Immutable God could not Act within Time.** Since God is eternal and unchanging, He could not react within our time-based universe, as in answering prayers or performing miracles. Divine intervention would be impossible, and in fact, He could not even have created the universe.

My Comment

This point is very specifically covered as part of the main thesis of **The God Franchise.** I can assure you that it does not disprove the existence of God.

6. **The Six Ways of Atheism.** Geoffrey Berg, a graduate of the University of Cambridge, published a book, *The Six Ways of Atheism*[181] in 2009, with six improved arguments for atheism.

---

181 Berg, G., *The Six Ways of Atheism: New Logical Disproofs of the Existence of God,* self-published, Prestwich, 2009.

The title of the book is, of course, a play on *"The Five Ways"* of St Thomas Aquinas, which we discuss in Appendix IV as part of The Theist's Case. Berg claims to have developed logical and *"new valid arguments against belief in a monotheistic God."*[182] He has summarised the arguments neatly in his book as well as expounded upon them, and has made the summary readily available on his website.[183] I will quote the summaries[184] in their entirety here. As before, I will comment after each one.

Argument 1: The Aggregate of Qualities Argument

1. *If God exists, God must necessarily possess all of several remarkable qualities (including supreme goodness, omnipotence, immortality, omniscience, ultimate creator, purpose giver).*

2. *Every one of these qualities may not exist in any one entity and if any such quality does exist it exists in few entities or in some cases (e.g. omnipotence, ultimate creator) in at most one entity.*

3. *Therefore it is highly unlikely any entity would possess even one of these qualities.*

4. *There is an infinitesimal chance that any one entity (given the almost infinite number of entities in the Universe) might possess the combination of even some two of these qualities, let alone all of them.*

5. *In statistical analysis a merely hypothetical infinitesimal chance can in effect be treated as the no chance to which it approximates so very closely.*

6. *Therefore as there is statistically such an infinitesimal chance of any entity possessing, as God would have to do, all God's essential qualities in combination it can be said for all practical and statistical purposes that God just does not exist.*

---

182 Berg, Pg. 7
183 www.thesixwaysofatheism.com
184 Berg, Pg. 173 for all the summaries, reproduced here with the kind permission of the author.

My Comment

The argument here would be true if you were trying to find *"all God's essential qualities in combination"* in one being today, amongst *"the almost infinite number of entities in the Universe."* However, since God is defined as the Prime Source of the universe, there was only one being at the time when God became God, so all these qualities would have been readily available in Him. The Creation and the multitude of entities only came afterwards. Of course, I use the words "the time when God became God" with tongue in cheek since, of course, He is defined as being eternal.

Argument 2: The Man and God Comprehension Gulf Argument

1. *Man is finite (in time, space and power, etc.).*
2. *God, if he exists, is infinite (in time, space and power, etc.).*
3. *Therefore, mankind cannot possibly recognise God or even know that God exists.*

My Comment

This is all very well, but is rather lame. If God can see all times from the past, through the present, and into all times in the future, then Man is able to meet Him in the present, which is Now. The past and the future don't matter to us, as for us they do not exist and are but a memory or a dream. In this moment of Now, if God so desires, He may reveal Himself to whomever He chooses. This may come as inspiration or revelation or in some other form.

Likewise, if God is in every place as an omnipresent being, then He is here right now. He is here and is able to inspire me here and now. Other places don't matter to me, only where I am right now. As it happens, God is here too.

The argument that God does not exist because Mankind cannot possibly recognise Him is meaningless. God's existence is not dependent on Mankind, or on recognition by us.

Argument 3: The 'God Has No Explanatory Value' Argument

1. *God, if he exists, must be the ultimate being and provide the answer to all our ultimate questions - otherwise he is not really God.*

2. *Yet even supposing as a hypothesis that God exists, the questions that God was supposed to finally answer still remain (though in some cases God is substituted in the question for the Universe).*

3. *Therefore, hypothesising God's existence is only unnecessarily adding an extra stage to such problems and has no real explanatory value.*

4. *Therefore, according to Logic (Occam's Razor Law - 'that entities are not to be multiplied beyond necessity'), we should not postulate God's existence and there is no adequate reason to suppose that God exists.*

5. *Therefore, we should suppose that God does not exist.*

My Comment

Once again, this is a very limited viewpoint. The complexities of the universe are slowly being revealed, and of course, many of the big questions remain unanswered — questions such as: What exactly is life? How did the universe begin, as in the time before the first seconds of the Big Bang? How did life originate? How did consciousness evolve?

In terms of Occam's razor principle (it is **not** a Law), we are looking for a simple, succinct solution. Having God as the Creator of everything in the universe cannot get much simpler as an explanation. Through that everything is explained. If it is too complex for science to explain, or for human logic, why blame that on God? So far as our understanding of God is concerned, logically, do we need to? Just because we don't know why or how life exists does not make us all dead (or inanimate).

Argument 4: The 'This Is Not The Best Possible World' Argument

1. *God, if he exists, must be omnipotent, supremely good, and our ultimate creator.*
2. *Therefore, an existent God (being supremely good and competent) would have created the best possible world (if he created anything).*
3. *As the world is inconsistent (between ages and people), it cannot all be the best possible world.*
4. *Therefore, as the world is not the best possible world, God cannot exist.*

In the detail of his argument, Berg argues this is not the best possible world (Step 3) because: *"Either it is the best possible thing to live in the modern, technologically developed world or otherwise to live in a primitive world or neither but not both."*[185] Therefore, God has not created the best possible world, and therefore, He does not exist.

Likewise, he points out it is inconsistent that some people should be born blind (for example) while others are born sighted. Since both conditions cannot be the best possible condition, God has not created the best possible world, and therefore, He does not exist.

My Comment

When a man and a woman create a child together, the child is born weak, ignorant, sleepy, greedy, and with no control of its excretions. Have these parents not produced the best possible baby? Of course they have, and over the years, that baby grows into a fine, strong, intelligent, creative, conscious, and civilised adult, who also usually has total control over his or her excretions.

The world was created as the best possible world, and it has had to go through the infant stage, the child stage, the teenage stage, and so on. I would like to think perhaps this best possible world is just beginning to come into its adult stage and all its fantastic potential is starting to come together in a rather wonderful adult. We are not there yet, as can be seen by the *evil* in the world around us. We are, however, moving in the right direction.

---

185   Berg, Pg. 79

Another point worth considering is whether our human concept of what is the best possible world is, in fact, the best possible world. For instance, if everything was lovely and easy, would there be enough reason to strive for the technological advancements we have seen, and that will continue? Remember, necessity is the mother of invention. If all our needs were satisfied by a best possible world, there would be no invention or development at all. How boring and imperfect would that be?

One could say the best possible jigsaw puzzle would be the perfect picture of an outstanding scene, framed and complete, with no ugly cuts in it. One could sit and admire it with nothing further to do. Or one could say that the best possible jigsaw puzzle would be the perfect picture of an outstanding scene, cut into 1,000 pieces placed in a plastic bag, and with no picture accompanying it to show what the outstanding picture is. Then, the discovery of the outstanding scene by painstakingly putting together the puzzle will prove this truly is the best possible jigsaw puzzle.

Regarding whether a person has been born blind (or crippled, or destitute, or dead), if one looks at the bigger picture, which some beliefs do, and takes into account reincarnation and karma, then any disabilities or encumbrances we start off with in the world are there to enable us to learn and grow. Helen Keller (1880–1968) is a shining example of someone who was, through illness at the age of 19 months, blind and profoundly deaf, and consequently dumb. Nevertheless, she went on to learn to speak and to communicate, to read and to write, and subsequently, become a renowned speaker, traveller, author, and political activist. Would Helen Keller have become the same force of inspiration and self-worth if she had not been struck blind and deaf as an infant?

There are many cases in literature and history books that are equally inspiring, as men and women overcome adversity to shine in the community, and add real benefit to the world. So, who can define what is the best possible world, and why should our current world not be the best possible world at this time? It is certainly no proof that God does not exist.

Argument 5: The Universal Uncertainty Argument

1. *An uncertain God is a contradiction in terms.*
2. *Everything in the Universe must be fundamentally uncertain about its own relationship to the Universe as a whole because there is no way of attaining such certainty.*
3. *Therefore, even an entity with all God's other qualities cannot have the final quality of certain knowledge concerning its own relationship to the Universe as a whole.*
4. *Therefore, God cannot exist because even any potential God cannot know for sure that it is God.*

Note: Stated as a logical paradox, this argument is *"God cannot exist because God cannot know for sure that it is God."* Berg also indicates this Argument 5 is his preferred and strongest argument.

My Comment

This is patently playing with words. The simple response is, if God is omniscient, as defined, He will know that He is God.

Further, if God knows everything except that He *"cannot have the final quality of certain knowledge concerning its own relationship to the Universe as a whole"* because that is illogical or impossible, then He still remains omniscient minus this one point. Why can He not be God if He is omniscient minus one point?

Again, if God is uncertain about His *"own relationship to the Universe as a whole,"* that is rather strange. At the outset, there was God and only God, so all He had to know was Himself. Later, He created the universe (as given in the definition of God), so He will be totally familiar with everything within His Creation through his omniscience.

Anyway, if it were impossible for God to *"know for sure that it is God,"* so what? That does not invalidate his Godhood, just as God's inability to make square circles cannot invalidate His existence. As C. S. Lewis wrote, *"[God's] omnipotence means power to do all that is intrinsically possible, not to do the intrinsically impossible. You may attribute miracles to him, but not nonsense."*[186]

---

186 Lewis, C.S., *The Problem of Pain*, Harper Collins, San Francisco, 2001, Pg. 18. Copyright © C.S. Lewis Pte. Ltd. 1940.

This disproof of the existence of God fails through a lack of looking beyond the human, beyond an anthropomorphic idea of God, into the very essence of what being an absolutely conscious, eternal, omnipotent, omniscient, omnipresent, omnibenevolent, purposeful, immutable Creator of the universe might entail. Frankly, it is beyond our comprehension (as Berg rightly points out), but we can take a stab in that direction.

We also cannot accept this attempted disproof of God as being remotely successful.

Argument 6: The 'Some of God's Defining Qualities Cannot Exist' Argument

1. *God must have certain characteristic qualities (such as providing purpose to life), otherwise he would not be God.*
2. *But it is impossible for any entity to possess some of these qualities (such as providing purpose to life since we can find no real purpose and therefore we in practice have no ultimate purpose to our lives) that are essential to God.*
3. *Therefore since some of God's essential qualities (such as being the purpose provider to life) cannot possibly exist in any entity, God cannot exist.*

My Comment

It is difficult to understand why, if a quality *"cannot possibly exist in any entity, God cannot exist."* Why does God need to have a quality that is logically impossible, in order to exist? While Berg does not push the point, he does imply that because God cannot create a square circle, he is not omnipotent, and therefore, does not exist.

While he discusses all the expected essential qualities of God, Berg homes in on the quality of God as the purpose giver to life. Berg states: *"I venture to state that there is no ultimate purpose to life. … At any rate, no purpose to life is readily apparent to us humans who are living life. As we know of no purpose to life, a purpose of life might as well not exist so far as we are concerned because we cannot then consciously be fulfilling that purpose, nor even living our lives in the knowledge of that or any purpose!"*[187]

---

187 Berg, Pg. 157

There are many people who would disagree with this statement as, personally, they have found a purpose in their lives. They know what it is and they go out of their way to fulfil it. Many people may feel lost for years until they do discover that purpose for their life, and then become focussed and purposeful.

If purpose is possible for some people at least, then surely God must be able to have a purpose for His Creation — or else He would not have bothered to create it. God's purpose and our purpose as humans are spelt out in a number of chapters in this book, culminating specifically in the chapter *So, What is the Purpose of Life?*

And so we conclude the case for the atheists. While I accept that hidden in the arguments there might be proof that a God as envisioned by some worshippers might not exist, and also that it might be illogical to believe in God, I do not accept there is any proof that God does not exist in reality. Perhaps the atheists are disproving the wrong God and then deducing from there that the real God does not exist either.

The God we describe in the main text of this book does very much exist. He is a God even atheists might accept if they allow their denials to rest for a while, and open their minds to a glimpse of the Truth. They might use their minds and logic to extrapolate from there.

Now let us take a look at the scientists' case.

APPENDIX II

The Scientists' Case

Many scientists who consider the big questions of Life, the universe, and God, fall into the atheists' camp. The reason scientists may become atheists, or at least sceptics, is they believe what their scientific research tells them, rather than what remains unproven in the scriptures. This is understandable. They are trained to be accurate, specific, and logical, and deal in objective reality. If what they see and prove appears to contradict what religion says, they will naturally go with what their own eyes and intellects tell them. They write against religion because they feel the need to enlighten the people whom they see as being hoodwinked by religion and superstition. Some writers have become almost scientific fundamentalists and missionaries in their zeal.

So let's take a look at the arguments three specific scientists have raised.

1. **The Dawkins Argument.** Here is the main argument raised by Richard Dawkins in his controversial book, *The God Delusion.*[188] I will quote his premise:

> The God Hypothesis is *"there exists a superhuman, supernatural intelligence who deliberately designed and*

---

188 Dawkins, R., *The God Delusion*, Bantam Press, London, 2006. (Copyright © 2006 by Richard Dawkins. UK and Commonwealth: Published by Bantam Press. Reprinted by permission of The Random House Group Limited. Rest of the world: Used by permission of Houghton Mifflin Harcourt Publishing Company. All rights reserved.)

created the universe and everything in it, including us. This book will advocate an alternative view: any creative intelligence, of sufficient complexity to design anything, comes into existence only as the end product of an extended process of gradual evolution. Creative intelligences, being evolved, necessarily arrive late in the universe, and therefore cannot be responsible for designing it."[189]

Dawkins also raises the subsidiary question: *Who made God?*

Dawkins looks at the intricacies of nature and agrees these could not come about by chance. However, neither does he see them as designed by God. The solution is Darwin's natural selection theories — the theory of evolution. While there may be some gaps in science's knowledge of the evolution of a particular organ or species, we should not automatically fill this gap with *God*. While the discovery of a truly *"irreducible complexity"*[190] would sink the evolutionists' case, the question of who made God would still pose a problem.

This leaves the question of what the origin of life is, the impetus that kick-starts the evolution process. Dawkins uses the anthropic principle to indicate life started on Earth simply because the conditions on Earth happened to be perfect to sustain life. The opposite view, that Earth was designed (by God) specifically to support life, is not the necessary answer, and is statistically less probable.

Life only needs to have originated once, of course, and from then natural selection will have taken over to provide the vast variety of forms that life has taken since. Dawkins admits the existence of other major gaps (apart from the origin of life) in scientific theory so far, including the origin of the eukaryotic cell (the complex cells of plants, animals and humans) from the original prokaryotic cell (essentially a single cell organism like a bacterium), and the development of consciousness.

Dawkins dismisses God as a solution because

---

189 Dawkins, Pg. 52
190 Dawkins, Pg. 144-161. The term was coined by Michael Behe in 1996.

"A God capable of continuously monitoring and controlling the individual status of every particle in the universe cannot be simple. His existence is going to need a mammoth explanation in its own right. Worse (from the point of view of simplicity), other corners of God's giant consciousness are simultaneously preoccupied with the doings and emotions and prayers of every single human being ..."[191]

Dawkins raises the classic argument against the probability of the universe being explained as the result of chance — the so-called *"Ultimate Boeing 747 Gambit."* This is usually used by theists to prove there needs to be a designer of the universe, whereas Dawkins believes it proves his case. The argument, originated by Fred Hoyle (the well-known astronomer) and now also called Hoyle's Fallacy, is that the chance development of life in the universe is just as likely as a tornado sweeping through a junkyard and assembling a Boeing 747 from the materials available there. Therefore, a designer or God must exist.

In contrast, Dawkins argues, *"God is the Ultimate Boeing 747."*[192] The fallacy in Hoyle's argument is it tries to show the odds against a complex form coming about by chance are too high to be probable. In contrast, natural selection shows living things start out very simply and through natural selection evolve to more complex organisms. Dawkins anticipates similar processes in cosmology, physics, and chemistry will be discovered to explain the major gaps regarding the origin of life, the origin of the eukaryotic cell, and the development of consciousness. Dawkins insists God is not an explanation, as He would need to be ultimately complex, and therefore, is ultimately improbable. This makes God the Ultimate Boeing 747.

This, in essence, is Dawkins' argument against the existence of God, although I am pleased to see he does word his conclusion, *"God almost certainly does not exist."*[193]

---

191 Dawkins, Pg. 149
192 Dawkins, Pg. 114
193 Dawkins, Pg. 158

My Comment

Dawkins discredits the idea of God existing due to the great odds against this being the answer. Nevertheless, he assumes the origin of life is easily explained despite the huge odds of that occurring. He expects some unique chemical reaction must have occurred to create life. He writes,

> *"We can deal with the unique origin of life by postulating a very large number of planetary opportunities. Once that initial stroke of luck has been granted – and the anthropic principle most decisively grants it to us – natural selection takes over: and natural selection is emphatically not a matter of luck."*[194]

He does not even try to plug the gaps of the origin of eukaryotic cells and consciousness.

Another assumption is God had to have been created and could not have been eternally present. There is no real reason, and he offers none, as to why an eternal being is not possible. Why could God not be an eternal being who decided at some point to create the universe? If Dawkins believes the universe does not need to have been created, why does he believe God needs to have been created?

A further serious assumption Dawkins makes is God has to be complex and would need *"a mammoth explanation in its own right."* I do not believe God is at all complex. He is naturally at a different and vastly superior level to us. While we might need complexity to explain our most powerful and clever creations or the powerful and clever things in nature, this does not necessarily mean omnipotence, omnipresence, eternal being, consciousness, and the other attributes ascribed to God are necessarily complex. I expect God, in His Godness, is very simple.

In his arguments, Dawkins does not allow for consciousness, or for the fact that God might be consciousness. I believe consciousness is the key that unlocks this whole argument regarding the existence of God. Any argument from a purely

---

194 Dawkins, Pg. 140

materialistic foundation is bound to come to areas it cannot explain, and so, arrive at a false conclusion. Its most serious false conclusion is that God does not exist.

Rather than tackle the really hard questions as indicated above, Dawkins keeps pushing the natural selection barrow. I have no objection to evolution being exactly as Darwin, Dawkins, and every other scientist have proved it to be. It does not prevent there being a God up front who designed it and set the whole evolutionary process in motion. The existence of God also very satisfactorily explains the origin of life, eukaryotic cells, and consciousness, as everyone — except atheists — understands.

2.   **The Stenger Argument.** Victor Stenger is a physicist, philosopher, and author of many books, including the recent *God: The Failed Hypothesis*.[195] Here, he meticulously explains the scientific method and shows how science proves (to his satisfaction) that God cannot or is extremely unlikely to exist. He approaches the argument from many different angles, too many to comment on here, so we will need to be satisfied with just a few of the points he makes.

If God exists, there would be evidence of Him and His presence, and science would be able to confirm this through its methods. No such evidence exists.

Stenger accepts that science does not know everything, and that there are some fundamental gaps in its knowledge. However, he does not accept *the God of the gaps*, that is, the argument that God is proved to exist by those very fundamental gaps in human scientific knowledge.

Like many scientists, Stenger refutes the *Argument from Design* on the basis that evolution and natural selection account for all aspects of the complexity we observe in the natural world. The continuing development of Charles Darwin's original theory has filled in some of the gaps and proved many of his predictions.

---

195 Stenger, V., *God: The Failed Hypothesis – How Science Shows That God Does Not Exist*, Prometheus, New York, 2007.

The theory of evolution is alive and well, and it is clear, not least due to the work on DNA, that Man is a direct descendent of members of the animal kingdom rather than being a separate life-form specifically created by God.

Stenger also sees no evidence of design. In fact, he quotes other scientists who believe that we, as humans, are badly designed, and offer various improvements that could be made. *"Indeed, Earth and life look just as they can be expected to look if there is no designer God."*[196]

He also can find no evidence that we are more than a physical body. Since chemicals and brain diseases can alter a person's experience and behaviour, it implies our thoughts and memories are a function of the physical brain. MRI and similar scans can see the changes in the brain when the subject is having particular experiences, and this confirms what science knows and can predict. Religious, spiritual, and out-of-body experiences can all be induced by chemicals and the effects can be observed in the physical brain. Neither these experiences nor ESP (extra-sensory perception) have been proved to occur naturally under proper scientific controls and observation. Likewise, alternative therapies and prayer have not been proven to work by science and so can be dismissed. As Stenger concludes,

> *"In short, after over a century of unsuccessful attempts to find convincing scientific evidence for the almost universally desired immortal and immaterial soul, it seems very unlikely that it, and a God who provides us with such a gift, exists."*[197]

Next, Stenger looks at the universe to see whether this needs God as a Creator. Energy and matter are interchangeable (Einstein's $E=mc^2$), and according to Stephen Hawking, the total energy in the universe is zero. This is because the negative gravitational energy equates to the positive energy/ matter in the universe. Thus, the universe could emerge from nothing at the

---

196 Stenger, Pg. 71
197 Stenger, Pg. 105

time of the Big Bang 14 billion years ago, and so there is no need for a Creator God.

On the fundamental question of why there is something (i.e., a universe) instead of nothing, Stenger argues that since simple systems of particles are very unstable, and *nothing* is the ultimate simplicity, the state of nothingness is inherently very unstable and so can easily flip into something! The transition from nothing to something is, therefore, natural. He then says, and I must quote this:

> *"Only by the constant action of an agent outside the universe, such as God, could a state of nothingness be maintained. The fact that we have something is just what we would expect if there was no God."*[198]

There are arguments on both sides with regard to the uniqueness of Earth. Some scientists say that Earth is extremely rare in that there are so many conditions that need to be in place in order for complex life to exist. Stenger mentions physicist Hugh Ross' statement that there are 33 characteristics a planet must have to support life, and that the probability of this combination is *"much less than one in a million trillion."*[199]

This brings us to the question of the universe being fine-tuned. Stenger identifies the five most significant factors, but then dismisses their significance. He argues that if God had created the universe for human life, we could expect it to be congenial to human life, which it clearly is not, except in a portion of one tiny planet in a huge and wasteful universe. Not only wasteful in space, God, if He existed, was wasteful with time too, taking nine billion years to make Earth, a further billion years to make life, followed by four billion years to make Man. On top of that, is the huge waste of energy in the universe. The fact there are few signs of complexity, little structure, and no signs of design in the universe, other than on Earth, as well as all this wastefulness proves to Stenger that there is no Creator, no God.

---

198 Stenger, Pg. 133
199 Stenger, Pg. 138

Even the moral argument does not stand up to scientific empirical evidence. There is no evidence that religious people are more moral than atheists. Even animals often show signs of moral behaviour, and it appears that our moral sense has developed by natural selection. There is no sign there is a God who told us how to be good. By contrast, the Old Testament, the New Testament, and the Koran are full of violence and instructions to do things which modern Man would not consider either moral or good.

Having looked at the evidence for and against God from many different angles, Victor Stenger concludes simply that God does not exist.

My Comment

Even this brief summary of Stenger's thesis contains a barrage of argument and would take considerable time and space to dispute point by point. I leave it to you to consider what points might have specific merit. Stenger does not consider consciousness as an important factor in this matter.

I accept that Stenger's arguments are mainly against the Judeo-Christian-Islamic God, rather than another type of God. Like many atheists and scientists, Stenger has focussed on this aspect of God, and has then extrapolated from there that there is no God at all.

The God Franchise shows that God is alive and well and is so present and so evident that the scientists have not seen the wood for the trees. They have looked for God but have not seen Him, even though He was standing right in front of them.

Because the universe could have derived from nothing, Stenger sees no need for God. I cannot get past the thought that there had to be some motivation for the Big Bang to occur, and that motivation was God.

As to Stenger's argument that if there was nothing it would prove the existence of God, but since there is something (a universe) this disproves Him, well, with all due respect, that is utter nonsense.

3. **The Hawking Argument.** Stephen Hawking[200] is particularly open in *A Briefer History of Time*[201] with regard to the question of God. The book provides a very clear (well, comparatively clear anyway) exposition of scientific thoughts about the universe. It follows and explains the theories of Newton, the general theory of relativity (Einstein), the Big Bang, black holes, the quantum theory, Heisenberg's uncertainty principle, Planck's constant, quantum mechanics, string theory, and the search for a complete unified theory that would explain the whole universe. This is all very well, but he does not answer the really hard questions with science, but allows God to be the answer.[202] He indicates it is difficult to explain why the universe is as it is without recourse to a God. He alludes to the intention of God, and even ends both the Brief and Briefer versions of the book with the much-quoted words, "mind of God." I see in Hawking's book the openness of an eminent present-day scientist prepared to admit that God is a viable Creator of the universe.

I also notice that Hawking fudges the science on the question of how life started. In one paragraph,[203] he covers the time period from when Earth was first formed through until today. He moves through evolution and natural selection to today's higher forms of life including human. As to what caused the initial spark of life, where matter moved from molecules of inert matter to living organisms, he is noticeably silent.

In his new book, *The Grand Design*, Stephen Hawking does attempt to dismiss God by saying: *"Spontaneous creation is the reason there is something rather than nothing, why the universe exists, why we exist.*

---

200 I use the name Hawking to simplify reference to the authors, who are Stephen Hawking **with** Leonard Mlodinow in the first book, and Stephen Hawking **and** Leonard Mlodinow in the second one, referenced shortly.

201 Hawking, S. with Mlodinow, L., *A Briefer History of Time*, Bantam Press, London, 2005. This is a clearer version for the layman of *A Brief History of Time* originally published in 1988, so written 17 years later.

202 Hawking, S. with Mlodinow, L., Pg. 73, 134 and 142 are good examples, which unfortunately I am unable to quote here.

203 Hawking, S. with Mlodinow, L., Pg. 83 – 84

It is not necessary to invoke God to light the blue touch paper and set the universe going."[204]

Let's take a brief look at some of the steps that Hawking takes to arrive at this conclusion. He is quick to clarify that realities can be described from different perspectives, and these are equally valid. As an example, he uses Ptolemy (c.85–c.165) and his geocentric (Earth at the centre) model of the universe as compared with Copernicus' (1473–1543) heliocentric (Sun at the centre) model. The real difference between the two models is the heliocentric model is far simpler. Hawking concludes, *"there is no picture- or theory-independent concept of reality."*[205]

Using the example of a goldfish, there is no reason why a goldfish could not formulate physical laws that describe its view of reality from inside a goldfish bowl. So, for example, an object following a straight line outside the bowl would appear to move along a curved path from the goldfish's viewpoint. *"Their laws would be more complicated than the laws in our frame, but simplicity is a matter of taste. If a goldfish formulated such a theory, we would have to admit the goldfish's view as a valid picture of reality."*[206]

An atom is the smallest part of physical matter you can see, even using the best modern equipment. Smaller particles such as electrons, protons, neutrons, and quarks are literally models of what may occur at the subatomic level. Scientists' observations and measurements have determined the best way of explaining how matter behaves is through the use of such a model, but one cannot say that is objective reality. Once again, the simpler the model, the more comfortable scientists are with its explanation of reality.

At this stage, there is no single theory of everything. For instance, Newtonian Laws and the theories of quantum physics

204 Hawking, S. and Mlodinow, L., *The Grand Design*, Bantam Press, London, 2010, Pg. 180 (UK and Commonwealth: Reprinted by permission of The Random House Group Limited. Rest of the world: Copyright © 2010 by Stephen W. Hawking and Leonard Mlodinow. Used by permission of Bantam Books, a division of Random House, Inc.).
205 Hawking, S. and Mlodinow, L., Pg. 42 (With permission)
206 Hawking, S. and Mlodinow, L., Pg. 39 (With permission)

are in conflict with each other. The unified theory of everything is the physicists' Holy Grail, a goal with which I completely identify (see this book's sub-title).

A commonly accepted model of the creation of the universe is the Big Bang theory that the universe started about 14 billion years ago. This seems to be a model that explains scientists' observations best. Hawking identifies that Newtonian Laws did not apply in the instant the universe started. However, applying quantum physics in the way described by Hawking just does not make sense. At the level of the particle, *"quantum physics tells us that no matter how thorough our observation of the present, the (unobserved) past, like the future, is indefinite and exists only as a spectrum of possibilities. The universe, according to quantum physics, has no single past, or history."*[207] The universe has no single past or history? I honestly don't know what to say ...

The theory is that a particle travels along all possible paths simultaneously, and it is possible to affect its destination retrospectively. The mathematics behind this is proved by empirical research. The data proves the theory. I cannot see how, even if particles behave that way, it means the universe on a macro level behaves that way. Newtonian theories are still valid at a macro level, and the past, therefore, can be expected to be a continuous sequence of specific events. I can't help but think these complex theories are similar to Ptolemy's geocentric model of the universe. This was proved by the data 1400 years later with the advent of Copernicus' heliocentric model, and turned out to be more complex than it needs to have been.

The quantum theory of electromagnetism, called quantum electrodynamics (QED), ends up with some infinite numbers in its formulae; to resolve that, renormalization is applied. As Hawking says, *"Renormalization is indeed, as it sounds, mathematically dubious."*[208]

As we delve deeper into quantum theory, we discover

---

207 Hawking, S. and Mlodinow, L., Pg. 82 (With permission)
208 Hawking, S. and Mlodinow, L., Pg. 107 (With permission)

baryons and mesons, made up of quarks, bosons (force-carrying particles), and W^+, W^- and Z^0 particles. Mesons are an unstable particle consisting of a quark and an anti-quark. The stable baryons (including protons and neutrons) consist of three quarks (with three anti-quarks forming the anti-particles of the baryons). Where does the complexity end?

In the search for a unified theory covering all four forces of nature (gravity, electromagnetism, weak nuclear force, and strong nuclear force), physicists have bumped up against imponderable difficulties. Infinite numbers get in the way again and again. String theory tries to come to the rescue, but it also requires many infinities, which hopefully cancel each other out. String theory requires that there be ten dimensions to space-time, but fortunately, those extra six dimensions are curved up into a very small space so we don't notice them! According to Hawking, there are millions of ways the extra dimensions could be curled up.

Resolving the five different string theories and the different ways the dimensions present themselves is a new theory called M-theory. With M-theory, physicists discovered that the calculation of ten space-time dimensions was incorrect. In fact, there are eleven! Because there are millions of ways to curl up the extra dimensions, it is necessary for M-theory to expect there to be multiple different universes with different laws in place. There could be up to 10^{500} universes — that is 1 followed by 500 zeroes, or in other words, the biggest number you have ever heard of other than infinity. It doesn't take much of a leap of faith to accept that one of those 10^{500} universes is our one, with the physical laws and constants we know and love. So why would we need God?

Hawking accepts that

"The emergence of the complex structures capable of supporting intelligent observers seems to be very fragile. The laws of nature form a system that is extremely fine-tuned, and very little in physical law can be altered without destroying the possibility of the development of life

as we know it. Were it not for a series of startling coincidences in the precise details of physical law, it seems, humans and similar life forms would never have come into being."[209]

He continues: *"Our universe and its laws appear to have a design that both is tailor-made to support us and, if we are to exist, leaves little room for alteration. That is not easily explained, and raises the natural question of why it is that way. Many people would like us to use these coincidences as evidence of the work of God."*[210]

However, Hawking explains that since all possible options of physical laws, universal constants, and environment are implicit in the 10^{500} universes available, as well as in the many billions of solar systems available in just our universe, there is nothing extraordinary about our universe springing from nothing 14 billion years ago. Nor is it surprising that just the right conditions were available to generate carbon from helium and then disperse it. Once our planet (and solar system) had formed, there was an opportunity for life to commence and for evolution to develop *Homo sapiens,* and subsequently, the intelligence and consciousness we have today.

It is true Hawking doesn't spell it out quite that way, but that is the implication. He sees the huge force of gravity present in the moments before the Big Bang as sufficient to set the process in motion. He also infers there was no time prior to the Big Bang since time is curved. You can't go further south than the South Pole due to the curvature of Earth, and so with time — you can't go back before the Big Bang due to the curvature of time. This is called the no-boundary condition.

My Comment

Hawking describes the universe as deterministic, that all physical events and conditions are determined by natural laws, and there is no room for intervention by God or other agencies. He does not consider the intervention of Man (and other living

---

209 Hawking, S. and Mlodinow, L., Pg. 161 (With permission)
210 Hawking, S. and Mlodinow, L., Pg. 162 (With permission)

things) who affect the environment through their own free will and consciousness. Consciousness is not a concept he takes into account at all. For the purposes of this discussion, I agree there is no need for the intervention of God to overrule the laws of nature. They are designed so well there is no need for intervention at a universal level. Whether God intervenes at a personal level is another discussion we have elsewhere, and even if He does, this does not invalidate the scientific view of the world. There is only one issue here: did God set the universe in motion or did it set itself in motion without any God being needed, or indeed existing?

It is interesting that Hawking concludes his book *The Grand Design* with the words,

> *"M-theory is the unified theory that Einstein was hoping to find. … If the theory is confirmed by observation, it will be the successful conclusion of a search going back more than 3,000 years. We will have found the grand design."*[211]

Whatever he specifically means by this, the words and book title *"The Grand Design"* implies a designer. M-theory may be true, but I, who am totally ignorant in such erudite science, doubt it is the final unified theory scientists have been searching for. However, this does not mean there was no designer or no need for a designer to conceive this grand design. On the contrary, it just confirms the complexity, clarity, and precision needed when designing a universe (or multiverse). Who better equipped to do this than God?

At this moment, I feel like the little boy who is about to point out that the emperor is naked. It appears to me that scientists often formulate their theories of the universe from a goldfish perspective. They come up with more complex theories than reality naturally demands. The M-theory is just one of those complex theories. Like Aristotle, scientists paste over inconsistencies in their laws. Rather than accept God as a simple

---

211 Hawking, S. and Mlodinow, L., Pg. 181 (With permission).

explanation, they come up with ever more complex theories to explain the universe in scientific terms.

Hawking started his book by stressing the importance of a simple elegant solution, and ends up with the unproven M-theory that has seven curved up dimensions we don't see. It also allows for 10^{500} universes of which our universe happens to be one because of the lucky happenstance that the laws of physics, universal constants, and environmental conditions matched the narrow band of requirements that make life, as we know it, possible and sustainable.

Occam's razor (the principle that entities are not to be multiplied beyond necessity) is a valued scientific principle. I ask, which is simpler here: an unproven M-theory with seven curved up dimensions we don't see, and allows for 10^{500} universes of which our universe happens to be one — or God, a single original Source of everything?

Before we move away from science, I would like to discuss the theory of evolution as that seems to be the mainstay of the scientists' argument. I will also introduce you to Kenneth R. Miller and his book *Finding Darwin's God*,[212] which after all my research, is the book that best describes the scientists' position and still leaves room for God. If you desire a clear understanding of the scientific arguments written in simple language, and without any apparent bias, I can offer no greater recommendation than Professor Miller's masterpiece.

---

212 Miller, K., *Finding Darwin's God: A Scientist's Search for Common Ground between God and Evolution*, HarperCollins, New York, 1999.

APPENDIX III

The Theory of Evolution

Through the ages, ever since scientific thought came on the scene and started to prove the universe was not quite as the Church had portrayed it, there has been friction between religion and science. Religion does not like being proved wrong, and in many cases cannot accept it is wrong. Apart from that, traditionally, the Church (Synagogue, Mosque, Temple) has had tremendous power over the hearts and minds (and purses) of the people, and they see that power being seized by science.

On the other hand, scientists have established the irrefutable proof of their theories, and so have determined the beliefs and teachings of the Church are misleading. Because they are men and women of intellect and logic, they see the beliefs and teachings of the Church as dangerous and mistaken, even as superstition. So the rift has grown. This difference in opinion has been intensified through distrust and misunderstanding, not only of the other side's position, but often of one's own side as well. Untenable beliefs, dogmas, theories, and positions have been adopted by both sides.

Let's discuss one of the most significant scientific discoveries, the theory of evolution. This theory[213] is accepted, as modified and developed over the past 150 years, by virtually everyone with any

---

213 A scientific theory is not what the layman often supposes, i.e., speculation. It is *"a set of hypotheses related by logical or mathematical arguments to explain and predict a wide variety of connected phenomena in general terms"* (*Collins English Dictionary*).

knowledge of science. Most of the opponents of the theory of evolution are those who misunderstand what it is saying, or who stubbornly believe it is contrary to a belief in God as Creator. It is not, but we will come to that shortly.

Charles Darwin

When Charles Darwin published *The Origin of Species*[214] in 1859, it caused an uproar, not least amongst the churchmen of the day. He continued to fine-tune his theories as well as answer his critics in subsequent editions. The final edition of the book in his lifetime, its 6th edition, was published in 1872, with final corrections made in 1876. Today, with some minor corrections, his theories still hold true and have been largely proved by continuing advances in biological and DNA research and discoveries. While the theory of evolution had already been broached by others, Darwin was the one who meticulously researched the evidence and presented it in detail. He also provided the mechanism by which evolution proceeds — natural selection.

Before Darwin, the idea generally held was that the various species of animals and plants were fixed species as set by God at the Creation. Darwin showed that new species could develop as modifications from previous species. What's more, nineteenth century geologists and palaeontologists had already proved through their research and fieldwork that Earth was millions of years old rather than the 6,000 years[215] of the Bible's account. This gave Darwin a suitably broad timeframe in which evolution could operate. Although some felt the biblical story related to just the last of a sequence of worldwide creations and extinctions, this idea was soon disproved by the discoveries that Man too had existed much longer than 6,000 years.

Let's get a little technical now, and discuss how genetics works in simple terms. Each species of plant or animal has a specific number

---

214 Darwin, C., *The Origin of Species by Means of Natural Selection, or The Preservation of Favoured Races in the Struggle for Life*, 6th Ed., John Murray, London, 1876 (Available: http://darwin-online.org.uk).

215 Bishop Ussher (1581-1656) calculated that the time of The Creation was at nightfall on the day before 23 October 4004 BC. Many others, including Sir Isaac Newton, have made similar calculations with similar results.

of chromosomes in its cells (e.g., fruit flies have four pairs and human beings have 23 pairs). The sex cells, however, only carry one chromosome of each pair. This means the offspring obtains one set of genes from the male and the other from the female, to make up the full complement. While 22 pairs of chromosomes are the same for men and women, the twenty-third pair is XX for women and XY for men. Thus, when the sex cells (gametes) are produced, the female ones (eggs) always have an X in this position, whereas the male ones (sperm) might be X or Y. The male thus determines the sex of the offspring through either an X sperm (daughter) or Y sperm (son). This principle is true for all mammals.

During meiosis (the cell division to produce the sex cells) there is a reshuffling of the chromosomes from those received from the father and mother (crossing over) so that the new sex cells in the offspring are a combination of the received chromosomes, rather than a duplication of either the father's or the mother's specific genes. Thus, variety is added through successive generations, while the overall species remains true to its essential characteristics. From time to time, mutations occur. These mutations are the fuel of evolution. Usually mutations are bad for the organism so the organism is unlikely to reproduce and pass it on (i.e., this is an element of natural selection). However, beneficial mutations enhance the organism so these benefits are likely to be passed on to new generations. New species form as these changes gradually accumulate through genetic variation and natural selection. Thus, all evolution is a combination of chance and the effects of natural selection (i.e., the process of useful variations tending to continue genetically as they have made the organism more successful economically, environmentally, and/or reproductively). Useless or impeding variations will naturally die out. Darwin wrote in his Introduction: *"I am convinced that Natural Selection has been the most important, but not the exclusive, means of modification."*[216]

Darwin also acknowledged the term "survival of the fittest" as an alternative to "natural selection." In the struggle for life, any genetic variations in an individual, which are advantageous, will naturally aid

---

216 Darwin, Pg. 4

the preservation of the individual, and will generally be passed on in the genes to the offspring. Thus, offspring will have the same advantage, and since only a comparatively small number of a species survive due to competition for limited food and other resources, those with the advantage are more likely to survive, and the variation is more likely to be passed on to subsequent generations. By the same token, a variation which gives a disadvantage would, for similar reasons, die out.

Virtually all plants and all animals have another species that either feeds on it or causes it to diminish by brute force. So there is a natural balance at play at all times, influenced by climatic conditions. This happens not only in the wild, but also in our backyards.

Darwin gives a great example in his research of bumblebees in his locality. These are essential to the fertilisation of heartsease and some kinds of clover. The number of bumblebees is often determined by field mice as these destroy their combs and nests, and the number of mice, in turn, is determined by the number of cats in the locality. *"Hence it is quite credible that the presence of feline animals in large numbers might determine, through the intervention first of mice and then of bees, the frequency of certain flowers in that district!"*[217] One can imagine how this plays out on a huge scale throughout nature.

Darwin clarified that it is not the natural selection that causes evolution: *"Several writers have misapprehended or objected to the term Natural Selection. Some have even imagined that natural selection induces variability, whereas it implies only the preservation of such variations as arise and are beneficial to the being under its conditions of life."*[218]

Philosopher and ex-atheist, Antony Flew, concurs in writing: *"... natural selection does not positively produce anything. It only eliminates, or tends to eliminate, whatever is not competitive. A variation does not need to bestow any actual competitive advantage in order to avoid elimination; it is sufficient that it does not burden its owner with any competitive disadvantage."*[219]

These two quotations clarify how mistaken the concept is that

---

217 Darwin, Pg. 58
218 Darwin, Pg. 63
219 Flew, A., *There Is a God: How the World's Most Notorious Atheist Changed His Mind*, HarperCollins, New York, 2007, Pg. 78. (Copyright © 2007 by Antony Flew. Reprinted by permission of HarperCollins Publishers.)

natural selection can, of itself, explain the complexity of life on Earth, including Man. If natural selection only eliminates what doesn't work, there needs to be some other force driving what does work. Rather than there being some sort of random trial of everything that might work and then eliminating what doesn't, there is far more likely to be a Designing Hand that impels the changes.

This is a brief discussion of evolution and natural selection as viewed by Darwin, and by and large, modern science continues to endorse his views. Some of the mechanisms had not yet been discovered, but in general, he was on the right track.

So, what did Darwin believe about God as Creator? He appeared to have given the Genesis account of the Creation a knockout blow, and that legacy has continued to this day as the two main camps of thought about the source of the universe seem to revolve around creationism (God) and Darwinism (no God).

In his conclusion to *The Origin of Species*, Darwin says, *"… science as yet throws no light on the far higher problem of the essence or origin of life."* He continues, *"I see no good reason why the views given in this volume should shock the religious feelings of anyone."*[220]

He subsequently quotes,

> *"A celebrated author and divine has written to me that 'he has gradually learnt to see that it is just as noble a conception of the Deity to believe that He created a few original forms capable of self-development into other and needful forms, as to believe that He required a fresh act of creation to supply the voids caused by the action of His laws.'"*[221]

Darwin concludes *The Origin of Species* with the following words:

> *"Thus, from the war of nature, from famine and death, the most exalted object which we are capable of conceiving, namely the production of the higher animals, directly follows. There is grandeur in this view of life, with its several powers, having been originally breathed by the Creator into a few forms or into*

---

220 Darwin, Pg. 421
221 Darwin, Pg. 422

one; and that, whilst this planet has gone cycling on according to the fixed law of gravity, from so simple a beginning endless forms most beautiful and most wonderful have been and are being evolved."[222]

Darwin was not arguing against the existence of God nor of His role as Creator of the universe. His main point was that from his study of plants and animals it was obvious God had not created individual species at a comparatively recent time (i.e., 6,000 years ago according to the Bible). Rather, He had created the original source of life, and that evolution, with natural selection and other factors, had evolved the world into the one we know today.

There is no reason for religious people or those who believe in the Creation to fear the theory of evolution. In truth, it shows what an awe-inspiring event Creation was. Instead of creating a vast number of different species individually, God created the mechanism whereby creatures that best suited the environment were able, through evolution and natural selection, to develop into the vast array of species and individuals we see today. The theory of evolution is recognition of an extremely important aspect of the feat of Creation.

Richard Dawkins

In 1976, Richard Dawkins, confirmed atheist and then University Lecturer in Zoology at New College, Oxford, burst onto the scene with the first of his popular science books, *The Selfish Gene*. This book developed Darwin's theory of evolution from the perspective of the gene, showing that its success is of primary importance, even more so than the success of the organism itself. It popularised aspects of Neo-Darwinism that had been pioneered in the 1930s and developed in the 1960s.

In *The Selfish Gene*, Dawkins offers a view of how the universe started. While the theory of evolution explains what happened after the first life form began life, it does not explain what happened to get to that first step. He says:

"In the beginning was simplicity. It is difficult enough explaining how even a simple universe began. I take it as agreed that it would be even harder

---

222 Darwin, Pg. 429

to explain the sudden springing up, fully armed, of complex order – life, or a being capable of creating life."[223]

This is an interesting start to the subject. Dawkins says, *"In the beginning was simplicity."* Genesis says, *"In the beginning God created the heaven and the earth."*[224] This seems like (and is) the simple answer. Dawkins then assumes that we, the reader, would agree it is harder to explain the sudden appearance of *"complex order – life, or a being capable of creating life."* While I agree it would be hard to accept the sudden appearance of life, this appears to me to be exactly what Dawkins and other scientists want us to believe — that a group of molecules at some stage did spring into life and that life was able to evolve into the complex beings in the world today, including Man. We will discuss this further shortly.

The other point, though, is Dawkins sees it as *even harder to explain the sudden springing up, fully armed, of … a being capable of creating life.* Once again, I agree; it would be. However, he overlooks the only other possibility: God already existed before the start of life on Earth, and He had no need to spring up as He is eternal. He would then be in a position to enable life to begin on Earth, even if He used the tools of evolution and natural selection to achieve it.

Evolution is all about genes, so let's briefly talk about them. All living things (all plants and all animals) are built up from cells. An amoeba is a single-celled creature, whereas Man is made up of about 50 to 100 trillion (50 to 100 million million) cells depending on the source you look up, and the size of the person, since a big person doesn't have bigger cells, just more of them.

There are about 200 different cell types in the human body, each differing in its size, shape, and function. Each cell has many different components, each with their own purpose. One of these components is the nucleus, and within that is the chromatin made up of DNA (a double helix) and histone proteins. The purpose of DNA is to store and replicate genetic information accurately, and to provide instructions for building protein (including enzymes). This is the genetic code. Within

---

223 Dawkins, R., *The Selfish Gene*, (30ᵗʰ Anniversary Edition), Oxford University Press, Oxford, 2006, Pg. 12 (By permission of Oxford University Press).
224 *Genesis* 1:1

a species, there is about 99.9 percent commonality of DNA structure as that is what determines the species, but no two individuals in that species have identical DNA, unless they are identical twins. This is why DNA profiling in criminal or paternity cases is possible.

The point I want to make is that DNA is incredible in the way it works. If you study any detailed book of biology, anatomy, and/or physiology, you will be struck with wonder at the level of complexity in the way things work. Take a look at how muscles work, or the eye, or the ear. It is difficult to consider that this universe is the result of random mutations and natural selection rather than the result of deliberate design. Sure, we can tweak the genetics of wheat to make it more disease resistant, or of cattle to make them grow faster. However, left to nature, most mutations or genetic hiccups are not helpful, but leave the plant or animal disabled in some way. DNA is stable and is not likely to mutate unless something goes wrong. Even then, the error is naturally corrected if possible.

Look at the different animals that are around today. There are many with four limbs such as mammals, including humans. There are birds with two wings and two legs, and there are insects with six legs and arachnids with eight legs. There are slithering things like snakes and worms. There are similar things with lots of legs like caterpillars and millipedes. There are fish with fins and gills. If you look at these classes of creatures, you see extensive similarities. Didn't dinosaurs have four legs with a head at one end and a tail at the other? Aren't insects ancient creatures? Ancient plants are, in essence, not much different from modern plants. Could we not expect them to be very different? If random mutations caused these creatures and plants, why are they not more diverse after 3.5 billion years of evolution? And why are they not more bizarre by now?

Kenneth Miller

While it is tempting to look at a Creator or Designer for the incredible complexity and functionality we see in the world around us, it is extremely interesting to read the view of Professor Kenneth Miller. He is a cell biologist and has a personal interest in bridging the apparent gap between an acceptance of the scientific truths of evolution and an acceptance of and faith in God. Miller concludes in his fascinating book, *Finding Darwin's God*,[225] that the answer to the question whether God and evolution can coexist is a resounding **yes**.

One reason religionists find evolution repugnant is that it shows our own species *Homo sapiens* evolved from the same roots as chimpanzees, gorillas, and other apes, and even further back to the same branch as monkeys, and of course other mammals. Our nearest living relatives are the chimpanzee and the bonobo, the pygmy chimpanzee. We share between 96 and 98.6 percent of the same DNA with them, depending on how you interpret the data. Christians, for instance, like to believe the Bible, the Word of God, is correct in saying *"God created man in his own image."*[226] So how could he be the subject of evolution like any other animal? We know we are more special than that!

As a researcher in cell biology, Miller can say with authority, *"evolution can generate lots of beneficial mutations — so many, in fact, that we can say that the evolutionary mechanism is not only real, but a downright nuisance."*[227] He cites as an example the ability of bacteria to mutate and then allow natural selection to ensure only bacteria resistant to antibiotics survive. This is true too with unwanted plants that become resistant to pesticides, and the HIV virus (that causes AIDS) which spontaneously mutated varieties that are (HIV-protease blocker) drug resistant.

As Miller sees it, the creationists are proved wrong by the sheer force of data establishing that Earth is about 4.5 billion years old; life has been around for about 3.5 billion years, and Man (*Homo sapiens*) for about 150,000 years. The process of evolution has been recorded consistently in rock strata. Contemporary species have been preserved and fossilised leaving a clear record of their chronology. If, as creationists would have it, these layers were laid down after Noah's Flood (c.2300 BC) the sequence of animals and plants would not have been consistently layered. Such geological layering would have been impossible. Instead, a credible record of evolution has been preserved.

---

225 Miller, K., *Finding Darwin's God: A Scientist's Search for Common Ground between God and Evolution*, HarperCollins, New York, 1999. (Copyright © 1999 by Kenneth R. Miller. Reprinted by permission of HarperCollins Publishers.)
226 *Genesis* 1:27
227 Miller, Pg. 49

The only way this data could be consistent with the Creation would be if God set out to deceive us, and that would make God a charlatan.

Intelligent design is a tempting solution to the creation vs. evolution argument. For those who find the six-day creation scenario of the Bible just a little hard to take, and still cannot believe we are nothing more than chance clusters of cells that somehow managed to evolve into the complex human and natural kingdoms we see around us today, intelligent design appeals. There is an intelligent designer who created us over millions of years without the need for evolution. This resolves the irreducible complexities such as the eye and ear, where there are a number of components needed to carry out a function, so apparently these could not be the result of evolution. Likewise, the complexity of DNA indicates an intelligent designer rather than a result of natural selection.

Unfortunately, it is not that simple since there are many signs in present day animals and humans of the evolutionary steps the species have taken. There are also many similarities between different species along with apparently redundant *technology*. It would be logical that an intelligent designer would be able to develop each species from a clean slate with a unique and proficient set of *components*. For instance, the human backbone is more suited to a four-legged animal than to an upright two-legged human. Evolutionists have identified many flaws in the human body and feel they could do a better job of designing the human body themselves. This is one of the reasons they disparage both creationism and intelligent design — they don't think God did a particularly good job, so why believe that He exists?

It is interesting that when species die out, they are replaced by species that seem to be based on the previous species. This fact makes sense under evolution, but does not when an intelligent designer would have the opportunity to design a new species from the ground up. Ninety-nine percent of species have already died out, and the average mammalian species lasts about two million years. Insect species last about 3.6 million and marine invertebrates 3.4 million years.[228] Also, why would an intelligent designer focus on specific groups of species in

---

228 Miller, Pg. 102

the specific geological periods? There seems to be a definite sequence of plant, fish, and animal species that point to evolution rather than the free will potential of an intelligent designer.

Throughout the chapter on intelligent design, Miller produces numerous arguments for evolution and against intelligent design. Having reviewed intelligent design in detail, he has found it wanting. As he concludes,

> *"Intelligent design does a terrible disservice to God by casting him as a magician who periodically creates and creates and then creates again throughout the geologic ages. ... Why did this magician, in order to produce the contemporary world, find it necessary to create and destroy creatures, habitats, and ecosystems millions of times over?"*[229]

Miller continues systematically through the alternative theories in his book. His next topic is God, the mechanic, where he discusses and refutes the arguments that there are irreducibly complex systems in the body. If there is a system where the parts all had to be present in order for the system to work, and there was no purpose for the intermediary steps, then, so the argument goes, natural selection could not have produced the complex system. Even Darwin could not explain this. This is a good argument, but as Miller points out, there is no evidence that points to irreducibly complex systems. An example is the five-component system of malleus, incus, and stapes (hammer, anvil, and stirrup) between the eardrum and the oval window, which passes sound from the eardrum to the inner ear while protecting the inner ear from excessively loud sounds.

Miller shows how these various components have been seen in fossils over millions of years, and that these early ears worked more simply than ears do now. They slowly adapted using nearby components to improve the hearing system. Evolution can certainly account for this apparent irreducibly complex system, and Miller indicates the same is true of all other examples put forward. Further proof has been demonstrated in the laboratory under the careful eye of biochemists. Even the complex eight-step Krebs cycle (citric acid

---

229 Miller, Pg. 128

cycle), which oxidises glucose to provide energy to the cells of the body, as well as producing various useful by-products, has been explained in evolutionary terms.

So why do we need God? Doesn't evolution explain everything? Could God have created the universe, including setting up the resources for evolution to progress, and then retired? Or died? The deist believes the universe was created, but God no longer takes an active role in it. Religion naturally rejects this idea, as they believe God is still available as an active part of our daily lives. The danger too of a deistic universe is that the result is too mechanistic and predictable, working as clockwork.

The development of quantum theory showed physics at a micro level is far from mechanistic, and the effects of unpredictability flow into the macro universe in which we live and move. Mutations in DNA are random events triggered by events at a quantum level, which means that evolution is driven in an unpredictable fashion.[230] As Miller clarifies, randomness is not the same as unpredictability. It is not a case that anything can happen, but rather that we cannot predict what will happen from a specific number of possibilities. This situation, far from being unpalatable, is in fact, the only thing that saves us from living in a totally predictable and clockwork-like world. Quantum theory principles prove events are not predictable, and while this does not prove the existence of God, it does allow for God to be working through the medium of these principles.

Science has slowly but very surely chipped away at all the principles held dear by anti-evolutionists. This has only made them dig their defences more deeply. At each step, the apparent inability of science to explain some aspect of the process of evolution has given them the opportunity to use God as the only possible explanation. When science has moved on and discovered the physical mechanism involved, the anti-evolutionists have just pointed to other gaps in scientific knowledge. God became a *God of the gaps*. Now, in the twenty-first

---

230 Perhaps, just perhaps, the quantum level unpredictability which is driving evolution is, in truth, being driven by God. Perhaps, this is one way in which He can choose to interfere in the evolution of life on Earth without being noticed by scientists!

century, it has become untenable to disregard the theory of evolution.

Unfortunately, there still remain opposing points of view. Atheists see no need for God, and believe evolution has conclusively explained how life has developed without God's interference. Creationists still hold to the view that God created the various species of plants and animals, as well as Man himself, as a specific individual creative act, or series of such acts. As Miller points out, these creationists accept the biology of today; for example, the development of a single fertilised egg cell into a complex multicellular organism such as a human, without any need to call on the direct interference of God in the process.

While they accept that a purely material explanation of this process is possible today, and maintain that God is all powerful and omnipresent today, they cannot accept that the scientifically described processes of the theory of evolution, a purely material explanation for the evolution of life, could have been designed or initiated by the same omnipotent and omnipresent God in the past.

Neither Miller nor I can accept that either of these views adequately explains reality. Rather, we have joined the many who believe the theory of evolution merely explains the methodology God has used to diversify the many forms of life that exist and have existed since life first appeared on Earth 3.5 billion years ago. Science and the theory of evolution cannot be dismissed. While there may be errors in some of the details, over time, these will be resolved. This is the nature of the scientific method. Therefore, we can accept the theory of evolution as being true, and still see a role for God in the design and *creation* of the universe. A role? As explained in the main text, without the Will of God, there would be no universe, and you and I certainly wouldn't be here debating it.

While we have only touched the surface of Professor Miller's *Finding Darwin's God*, I genuinely hope this taster will encourage you to read and contemplate his work. It is fascinating and sensible, and lots of fun along the way. While his conclusion with regard to the nature of God and the universe differs from **The God Franchise** concept, he very clearly demonstrates there is a place for both evolution and God.

Now let's see what the theists have to say about God and the universe.

APPENDIX IV

The Theists' Case

Now that we have covered (and largely refuted) the case against there being a God, let's take a look at a few of the proofs that have been offered to support the existence of God. A *theist* in the loosest sense is someone who believes in God or multiple gods, or says that God does exist. Granted, there are numerous belief systems to choose from today, and theoretically, they cannot all be correct, as there should be only one Truth — however, which one it is remains a question of personal opinion. We will take a broad approach, and then take a look at the arguments for God raised by Keith Ward, one of Britain's leading philosopher-theologians.

1. **The Five Ways** of St Thomas Aquinas (1225-1274) were set out in his book *Summa Theologica*. They are:

    +   **The Argument of the Unmoved Mover**. Everything in the universe with the potential to move can only actually move when something else causes it to move. If this is sequentially followed back to the beginning of time, there could be no first initiating cause of movement. Therefore, there has to be a first mover, and that first mover is known as God.

    +   **The Argument of the First Cause**. Every effect has a cause, and if this is sequentially followed back to the beginning of time, there could be no first cause to set the sequence going. There needs to be a first cause, and that first cause is known as God.

+ **The Argument from Contingency.** All things can possibly be or not be, and in order for them to be, they need to be generated. If at any time nothing existed, there would have been no starting point. Also as said above, if each thing coming into being is dependent on a prior thing, and this is sequentially followed back to the beginning of time, there could be no initiating cause to generate the first thing. There needs to be a first generator, and that first generator is known as God.

+ **The Argument from Degree.** Every being has degrees of good qualities. The being with the best of all these qualities, which are able to be passed on to others, is the one we call God.

+ **The Teleological Argument (or Argument from Design).** Things that lack intelligence still act towards an end. This is not fortuitous, but must have been through intelligent direction. Therefore, an intelligent being must exist that directs all natural things to their end, and this we call God.

The Five Ways of St Thomas Aquinas is the essential argument for God and is quoted or commented on by many (if not most) writers on this subject. Richard Dawkins pours scorn on the arguments in *The God Delusion*,[231] however, he achieves his points by restating the arguments in his own terms and then shooting them down. Keith Ward in his book, which we cover in some depth shortly, devotes a whole chapter to supporting the Five Ways arguments.

My Comment

The first three arguments are infinite regresses, and St Thomas Aquinas accepts that God is the only possible terminator of this sequence. Since there has to be an initiating mover, cause, and generator or we would not exist, there has to have been one. As science has proved, there needs to be an initiating factor to every movement and effect, and also to being itself. This initiating

---

231 Dawkins, R., *The God Delusion*, Bantam Press, London, 2006. Pg. 100 – 103.

factor cannot have been moved, caused, or generated itself as it is the first initiator; therefore, it needs to be something greater than subsequent movements (or movers), effects (or causes), and being (or generators) in order to be the first one.

This first initiator also needs to have the potential of all subsequent steps built into it. It is, therefore, more powerful than any subsequent step and can thus be called omnipotent. Even if it cannot do absolutely everything, as Dawkins claims it couldn't, being the most powerful possible thing is a force worthy of our awe. One could, therefore, reasonably call it God. Since an initiating force is before time (since time implies change), and is uninitiated itself, it has to be eternal and outside time.

Since all physical things have a physical initiator, well at least once they are started, it makes sense that the prime initiator is non-physical. Anything that is held as a concept rather than as a physical entity is mind, or rather, consciousness. Since the initiating consciousness seems to have initiated a rather special and coherent universe, to expect it to have omniscience and intelligence is not unreasonable, and we can reasonably call it God.

Naturally, the words omnipotence and omniscience can sensibly be limited to what is logical or reasonable for them to mean. Thus, as Ward points out, God cannot commit suicide or change the past.

"Which came first, the chicken or the egg?" is not a childish question — it is conceivably the deepest question that can be asked. There is only one possible answer — God came first.

2. **The Fine-tuned Universe** is the concept that the conditions required to allow life and the physical structure of the universe to exist are in fact supported by a number of fundamental scientific constants that lie within a small range of possibilities. Martin Rees (the Astronomer Royal) discusses six of these in his absorbing book *Just Six Numbers*.[232] Therefore, it is claimed,

---

232 Rees, M., *Just Six Numbers: The Deep Forces that Shape the Universe*, Basic Books, New York, 2001. These are discussed in detail in Chapter 15.

God must exist as He must have fine-tuned the universe, and it could not have happened by chance. This argument is used by the intelligent design proponents as well.

3.   **The Argument from Morality** states that most people have a moral ethic, and the original source of that morality and our conscience is more likely to be God. So God must exist. There are similar arguments for beauty, love, and religious experience.

4.   **The Argument from Reason** states briefly:

+   To be able to assess truth, one needs to be rational.
+   A being of purely physical origin cannot be rational.
+   A human can assess truth, so is more than physical matter.
+   The ability of humans to assess truth must come from a rational source that is also not just physical.
+   Rationality cannot arise from non-rationality, nor can it arise from nothing.
+   There must be a rational being from which humans obtained their rationality.
+   This being is called God.

5.   **The Argument from Personal Experience** is a hard one to counter, but unfortunately cannot be given much weight. The individual who has received a visitation or heard a voice and firmly believes this was God or Jesus or the Virgin Mary, is unable to be swayed from this view. However, unless there were witnesses who could honestly corroborate each other's stories, or some other evidence, it is understandable there will be many others who will not believe this is proof of the existence of God. The mind can be tricky.

6.   **The Argument from the Scriptures** is that the scriptures are the Word of God and, therefore, must be taken as true.

Aside from **The Five Ways** of St Thomas Aquinas, which I find particularly compelling, these arguments are reasonable, but not particularly conclusive. However, for some particularly strong arguments supporting the case for the existence of God, I have found none better than the arguments of Professor Keith Ward.

Keith Ward

Keith Ward writes simply and in good humour in his book *Why There Almost Certainly Is a God*,[233] and I recommend this short book to anyone who doubts the existence of God. While it was written as a foil to Richards Dawkins' atheistic *The God Delusion*, which we have already discussed, it stands independently. Until you get the chance to read Keith Ward's masterpiece in logic and common sense, here is a taster of some of the points he makes.

Is intelligent mind or consciousness the ultimate nature of reality, or is it the unforeseen and unintended result of material evolution? Is there any evidence that consciousness could not exist without the material brain, or that consciousness has to be just as humans experience it? To the contrary, everything points to consciousness being beyond what can be explained by science.

The existence of a divine consciousness vastly superior to the human experience of consciousness is just as credible as consciousness having somehow arisen through evolution. *"The question of God is the question of whether conscious mind can exist without any physical body, and whether that mind could account for the origin and nature of our universe."*[234] Scientists allow for other universes, other space-time continuums, and other sets of physical laws outside our universe, so allowing for consciousness outside our physical universe should not be a stretch for them.

The argument comes down to whether the ultimate reality of all there is in the universe is *materiality* or *consciousness*. Scientists can measure and explain materiality to a large and increasing extent, but they cannot explain consciousness. They expect to explain God scientifically and fail. They, therefore, conclude He is unnecessary and

---

233 Ward, K., *Why There Almost Certainly Is a God: Doubting Dawkins*, Lion Hudson, Oxford, 2008. The title of this book is not an uncertainty in Professor Ward's beliefs but a play on the name of Richard Dawkins' chapter in *The God Delusion* entitled *Why there almost certainly is no God*.

234 Ward, Pg. 19 (Extract taken from *Why There Almost Certainly Is a God* by Keith Ward, published by Lion Hudson plc, 2008. Copyright 2008 Keith Ward. Used with permission of Lion Hudson plc.)

does not exist. On the other hand, if you take consciousness as the ultimate reality, and accept God as eternal consciousness, it is feasible that consciousness could have been responsible for designing and creating the physical universe, including all the laws and other aspects discovered and expected by scientists.

Keith Ward addresses the argument that the laws of nature ensure evolution occurs through the processes of random mutation and survival of the fittest. The explanation of God being the designer of those laws of nature to achieve that evolutionary aim is reasonable. It is also the only one that overcomes the immense improbability of the universe reaching its current state purely through a sequence of random steps, even if there are an incalculable number of small steps. Bear in mind too that evolution without God as a Designer would be purposeless, so there would be no goal in even one of the random evolutionary steps taken. As Ward says, *"The chances of [blind and gradual selection] doing so, given all the alternative paths of evolution there are, still seem to be astronomically small. Unless, that is, the laws governing the sorts of mutation that occur have been carefully worked out beforehand."*[235]

If physical laws, environmental conditions, and the universal constants that exist had been even slightly different, it would have been impossible for the universe to hold together, for life to exist, or for it to have evolved in the way it has. It is because of this, and the fact that it is so entirely improbable that things are as they are in the universe, that makes the simple explanation of a Designer so elegant.

As we have previously observed, Richard Dawkins says, *"any creative intelligence, of sufficient complexity to design anything, comes into existence only as the end product of an extended process of gradual evolution. Creative intelligences, being evolved, necessarily arrive late in the universe, and therefore cannot be responsible for designing it."*[236]

Keith Ward challenges that God is complex, firstly on the grounds that God is not made up of separate parts, but is one consciousness unhampered by physical form. Secondly, God is simple in that His Mind can be expected to work both elegantly and rationally. Thirdly,

---

235 Ward, Pg. 37 (With permission)
236 Dawkins, Pg. 52

since God is assumed to be the only cause of everything except Himself, and since God is eternal and not evolved, this satisfies Occam's razor in that this solution does not multiply entities unnecessarily.

Dawkins' concern that *"Creative intelligences, being evolved, necessarily arrive late in the universe"* is a fallacy. God is not evolved — He is eternal. This means the question of who made God is not relevant. He existed before time and will exist after time has ended. There is nothing illogical about this because why should consciousness, especially the most supreme consciousness, not be outside time? The principles of sequential cause and effect no longer apply since there is no need for a cause for something that has always existed.

One solution, offered by scientists to cover the need for very specific physical laws, environmental conditions, and the universal constants, is to allow that all possible universes exist. This is the multiverse solution. In that way, our universe with its specific needs is easily accounted for, and there is no need for there to be any designer. Even Dawkins baulks at the extravagant number of universes this theory presents, and I like Keith Ward's dry comment, *"I agree with Dawkins that it would be preferable to have a simpler, less extravagant theory, if we could. Luckily, such a theory exists. It is God."*[237]

Regarding the God of the Old Testament, Ward makes the very valid point: to the sensibilities of those days, the God described was *"the best sort of God – the ideal of moral perfection – that the people of the time could imagine."*[238] So, our abhorrence today at the concept of a jealous, angry God who demanded sacrifices is unjustified. Those days are past, and the God of today is painted (in most churches) as a loving, caring, just, merciful, forgiving, and healing God. These concepts and beliefs are Man's of course, so let us not be indignant about what Man thought and believed in the distant past. In addition, let us not allow even today's supposed qualities of God to hijack this discussion.

The question of how anything can bring into existence something else is one that must be faced. This is most difficult to explain if one's starting point is purely physical. There is just no logical explanation.

237 Ward Pg. 57 (With permission)
238 Ward Pg. 64 (With permission)

However, if one starts from consciousness or the Mind of God, it is much more feasible that the laws and mechanisms necessary to cause that creation can be designed and executed. As we know, with the human mind, any number of possibilities can be devised and the best possible solution can be executed and materialised. Therefore, with the vastly superior consciousness and mind that would be God's, it is easy to understand there would be few if any constraints placed upon what could be achieved.

As I have said, I find Professor Keith Ward's ideas to be utterly conclusive and beautifully presented. If you are not convinced that God exists, in whatever *form* you like, I invite you to read his book, *Why There Almost Certainly Is a God*. That is, if you are brave enough.

You could also read the next appendix where we meet three men who were atheists for many years before realising that yes, there is a God after all.

APPENDIX V

Changing Horses

We have considered the atheistic, scientific, and theistic viewpoints on the existence of God. Scientists often sit in the space between atheism and theism because they believe strongly in what their science tells them, and they can find no specific evidence of God they can measure or include in their formulae and theories. God somehow seems to be redundant. Nevertheless, scientist/writers like Francis Collins and Alister McGrath have changed sides, from atheism to Christianity. Francis Collins has written the very interesting book *The Language of God: A Scientist Presents Evidence for Belief*.[239] He is a leading geneticist who was leader of the Human Genome Project. While he passed through the phases of being an agnostic and an atheist, he is now a committed Christian. Likewise, Alister McGrath was a researcher in molecular biophysics before studying Christian theology and becoming a committed Christian. However, it is Antony Flew's change of heart I would like to discuss first.

Antony Flew

Antony Flew is a renowned philosopher, and up until 2004, was a committed atheist. He has always followed the directive Plato attributed

---

239 Collins, F., *The Language of God: A Scientist Presents Evidence for Belief,* Simon & Schuster, London, 2007.

to Socrates to *"follow the argument wherever it leads."*[240] In following the facts and developing his understanding, Antony Flew finally came to the conclusion that God does exist, as expressed in his 2007 book, *There is a God.* I am unable to do his work justice here, but would like to mention some of the points he makes. I recommend this book to anyone who would like to follow the detail of his reasoning. It is a short book, providing an overview of his atheistic writings, followed by a detailed exposition of his theistic revelations. These are enthralling and utterly convincing.

Flew identifies three aspects of nature that indicate there is a God:

+ Nature obeys natural laws. How did the laws of nature arise?
+ The development of life and intelligent, organised, purpose-driven beings. How did life originate from non-life? What about reproduction?
+ The very existence of nature. How did the universe come into existence?

By the laws of nature, we mean there is regularity and symmetry in nature. This has led to the discovery of laws such as Newton's Laws of Motion, The Laws of Thermodynamics, and the General Theory of Relativity — indeed, this regularity applies to all laws of physics and chemistry. As Flew says, *"The important point is not merely that there are regularities in nature, but that these regularities are mathematically precise, universal, and 'tied together'."*[241] So, what has caused this regularity and symmetry? The only answer anyone has been able to muster is, *The Mind of God.*

The fine-tuning of the physical attributes of the universe seems remarkable, and not by chance. If the natural laws themselves somehow evolved, they would have had to follow some underlying

---

240 Flew, A., *There Is a God: How the World's Most Notorious Atheist Changed His Mind*, HarperCollins, New York, 2007, Pg. 23. (Copyright © 2007 by Antony Flew. Reprinted by permission of HarperCollins Publishers.)
Here Flew refers to Plato's *Republic* 394d: *"whithersoever the wind, as it were, of the argument blows, there lies our course,"* written c.380 BC.
241 Flew Pg. 96

laws for there to be the consistency we observe. We have already discussed this briefly, and the obvious answer is the universe has been designed specifically to be able to support life and the development of consciousness and intelligence. The only reasonable alternative is there are multiple universes (a multiverse) with different physical laws and ours just happens to support life and consciousness. This sounds like a complicated solution and explains nothing. Even if there are multiple parallel universes, this does not preclude the existence of a designer, God Himself.

Flew next asks: *"How can a universe of mindless matter produce beings with intrinsic ends, self-replication capabilities, and 'coded chemistry'?"* [242] Living beings have an inherent organisation to fulfil certain goals, whereas mindless matter does not. Likewise, the ability to reproduce is something that is unique to living beings, so how did this arise from matter that did not reproduce? DNA is the foundation of all living matter, but how did this complex genetic coding system start? No one has determined the underlying physical principles required to enable this to occur. Protobiologists may be trying to find the answers to these questions, but they have failed to do so yet. The only appropriate solution is that an infinitely intelligent Mind designed and created life. In other words, God.

The third big subject is, how did the universe apparently come out of nothing? Most scientists agree the universe did have a beginning, rather than it just being a fundamental and ultimate fact. If the universe did have a beginning, what caused it to spontaneously arise from nothing? Bear in mind that *nothing* has absolutely no qualities or content, but is a complete and absolute absence of anything. Flew quotes Richard Swinburne[243] to give a definitive summary of the cosmological argument. As he points out, it is more likely God exists uncaused than for the universe to exist uncaused.

As an appendix to his book, Antony Flew includes a paper by Roy

---

242 Flew, Pg. 124
243 Flew, Pg. 144 quoting Swinburne, R., *The Existence of God*, Clarendon, Oxford, 2004, Pg. 152.

Abraham Varghese.[244] This paper includes some very relevant points as a counter to the atheistic approach. Varghese argues that the *New Atheists* fail to make a case that there is no God, and also *"ignore the very phenomena that are particularly relevant to the question of whether God exists."*[245] He then lists the five phenomena that *"are evident in our immediate experience that can only be explained in terms of the existence of God."*

+ *"The rationality implicit in all our experience of the physical world"*
+ *"Life, the capacity to act autonomously"*
+ *"Consciousness, the ability to be aware"*
+ *"Conceptual thought, the power of articulating and understanding meaningful symbols such as are embedded in language"*
+ *"The human self, the 'center' of consciousness, thought and action."*[246]

While these phenomena we experience daily do not prove the existence of God, they can be said to presuppose the eternal consciousness we have called God. If atheists say there is no evidence of the existence of God, one might ask what more evidence does one need than these five phenomena that form a part of our everyday lives?

Varghese points out that we would never expect a marble table to gain consciousness, or a sense of self, even given infinite time to do so. *"But the atheist position is that, at some point in the history of the universe, the impossible and the inconceivable took place."*[247] The impossibility of this table suddenly, or gradually, gaining consciousness, a mind, and a sense of self, extends to all other matter on Earth and in the universe.

Francis Collins

Now, let's meet Francis Collins, a scientist who changed his beliefs from atheism to a belief in God. His recent book is *The Language of*

---

244 Varghese, R., *The 'New Atheism': A Critical Appraisal of Dawkins,* Dennett, Wolpert, Harris, and Stenger, published as an appendix to Flew, A., *There Is a God: How the World's Most Notorious Atheist Changed His Mind,* HarperCollins, New York, 2007, Pg. 161 – 183. (Copyright © 2007 by Antony Flew. Reprinted by permission of HarperCollins Publishers.)
245 Varghese, Pg. 161
246 Varghese, Pg. 161-162
247 Varghese, Pg. 163

God: A Scientist Presents Evidence for Belief[248] The book follows many of the arguments we have already covered, although Collins brings considerable scientific detail to the table. It was the beauty and depth he saw in the universe through his scientific studies and research that led him to re-evaluate his faith. He literally came to the stage where he could not accept that the universe he was seeing could have come into being without a Designer God behind it.

Nevertheless, Collins sees that if there is only one Truth, then both religion and science should be compatible with it. To support this view, and following the mass of e-mails and support he got for his book, *The Language of God,* in 2009, he founded The BioLogos Foundation[249] to bring science and religion closer together.

The historic term for his philosophy is perhaps *Theistic Evolution,* since it is evolution with the guiding hand of a loving God behind it. However, Francis Collins coined the name BioLogos as he felt the terms *theistic* and *evolution* perhaps came with too many preconceptions.

Alister McGrath

Finally, let's refer to Alister McGrath's 2007 book, *The Dawkins Delusion?*[250], written with his wife, Joanna Collicutt McGrath. McGrath, a professor at Oxford University, as is Richard Dawkins, felt it was necessary to provide a rebuttal of Richard Dawkins' *The God Delusion,* as its aggressive, anti-religious, atheist fundamentalism had strayed so far from Dawkins' usual, carefully argued writings.

Dawkins made the point that our existence is very improbable, and therefore, God, whose existence must be even more complex than ours, must be even more improbable. McGrath neatly points out that more complexity does not necessarily increase improbability. *"We may be highly improbable – **yet we are here**. The issue, then, is not whether God is **probable**, but whether God is **actual**."*[251] Commenting on the old chestnut

---

248 Collins, F., *The Language of God: A Scientist Presents Evidence for Belief,* Simon & Schuster, London, 2007.

249 Please see their website for more details of BioLogos — http://biologos.org/

250 McGrath, A. with McGrath J., *The Dawkins Delusion?: Atheist Fundamentalism and the Denial of the Divine*, Society for Promoting Christian Knowledge, London, 2007.

251 McGrath, Pg. 10 (Quoted with permission of SPCK and with Prof. McGrath's emphases).

of *God of the gaps*, he points out that it is not the gaps in our knowledge we should be focussing on, but rather the fact we are capable of having as comprehensive an understanding of the universe as we do have.

McGrath points out that Dawkins appears to believe science has disproved God. Of course, it has done no such thing. It also has to be accepted that there are some questions science just cannot answer. Likewise, Dawkins equates a belief in God with a belief in religion. He does not allow for the fact that there are many people who believe in God while avoiding religion — and even religions (e.g., Buddhism) that don't believe in God in the monotheistic sense.

McGrath's book serves the purpose of rebutting Dawkins' atheist fundamentalism. However, we will leave this commentary here, as we have no need for further rebuttal.

It is clear from all we have covered in these appendices to **The God Franchise** that we now have enough information to decide once and for all, for your purpose and mine, whether God exists — or not. As I have clearly shown throughout this book, I believe the case for God's existence has been well and truly proved.

If, at this juncture, you have not read the main text of the book, then allow me to direct you back to Chapter 3, where we discuss the nature of God. If you have now completed the whole book, I suggest that you return to the two chapters that make up Part Five. By rereading those, as an antidote to the complexities of the arguments laid out in the appendices, you will attain a clearer understanding of the significance and importance of **The God Franchise** in your own life.

BIBLIOGRAPHY

The Holy Bible, King James Version, 1611

Collins English Dictionary Complete and Unabridged, 6th Ed. 2003, © HarperCollins Publishers, Glasgow, 1991, 1994, 1998, 2000, 2003

Alexander, D. & P. (Eds), *The Lion Handbook to the Bible*, Lion Publishing, Berkhamsted, Hertfordshire, 1973

Bays, B., *The Journey: An Extraordinary Guide for Healing Your Life and Setting Yourself Free*, Element, London, 2003 (Originally published by Thorsons, 1999)

Bays, B., *Freedom Is: Liberating Your Boundless Potential*, Hodder & Stoughton, London, 2006

Berg, G., *The Six Ways of Atheism: New Logical Disproofs of the Existence of God*, self-published, Prestwich, Lancashire, 2009

Collins, F., *The Language of God: A Scientist Presents Evidence for Belief*, Simon & Schuster, London, 2007

Colman, A., *A Dictionary of Psychology*, 3rd Ed. , Oxford University Press, Oxford, 2009

Conner, K., *The Foundations of Christian Doctrine*, City Christian, Portland, Oregon, 1980

Darwin, C., *The Origin of Species by Means of Natural Selection, or The Preservation of Favoured Races in the Struggle for Life*, 6th Ed., John Murray, London, 1876 (Available: http://darwin-online.org.uk)

Dawkins, R., *The Selfish Gene*, 30th Anniversary Ed., Oxford University Press, Oxford, 2006

Dawkins, R., *The God Delusion*, Bantam Press, London, 2006

Devereux, P., *Living Ancient Wisdom: Understanding and Using Its Principles Today*, Rider, London, 2002

Eldredge, N., *Why We Do It: Rethinking Sex and the Selfish Gene*, W.W. Norton, New York, 2004

Flew, A., *There Is a God: How the World's Most Notorious Atheist Changed His Mind*, HarperCollins, New York, 2007

Fortune, D., *The Mystical Qabalah*, Ernest Benn, London, 1935

Greer, J., *Paths of Wisdom: The Magical Cabala in the Western Tradition*, Llewellyn, St.Paul, Minnesota, 1996

Halverson, D. (Ed.), *The Compact Guide to World Religions*, Bethany House, Minneapolis, 1996

Hawking, S. with Mlodinow, L., *A Briefer History of Time*, Bantam Press, London, 2005

Hawking, S. and Mlodinow, L., *The Grand Design*, Bantam Press, London, 2010

Hay, L., *You Can Heal Your Life*, Hay House, Carlsbad, California, 1984, 1987, 2004

Hewitt, P., *Conceptual Physics: A New Introduction to Your Environment*, 2nd Ed., Little, Brown and Company, Boston, 1974

Hinnells, J., (Ed.), *The New Penguin Handbook of Living Religions*, Penguin, London, 1998

Holliwell, R., *Working with the Law*, School of Christian Philosophy, Phoenix, 1964 (Revised edition published by DeVorss Publications, Camarillo, California, 2005)

Hopfe, L., and Woodward, M., (Eds.), *Religions of the World*, 8th Ed., Prentice Hall, Upper Saddle River, New Jersey, 2001

Humphreys, C., *A Popular Dictionary of Buddhism*, Arco, London, 1962

Marieb, E., *Human Anatomy & Physiology*, 6th Ed., Pearson Benjamin Cummings, San Francisco, 2004

McArthur, B., *Your Life: Why It Is the Way It Is and What You Can Do About It - Understanding the Universal Laws*, A.R.E. Press, Virginia Beach, 1993

McGrath, A. with McGrath J., *The Dawkins Delusion?: Atheist Fundamentalism and the Denial of the Divine*, Society for Promoting Christian Knowledge, London, 2007

Miller, K., *Finding Darwin's God: A Scientist's Search for Common Ground between God and Evolution*, HarperCollins, New York, 1999

Rees, M., *Just Six Numbers: The Deep Forces that Shape the Universe*, Basic Books, New York, 2001

Riso, D. and Hudson R., *The Wisdom of the Enneagram: The Complete Guide to Psychological and Spiritual Growth for the Nine Personality Types*, Bantam Books, New York, 1999

Shinn, F. Scovel, *The Wisdom of Florence Scovel Shinn*, Simon & Schuster, New York, 1989 (including *The Game of Life and How to Play It* [1925], *Your Word is Your Wand* [1928], *The Secret Door to Success* [1940], and *The Power of the Spoken Word* [1945])

Sinnott-Armstrong, W., *Morality ~~Without God~~?*, Oxford University Press, New York, 2009

Speller, J., *Seed Money in Action: Working the Law of Tenfold Return*, Robert Speller, New York, 1965

Stenger, V., *God: The Failed Hypothesis: How Science Shows That God Does Not Exist*, Prometheus, New York, 2007

Tolle, E., *The Power of Now*, Hodder Headline Australia, Sydney, 2004 (Originally published by Namaste Publishing, Vancouver, 1997)

Tolle, E., *A New Earth*, Michael Joseph (Penguin), London, 2005

Varghese, R., *The 'New Atheism': A Critical Appraisal of Dawkins, Dennett, Wolpert, Harris and Stenger*, published as an appendix to Flew, A., *There Is a God: How the World's Most Notorious Atheist Changed His Mind*, HarperCollins, New York, 2007

Ward, K., *Why There Almost Certainly Is a God: Doubting Dawkins*, Lion Hudson, Oxford, 2008

In addition, much information is available on the Internet, in particular in Wikipedia (www.wikipedia.org). I have found the Internet to be an encyclopaedic source of information. However, I have used nothing from there that might compromise the validity of this book by its inclusion, nor have I quoted opinions or passages verbatim without acknowledgment.

Books on the Law of Manifestation and Creating Your Own Reality

Anthony, R., *Beyond Positive Thinking: A No-Nonsense Formula for Getting the Results You Want*, Morgan James, Virginia, 2004

Braden, G., *The Spontaneous Healing of Belief: Shattering the Paradigm of False Limits*, Hay House Inc., Carlsbad, California, 2008

Byrne, R., *The Secret*, Atria Books, New York, *and* Beyond Words, Hillsboro, Oregon, 2006

Grabhorn, L., *Excuse Me, Your Life is Waiting*, Hodder and Stoughton, London, 2004

Hay, L., *You Can Heal Your Life*, Hay House, Carlsbad, California, 1984, 1987, 2004

Hicks, E. & Hicks, J., *Ask and It is Given: Learning to Manifest Your Desires*, Hay House Inc., Carlsbad, California, 2004

Hicks, E. & Hicks, J., *The Amazing Power of Deliberate Intent: Living the Art of Allowing*, Hay House Inc., Carlsbad, California, 2006

Hicks, E. & Hicks, J., *The Law of Attraction: The Basics of the Teachings of Abraham*, Hay House Inc., Carlsbad, California, 2006

Hill, N., *Think and Grow Rich*, Wilshire, Hollywood, 1966 (Originally published 1937)

Holliwell, R., *Working with the Law*, School of Christian Philosophy, Phoenix, 1964 (Revised edition published by DeVorss Publications, Camarillo, California, 2005)

Losier, M., *Law of Attraction: The Science of Attracting More of What You Want and Less of What You Don't Want*, self-published, Victoria, British Columbia, 2006

McArthur, B., *Your Life: Why It Is the Way It Is and What You Can Do About It - Understanding the Universal Laws*, A.R.E. Press, Virginia Beach, 1993

Goddard, N., *The Neville Reader*, DeVorss, Camarillo, California, 2005

Peirce, P., *The Intuitive Way: A Guide to Living from Inner Wisdom,* Axiom Publishing, Hillsboro, Oregon, 2000

Ray, J., *Harmonic Wealth: The Secret of Attracting the Life You Want,* Sphere, London, 2008

Rowland, M., *Absolute Happiness: The Whole Untold Story – The Way to a Life of Complete Fulfilment,* 2nd ed., Self Communications, Bondi Beach, New South Wales, 1994 (Also published by Hay House, 1995)

Spangler, D., *The Laws of Manifestation,* Findhorn Foundation, Forres, Scotland, 1975

Vitale, J., *The Attractor Factor,* John Wiley & Sons, Hoboken, New Jersey, 2005

GLOSSARY

Creation Frequency: The unique vibration you put out based on the totality of what you fundamentally believe in this moment (The *Fundamental You*). This attracts to you experiences, people, and things that resonate (vibrate at the same frequency). It is the attracting force between who and what you are on the one hand, and the things or experiences you desire or expect on the other hand.

Ego: The sense of individuality and separateness from God that has come from the misuse of free will. It is driven by preconceptions, limitations, fear, pain, and suffering. It is self-serving and is aligned with the mind and getting lost in justification, self-pity, blame, and superiority. The Ego could be described as a false sense of self, a self that is hidden beneath many *veils*. The Ego is the same as the *Lesser Self* and, as such, is an illusion (maya).

Free will: The freedom to make one's own choices and decisions without outside determination by God (as an implied outside power) or prior circumstances or causes.

Fundamental You: The sum total of all your beliefs, all your values, and all your attitudes, vows, promises, and rules. The Fundamental You, with all your core beliefs, is the source of everything you experience in your life.

God-Consciousness: A more accurate name for God. It implies that God is Consciousness: awareness, intelligence, and presence without any physical or other form. God-Consciousness can be described as conscious, eternal, omnipotent (all-powerful), omnipresent (present everywhere), omniscient (all-knowing), the Creator of the universe, having a purpose for His Creation, omnibenevolent (absolutely good), and immutable (unchanging through time). Although it is traditional to use the pronouns *He* and *Him* when referring to God, using *It* would be more accurate.

God Franchise: Granted to every individual person by *God-Consciousness*, it is the privilege or right to personally employ all God's qualities and powers to a greater or lesser extent in daily living. In particular, each person has the creative power and free will to create his or her own life experience. In practice, we all do this, either consciously or unconsciously, although the results are often corrupted by the *Ego*.

God Franchisee: You and me and everyone, individually. We each have a *God Franchise* as described above.

Higher Self: *God-Consciousness* with a blindfold on, incarnate as the individual person. The Higher Self expresses individuality and free will in their pure form, and displays all the qualities of *God-Consciousness* although to a reduced (manageable) level. These qualities are more than enough for us to live our lives fully and creatively as *God Franchisees*. It can also be called the True Self, and is Man made in the image and likeness of God. See also *Lesser Self*.

Law of Karma: The Law of Cause and Effect, one of the *Universal Laws*. We each reap what we sow in life. We may reap immediately (instant karma) or at some future time, or as expected by those who believe in reincarnation, in a future lifetime. All karma earned, whether good or bad, must be experienced, unless cleared through forgiveness or some act of genuine contrition.

Law of Manifestation: One of God's *Universal Laws*, The Law of Manifestation brings experiences into your life whether they are what you want or don't want, and whether they are beneficial or detrimental to you and your wellbeing. It attracts to you whatever you absolutely believe or focus on (that is not contradicted by a stronger law or force) without fail. This Law operates whether you apply it consciously or unconsciously. Your *Creation Frequency* determines what is attracted and how quickly. The Law of Manifestation is also known as the Law of Attraction.

Lesser Self: This is the *Ego* and as such is an illusion (maya). The Lesser Self is the Self covered with many *veils*, and it constantly struggles for its survival. It manifests as self-absorbed, self-pitying, and separate *Ego*, suffering in its ignorance. See also *Higher Self*.

Secondary Gain: The indirect social, interpersonal, or monetary gain that one might get from having a "disability" or living in an apparently unfavourable situation. This secondary gain may prevent you from healing or trying to improve your situation, as you could then lose the secondary benefits you receive.

Universal Laws: A Universal Law is *"an unbreakable, unchangeable principle of life that operates inevitably, all the time."*[252] The Universal Laws act impartially, justly, and equally for every single person. They are God's Laws, so cannot be broken, in the same way the Laws of Mathematics cannot be broken. Examples are the *Law of Manifestation* (Like creates like) and the Law of Cause and Effect (*Law of Karma*).

Veil: *"Something that covers, conceals, or separates; mask"*[253] The *Higher Self* is concealed beneath many veils, thus producing the illusion of a *Lesser Self*. Enlightenment is the stripping away of the veils to reveal the True Self, the *Higher Self*, the God-Consciousness which we truly are.

---

252 McArthur, B., *Your Life: Why It Is the Way It Is and What You Can Do About It - Understanding the Universal Laws*, A.R.E. Press, Virginia Beach, 1993, Pg. 5.

253 *Collins English Dictionary*

INDEX

Thank you

Thank you for purchasing *The God Franchise*. If you have enjoyed reading it, and feel, as I do, that this is a message that needs to be spread around the world, you can assist. Every voice helps, and you can create a greater awareness of **The God Franchise** that is available to every one of us, whether we realise it or not.

To help, you can:

1. Tell your friends.

2. Write a review for the online bookstore from which you purchased this book, and also you can put the same review on
   + Amazon.com
   + Google Books
   + Any other favourite online bookstore.

3. E-mail your mail list. If you belong to a society or organisation, or have a group of friends whom you keep posted with the latest news, let them know they are God Franchisees.

4. Comment on Facebook or Twitter to let your friends know.

5. Comment on the online blog at **www.TheGodFranchise.com** — click on the **Follow** button so you are advised of any new blogs.

6. E-mail me. See **http://Publishing.LifeMagic.co.nz** for details.

7. Buy *The God Franchise* as a special present for your favourite aunt and uncle, and all your best friends.

Yes, thank you very much for your help. As each person becomes aware of how they create the life they live, and how they are fulfilling the purpose of God-Consciousness in every moment of every day, the veils of limitation and ignorance in the world will start to slip away. Bless you.

Lightning Source UK Ltd.
Milton Keynes UK
UKHW011503170720
366712UK00001B/70